Homosexuality and Religion

Homosexuality and Religion

Richard Hasbany, PhD
Editor

Homosexuality and Religion was simultaneously issued by The Haworth Press, Inc., under the same title, as a special issue of the *Journal of Homosexuality*, Volume 18, Numbers 3/4, 1989/90, John De Cecco, Editor.

Harrington Park Press
New York • London

ISBN 0-918393-66-3

Published by

Harrington Park Press, Inc., 10 Alice Street, Binghamton, New York 13904-1580
EUROSPAN/Harrington, 3 Henrietta Street, London WC2E 8LU England

Harrington Park Press, Inc., is a subsidiary of The Haworth Press, Inc., 10 Alice Street, Binghamton, New York 13904-1580.

Homosexuality and Religion was originally published as the *Journal of Homosexuality*, Volume 18, Numbers 3/4 1989/90.

Cover design by Marshall Andrews.

Library of Congress Cataloging-in-Publication Data

Homosexuality and religion / Richard Hasbany, guest editor.
    p. cm.
    "Originally published as Journal of homosexuality, volume 18, numbers 3/4, 1989" – T.p. verso.
    Includes bibliographical references and index.
    ISBN 0-918393-66-3
    1. Homosexuality – Religious aspects – Christianity. 2. Homosexuality – Religious aspects – Judaism. 3. Homosexuality – United States. I. Hasbany, Richard.
BR115.H6H64   1989b
261.8'35766 – dc20
                                                  89-39799
                                                        CIP

CONTENTS

ABOUT THE EDITOR

Richard Hasbany, PhD, received advanced degrees in literature and has taught at universities in Michigan and California. He became involved in the current dialogue about religious thought and life and homosexuals and has served on the Presbytery of San Franciso's Special Committee on Homosexuality and its Task Force on Human Sexuality. He is a member of the national Executive Board of Presbyterians for Lesbian/Gay Concerns. Dr. Hasbany is a ruling elder at Seventh Avenue Presbyterian Church in San Francisco and is Administrative Assistant at the School of Humanities, San Francisco State University.

Preface

An exemplary incident provides a frame for the articles in this volume. Without this frame, the dialogue that is going on in the churches and temples and is recorded and furthered here appears to be parochial and academic, a tangential disturbance. Placed in this frame, the dialogue comes into focus as a crucial element in the contemporary inquiry into the nature and role of homosexuality and homosexuals in modern society. In 1984, after a number of attempts, a bill barring discrimination against gay men and lesbians passed the California legislature and lay on the desk of Governor George Deukmejian. During the 13 days it lay on the Governor's desk, the Sacramento-based Committee on Moral Concerns, led by retired Baptist preacher W. B. Timberlake, was able to generate 100,000 letters and calls against the measure, thought to be the most communications ever received by a California governor on a single subject. In addition, a coalition of pastors and the American Life Lobby mounted a large prayer rally on the steps of the capitol, showing up the much smaller congregation of gay activists rallying on the other side of the building. Whatever other factors may have influenced the governor's decision, the religious lobby had its way, and Deukmejian vetoed the bill. In gratitude, Senator H. L. Richardson called on ministers across the state to make the following Sunday a day of thanksgiving (Chandler, 1984).

In other cities and states where gay civil rights bills have been introduced and passed, opposition has been frequently if not usually led by local religious leaders, or itinerants like Anita Bryant. Though many mainline Christian denominations and the major Jewish bodies have made statements supporting civil rights for homosexuals, conservative religious groups and even some segments within the mainline groups continue to present the most vocal and unified opposition to those rights. In influencing political decisions, researchers in the physical and social sciences are hard pressed to

1

compete with the sheer numbers, organization, and tactics of religious people, whose opposition in the civil arena is a logical conclusion of beliefs that have led ecclesiastical judicatories to adopt policies denying gay persons access to ordination, the focal point of most controversies within the church. It is easy to understand why the relationship between the gay community and the religious establishment is a treacherous and unstable one; why attempts to alter the status quo of this bitter division touch profound sensitivities in each constituency.

Lesbian and gay believers' reactions to their religious opponents are necessarily more complicated than the unequivocal contempt, dismissal and opposition of gay nonbelievers. Gay and lesbian believers share a compelling experience of faith with the Reverend Timberlakes, and they share an identity (i.e., Jew/Christian). At the same time, they experience a compelling gay/lesbian identity. They cannot deny either one of these identities without violating their deepest knowledge of themselves.

It is probably accurate to describe gay/lesbian believers as isolated in both their identity communities. Within their faith communities they are castigated by religious conservatives and fundamentalists, who have successfully blocked the full participation of openly gay and lesbian believers in virtually every denomination. (Even in the United Church of Christ where the ordination of gay men and lesbians is permitted, nearly every gay and lesbian candidate for the ministry has been blocked at the congregational level. The summer 1988 vote by the United Church of Canada's 32nd General Council to accept gay men and lesbians as candidates for ministry may portend a significant breakthrough on the issue of ordination, though it is too soon after the vote at this writing to determine how the denomination's judicatories will implement its decision.) Outside the religious communities, on the other hand, many in the generally bitter lesbian/gay community see gay believer activists as dupes and masochists engaged in a neurotic and meaningless struggle. Some go even further and scorn the believers' activism as an obstacle to the building of a distinctive gay spirituality.

Those who critique the lesbian and gay believers' enterprise in their churches or temples raise important questions regarding the goal of a self-consciously gay/lesbian identity and presence; whether it is to assert normality, facilitate acceptance and secure rights, or to cultivate homosexual uniqueness and independence. Don Kilhefner, the first executive director of the Los Angeles Gay and Lesbian Community Services Center and a student of gay poets and writers, defined the dilemma facing lesbian/gay people as "our assimilation into the mainstream versus our enspiritment as a people" (Kilhefner, 1987, p. 123). "What passes for 'gay' politics, 'gay' religion, 'gay' psychology, et cetera," he wrote, "is really little more than hetero male evolved politics, religion, and psychology with the word gay mindlessly or opportunistically prefixed. So-called gay churches and synagogues are based largely on the same structures, values and consciousness as their patriarchally possessed prototypes" (p. 125). Kilhefner is quoted in Mark Thompson's collection, *Gay Spirit*, a significant collection of essays that stakes out a nonassimilationist ground based on a "quest for authentic inner experience, the awakening to other forms of reality" (Thompson, 1987, p. xiv) and critiques the allegedly inauthentic experience and self-destructive relationship Judaeo-Christian believers endure with their spiritual establishments. Even assuming the validity of Kilhefner and Thompson's formulations, however, I propose that the issues for gay and lesbian religious activists must be phrased differently to permit other possibilities. It may be that their quest will be blunted and diverted by a craven quest for acceptance and incorporation. On the other hand, it may be that the vision and values of the gay and lesbian activists will transform thei rreligious establishments, provoking a fresh and profound confrontation with scriptures and traditions, and making the establishments more open, more just, more inclusive, more feminist.

Some lesbians and feminist women have embarked upon a quest for a self-consciously feminist spirituality, similar in its stress upon uniqueness and authenticity to the spirituality described in Thompson's volume. The development of women's/feminist spirituality has probably progressed more rapidly than gay male explorations, and one is free to speculate on the reasons for that. Whatever the reasons, however, the result of the women's quest is a remarkable body of work from a broad spectrum of approaches and positions, including antipatriarchal stances that critique Judaeo-Christian traditions while remaining faithful to essential tenets and institutions, separatist strains that break with the traditional institutions but stay in the faith, and those that begin to recover or explore radically alternative spiritual paths. The feminist and lesbian feminist scholars and theologians whose works continue to address the traditional Judaeo-Christian bodies, such as Carter Heyward, Elisabeth Schussler Fiorenza, and Virginia Ramey Mollenkott, have begun to play a critical role in the dialogue about the place of women, lesbians, and gay men in their faiths. The discoveries, directions, and ramifications of the feminist/lesbian spirituality movement is sometimes evident in this volume, and always, I hope, implicit in it. Nonetheless, it deserves scholarly attention far beyond what it is accorded here.

This volume does not directly attempt to further the lively discussion among lesbians and gay men regarding assimilationist reform of traditional structures versus the quest for a unique and authentically gay spirituality, important and stimulating as that debate may be. The aims are modest, less speculative, and more historically specific. The assumption is that the dialogue between gay/lesbian believers and their religious establishments is an important and protracted historical event and, hence, well worth recording. The volume gathers concise and comprehensive surveys of the current lesbian/gay challenge to the ecclesiastical and theological traditions and to the polities of the Jewish and Christian faiths; it hopes to establish in a brief volume the historical record to date of this dialogical challenge.

The surveys of the Christian dialogue by Robert Nugent and Jeannine Gramick and the Jewish dialogue by Rabbi Yoel Kahn and Aaron Cooper demonstrate the complex interweaving of tradition, theology, and political strategy that is part of the struggle. Though not addressed directly, the synchronous relationship between the gay/lesbian religious debate and the struggle for civil rights is implicit in the Nugent/Gramick and Kahn/Cooper articles. The relationship is forged on one level by the vociferous opposition to civil rights by religious leaders, and on another level because the struggle within the ecclesiastical governing structures of various denominations and Jewish movements mirrors the external civil struggle. Each struggle will have an impact on the other's progress. There is a fine and subtle synchronicity at work.

This volume hopes to document and stimulate further investigation of the more personal dimension of this event as well. Several articles focus on the people who have been the catalysts, originators, and prosecutors of the dialogue, the gay/lesbian religious activitists and the gay clergy (generally closeted and often nonactivist), as they pursue both their visions of justice inside the church and ways to reconcile their conflicting personal identities. Clare Fischer is a sociologist of religion teaching at the Starr King School for Ministry (Unitarian). Her article, "A Bonding of Choice: Values and Identity Among Lesbian and Gay Religious Leaders," provides a more structured investigation of lesbian and gay clergy than the valuable but largely anecdotal accounts that have been available to date, such as *Lesbian Nuns* or the writings of Malcolm Boyd. Clare Fischer's findings, though based on a small sample, suggest some preliminary evidence on the value structures and self-imagery of gay/lesbian people already committed to their clerical calling. It also provides some evidence about the authenticity and enspiritment of gay men and lesbians in traditional spiritualities as opposed to those in nonassimilationist and nontraditional spiritualities. Gary Comstock's address to the national gathering of the United Church of Christ's Coalition for Lesbian/Gay Concerns defines some of the issues and documents the struggle of a gay man on the verge of committing to professional service in an ecclesiastical institution. It formulates some options and also points to the discussion within the gay/lesbian caucuses of the various denominations and the profound theological and existential issues that they commonly enjoin.

Four articles engage directly continuing and expanding dialogue within the Christian church. George Edwards, Professor Emeritus of New Testament at Louisville Theological Seminary, surveys the conduct of the debate in his own denomination, the Presbyterian Church, USA, over what the Genesis creation texts have to say about homosexuality. Edwards furthers the dialogue by placing the texts and the discussion in feminist and liberationist contexts, and by suggesting that a literalist hermeneutics neither has been fairly applied nor is necessarily appropriate. Professor of Religious Studies Ann Matter's article falls into the growing body of historical research on the gay/lesbian presence in the Christian church throughout its existence, research most prominently exemplified by

John Boswell and Judith Brown's work. Matter's article shares preliminary investigations into a 17th-century Cappucine nun, Maria Domitilla Galluzzi, and offers a caution regarding 20th-century terminology; it may be misleading to use the term "lesbian" for some same-sex expressions of spiritual ecstacy, she argues.

Two Catholic priests who are also professional therapists draw from different theoretical sources to develop models of pastoral therapy that integrate traditional Christian understandings and effective therapy for gay and lesbian clients. Father John Struzzo bases his model in a creation spirituality and transpersonal therapy. Father Michael Garanzini's model, based in object relations, looks more toward interpersonal functioning and the healing of early narcissistic wounds.

Although as Gramick and Nugent show, the dialogue between Judaeo/Christian institutions already has a history dating in decades, it has emerged as an open debate that has reached the consciousness and challenged the conceptions of the mass of believers only since the early 1970s. This volume attempts to be a kind of first update. The dialogue has progressed relatively rapidly, pushed ahead by the energy of the civil rights struggle, scientific research regarding homosexuality, the search for an appropriate response to the AIDS epidemic, and finally by an emerging body of religiously focused scholars, spokespersons, and activists devoted to its furtherance. It is hoped that this volume will be an encouragement to their scholarly activities and a stimulus to futhering that dialogue.

Richard Hasbany, PhD

REFERENCES

Chandler, R. (1984, April 20). Christian activists help kill a California gay rights bill. *Christianity Today*, p. 42.

Kilhefner, D. (1987). Gay people at a critical crossroad: Assimilation or affirmation? In Mark Thompson (Ed.), *Gay spirit: Myth and meaning* (pp. 121-130). New York: St. Martin's Press.

Thompson, M. (1987). *Gay spirit: Myth and meaning.* New York: St. Martin's Press.

Homosexuality:
Protestant, Catholic,
and Jewish Issues;
A Fishbone Tale

Robert Nugent, STM
Jeannine Gramick, PhD

SUMMARY. Homosexuality is compared to a fishbone caught in the church's throat that the church can neither eject nor swallow entirely. Authors in all denominations are questioning traditional church stances influenced by the model of clinical pastoral education. Most major denominations have made policy statements on homosexuality. Four such stances discussed here highlight some of the common issues denominations face in their reexamination of the subject. Homosexuals struggling for full acceptance in the church must confront the classical understanding of the human being and human sexual differentiation as these concepts have traditionally influenced the churches.

Robert Nugent is a Roman Catholic priest who has been involved in church-related ministry for homosexual people since 1971. He has a master's degree in theology from the Yale Divinity School and is a co-founder of New Ways Ministry. He edited *A Challenge to Love: Gay and Lesbian Catholics in the Church*, and is coordinator of the Center for Homophobia Education.
Correspondence may be addressed to 637 Dover St., Baltimore, MD 21230.
Jeannine Gramick received her PhD from the University of Pennsylvania and was an Assistant Professor of Mathematics at the College of Notre Dame of Maryland before beginning her full-time work in lesbian/gay ministry. She co-founded New Ways Ministry, and edited the books *Homosexuality and the Catholic Church*, *The Vatican and Homosexuality*, and *Homosexuality in the Priesthood and the Religious Life*.
Correspondence may be addressed to 6401 N. Charles St., Baltimore, MD 21212.

More than a dozen years ago the author of one of the first major treatments in the Catholic press on homosexuality compared an organization for Catholic homosexual people and their friends to a fishbone lodged in the throat of the Catholic Church. "The institution can't swallow it; and it just won't go away" (Rashke, 1976, p. 28). The fishbone analogy is an apt one for a larger discussion of homosexuality and U.S. mainline Christian denominations. The inability of the churches to "swallow" everything that some people claim for homosexuality, and the realization that neither these claims nor the lively debate they have generated will go away, means that the fishbone remains a central issue the churches will have to grapple with in the coming years. Simultaneously, the churches must attempt to respond to an increasingly sophisticated and articulate homosexual constituency that is supported by many in church groups who do not share the experience of being lesbian or gay themselves, but who share many of the goals of the religious gay and lesbian movement.

Although the situation has not changed substantially since the fishbone analogy was first employed, significant progress has been made among several church groups in opening up the topic for public study and discussion. In some instances the impetus has come from having to face the question of ordaining publicly self-affirming lesbian and gay candidates for church ministries. Many mainline Christian denominations are seeking better ways to respond to the pastoral needs and theological challenges of those lesbian and gay members who still retain some kind of denominational affiliation and practice, and who continue to seek some kind of official church recognition of their sexuality and its genital expressions and full and equal participation in all aspects of church life.

The AIDS crisis has confronted churches with life and death situations related to institutional and personal affirmation and acceptance of individuals who traditionally have been rejected by society and religion. What churches teach about homosexuality cannot be easily or comfortably divorced from their pastoral ministries to individual gay men coping with AIDS and ARC. During his 1987 visit to the United States, Pope John Paul II said that the church is concerned with the moral background of AIDS as well as with offering care and hope for the suffering and those caring for them. Other prominent church representatives who argue that AIDS is a punishment from God or nature for immoral behavior present a more obvious example of how the medical and moral issues are linked in the thinking of many people.

Traditionally, Roman Catholicism has had a precise and clearly articulated, though not unchallenged, theology of sexual ethics. This theology is based on an understanding of the meaning and purpose of human sexuality drawn primarily from a specific biblical anthropology. In this view, genital sexuality is good and moral only within a heterosexual, monogamous union at least potentially biologically procreative, based on mutual love and fidelity and sanctioned by some kind of covenanted marriage commitment. As recently as 1986, Catholic teaching, which condemns homogenital expression, was reiterated by Vatican authorities, who also categorized the homosexual "condition" as "objectively disordered" because it leads to genital acts which are nonprocreative. The document was severely criticized from many quarters for its particularly insensitive and unnecessarily harsh language and tone as well as for its arguments, which many found unconvincing. The document, in effect, seemed to be an attempt to close the door on any further discussion on other understandings of human sexuality or on theological developments that might lead to substantial modification of classical Roman Catholic opposition to homogenital expression.

The emergence of denominational caucuses such as Dignity, Integrity, Affirmation, Lutherans Concerned, Presbyterians for Lesbian and Gay Concerns, and so forth, has raised lesbian and gay issues in the churches. In addition, the Metropolitan Community Church, with a primary outreach to gay and lesbian people, and gay synagogues among some branches of Judaism in the United States, have provided much needed pastoral care and structured efforts to lobby for continuing institutional study and dialogue. Yet the tensions that exist among those who take different theological and pastoral stances, both personally and institutionally, are still formidable. This is so even in the presence of the best of intentions and good will to explore the topic and wrestle with the complex and emotional issues that the discussion of homosexuality and religion invariably generates. Fundamental theological issues such as a normative understanding of human nature, the binding elements in the classical biblical creation accounts of Genesis, the individual scriptural texts traditionally utilized to condemn homogenital behavior, the nature of particular denominational teaching authority, and biblical and theological traditions that lay claim to infallibility are all part of the underlying discussion of homosexuality in an ecclesial context. Serious efforts are being made in some church circles to address these and other related issues. Meantime, the more traditional norms, values, and beliefs still hold sway in most mainline Christian churches and among the large majority of Christian and Jewish faithful. Chandler (1987) reported that the Catholic church's position against homogenital behavior was supported by a ratio of more than 2 to 1 among the Catholics polled in a *Los Angeles Times* survey, 4 to 1 among the Protestants, and nearly 70% among all Americans.

Most organized religions have articulated official positions on homogenital expression, civil rights for homosexual citizens, the unacceptability of antihomosexual violence, the meaning of same-gender affectional relationships, and the criteria for church participation for gay and lesbian members. Some of these statements and positions have been modified over the years as a result of further knowledge and continued dialogue within the denomination itself. There is much more flexibility in the more private arenas of pastoral counseling and professional gatherings, and in the writings of certain influential people, both clerical and lay, in various denominations. These positions run the gamut from the Quakers, who view homosexuality as fully equal with heterosexuality, to Roman Catholic magisterial teaching, which continues to reject all homogenital expression and to resist any attempt to validate or sanction even the homosexual orientation. All church positions are open to serious questions and challenges on many levels. The vigorous debate, to which no end seems insight, continues in all of the churches. The fact that such a controversial and emotional discussion can be explored and continuously fueled from so many diverse quarters, although apparently never settled to anyone's complete satisfaction, is, perhaps, the one hopeful sign on the present horizon. By comparison, such debate is a giant step forward from a previously uncritical and fundamentalist condemnation of homosexuality and, in effect, a rejection of homosexual *people* that seems to have dominated the general religious scene for the last 6 centuries.

The thawing of the ice that froze the public discussion of homosexuality in church circles began in the U.S. in this century. Although the encouraging results of this thaw are tangible to us today, no one realistically expects that a dramatic breakthrough in official church positions will come either quickly or easily. In describing, for example, official talks between the leaders of Presbyterians for Lesbian/Gay Concerns, a caucus in the Presbyterian Church (USA), and Presbyterians United for Biblical Concerns, a group opposing any radical change in Presbyterian teachings on homosexuality, one participant (Anderson, 1986) noted that from the inception of the talks "it was clear the differences between PLGC and PUBC are real and profound" (p. 1). Nonetheless, it is important to recognize and applaud the emergence of an historical situation where many denominations are willing to encourage, support, and even fund continuing dialogue and official studies on an issue that was for most people in the past, and for many still today, simply closed once and for all.

In light of these introductory remarks, the purposes of this article are: (a) to highlight briefly some of the major figures in the mainline U.S. Christian denominations and branches of Judaism who have spoken publicly and urged study and reassessment of the traditional teachings and practices regarding homosexuality, (b) to present an overview of contemporary major church studies and policy statements of several Christian denominations, and (c) to outline and critique several possible ecclesial stances on homosexuality in order to articulate some of the common theological and pastoral concerns they share. In this way, we can also make some effort to suggest future directions in which an official dialogue might move. What is needed now is a serious effort to explore and develop those areas that for many remain formidable obstacles to an acceptance of homosexual identity and expression as potentially morally good and healthy as heterosexuality in the Judaeo-Christian scheme.

MAJOR FIGURES IN JUDAEO-CHRISTIAN DISCUSSION

In the first half of this century, the usual view of homosexuality on the part of religious thinkers and especially those involved in pastoral work was one based on a medical model. This evaluation considered the homosexual individual to be a person with a particular illness but not necessarily to be blamed because its origins were simply not understood or even known. Nevertheless, the person was generally advised to seek professional psychological help in order either to change the situation or at least to learn to control the impulses. A popular assumption was that for some reason the homosexual impulses were stronger and more difficult to manage than heterosexual ones. This evaluation represented a slight advance over a previous religious approach that categorized homosexuality as a direct result of personal, moral failure or of a deliberate sin for which the individual *was* held accountable, blameworthy, and sometimes even punishable either in this world or the next.

As long as the medical view dominated the study of homosexuality, both religious authorities and pastoral counselors could supply limited spiritual remedies, but these were always secondary and in support of more fundamental therapeutic remedies of various kinds that could address the real underlying problem. It was believed that psychiatry could "cure" homosexual people or at least help them channel their sexual energies into socially and religiously approved activities, projects, and behaviors. What physical punishments and ecclesiastical exorcisms had previously failed to accomplish, the new psychological remedies would attain. This early 20th-century approach has been described by Malloy (1979):

> The presumption was that once the causes of homosexuality could be found in some psychosexual dysfunction in the individual's personal history, a focus on individual therapy offered the best promise for a change in behavior. The moral dimension of the problem was ultimately subsumed under consideration of the purported sickness of the particular person under consideration. (p. 123)

Gradually, church people moved from the medical model to an essentialist model which incorporated increasing scientific evidence that in some cases the true homosexual orientation is established at a relatively early stage in the development of the individual, is permanent and generally impervious to techniques for radical change. The current debate between the essentialists and the social constructionists has not yet penetrated theological circles. Hiltner (1980) suggested that the clinical pastoral education movement (CPE), especially as initiated in Protestant circles, was a prime factor in this shift. CPE was a more professional attempt to equip pastoral ministers with better skills to undertake direct helping relationships in a variety of human problems and situations. One of these areas was the reality of homosexual people encountered by clergy in every denomination and religious group. The CPE model emerged in the early 1920s and gradually influenced Roman Catholic and Jewish educational programs, ministerial preparation structures, and theological schools. Whether individual clergy personally undertook the counseling of homosexual clients or made referrals to other professionals, they soon acknowledged the apparent fixity of a genuine homosexual orientation and identity in certain individuals. Seeing that even intense and prolonged psychotherapy would not alter a true homosexual orientation, many were faced with the personal decision of having to adopt a kind of prophetic stance in their churches about homosexuality or else to remain silent.

For Hiltner, one of the early prophets in this movement was H. Kimbell Jones (1966), who dispelled many erroneous ideas about homosexuality and argued persuasively for more understanding of the real nature of the problem as he saw it. Jones believed, however, that homosexual behavior was not a fulfillment of human sexuality. Citing the Genesis account of creation in the Christian scriptures, Jones concluded that homogenital acts were not what God intended for human sexuality. He also argued, however, that because all human life is involved in a sinful distortion of love, the real issues are not sexual acts that are "normal" and those that are not, but sex as a depersonalizing force versus sex as the fulfillment of human relationships. For Jones, this way of thinking, did not exclude the possibility of an ethical and fulfilling relationship for homosexual people. He also suggested that the churches should recognize such partnerships and should encourage fidelity and personal fulfillment within them.

Pittinger (1976), an Anglican priest-theologian, argued that he remained unconvinced of the sinfulness of all homogenital behavior and suggested that traditional religious arguments for that judgment contained little more than "special pleading, inherited or personal prejudice, outworn patterns of thought and inadequate or even erroneous factual data'' (p. 75). Another important contribution to the discussion was Weltge's (1969) anthology of articles from various disciplines asserting that no valid scientific evidence existed to prove that homosexuality belongs per se to the realm of mental health, and that homosexuality, like heterosexuality, should be considered moral in the sense of being positive, good, right, and even desirable.

One of Weltge's contributors, Secor (1969), in his brief for a new homosexual ethic, stated that human sexual identification and behavior patterns are morally neutral regardless of their preferred gender object. He wrote that the moral quality of any particular sexual pattern depends rather on whether or not it meets the Christian standards for all human relational behavior. Ethical concern for homosexual persons is warranted on the basis that homosexual people are persons, not on the basis of their sexual inclinations. One cannot make a priori ethical judgments on sexual behavior simply by reason of the object of the sexual behavior, the sexual behavior itself, or behavior as socially aberrant. Secor's thinking anticipated and reflected a trend among many moralists in all denominations today who question whether there are any human acts that can be labeled intrinsically evil when judged apart from other considerations such as consequences, the intention of the acting person (the act-or or moral agent), and the tensions between the moral values and disvalues associated with all human acts.

Among other Protestant writers who were early pioneers in exploring the topic of homosexuality and church teachings were Oberholtzer (1971), and Wood (1960). Among the more scholarly works of this genre was Bailey's (1955) truly foundational work that dealt both with key biblical accounts and the history of the church's treatment of homosexuality from both Protestant and Roman Catholic traditions. Bailey attempted to demonstrate how the "crime against nature" judgment developed historically and argued for a radical change in light of contemporary scientific knowledge of the homosexual orientation. All subsequent and reputable studies of the biblical data on homosexuality, including both McNeill (1976) and Boswell (1980), were indebted to Bailey's initial attempt to mount the first serious challenge to traditional interpretations of classical scriptural passages purportedly related to homosexuality. In the Protestant community before 1970, the situation was best described by Hiltner (1980):

> Even though the churches said as little as possible about homosexuality, they had acquired an uneasy conscience about the older attitudes on three kinds of grounds. First, a better informed pastoral care had revealed much unnecessary suffering. Second, the issues of human and civil rights could not be ignored. Third, even though scholarly work on the tradition was small in quantity, it pointed in the direction of inadequate scholarly bases for the traditional positions. (pp. 222-223)

During this same period, there was a parallel movement in the Roman Catholic scholarly community urging a reexamination of traditional church teachings. McNeill (1970), a Jesuit theologian, had published several exploratory articles in a Catholic clerical journal that formed the basis for a later full-length work on the same topic. McNeill questioned Church teaching that any use of sex outside of marriage or in a way that prohibits procreation is always objectively wrong. In the context of Vatican II's abandonment of "primary" and "secondary" language when speaking of the procreational and unitive aspects of heterosexual intercourse in marriage, some contemporary moralists had begun to question the value and viability of an act-centered morality and encouraged the use of more personal criteria such as the relational aspects of human sexuality. McNeill also applied the traditional Catholic moral principle that allows for one to tolerate the lesser of two evils when faced with a necessary choice between two disvalues. He argued for the acceptance of a stable and permanent homosexual relationship as a lesser evil than promiscuity. McNeill's assumption was that a life of total sexual abstinence is not always a viable alternative for particular homosexual individuals. A life of complete genital abstinence is a pastoral standard that is proposed not only for homosexual Christians, but, by traditional Christian teachings, for all unmarried individuals. In 1988 an Episcopal bishop challenged the church to reconsider this standard in particular cases (Spong, 1988).

Charles Curran (1971) criticized several Protestant approaches as well as McNeill and from his ethical theory of compromise offered a mediating position between total condemnation of all homogenital behavior and total acceptance. This position states that homosexual acts are not normative and always lacking something necessary for full human sexuality. But it also acknowledges that for some people such behavior can be both objectively good and moral because, in the face of the human condition and the presence of sin in the world affecting sexuality, the ideal or norm of heterosexuality can be compromised since this is the best that true homosexual people can do in the present situation. Curran acknowledged that the Catholic tradition is logically more compatible with an understanding of sexuality structured in terms of the love union of male and female, and he conceded that his argument was one of "fittingness rather than proof" (p. 471). He also remained open to new evidence from many sources that would demand a change in his position.

Several other Catholic writers contributed to the general discussion of homosexuality, especially under pastoral considerations, in the 1950s and 1960s but none of them moved much beyond the traditional call for "understanding and compassion" coupled with a plea for more psychological investigation and study of causes and cures. Many of them also urged a generous application of the traditional Catholic principle that, in matters of sexual behavior, other factors could often impede or even completely destroy one's personal freedom to act and thus reduce both personal responsibility and culpability. These included the force of habit, particular compulsions, overpowering sexual attractions and impulses, and so on.

A striking exception to this stance was the publication of "Ministry/USA, A Model for Ministry to the Homosexual Community" (Salvatorian Gay Ministry Task Force, 1974). These guidelines for extending a Christian ministry to homosexual persons simply assumed that homosexuality was in every way as valid as heterosexuality. Although commissioned officially by the National Federation of Priests' Councils, they were not formally accepted by the group and were only later published privately.

Other contributors in this volume will address Jewish perspectives and developments in much greater depth; thus, only brief mention will be made here of a few of the major advances in that faith community. Until very recently, there was little evidence of any serious public discussion of homosexuality, much less any significant shift in teachings and attitudes, in the major branches of Judaism. According to Soloff (1983), "No article entitled 'homosexuality,' appeared in the *Jewish Encyclopedia* of seventy-five years ago, and no article entitled 'homosexuality' appeared in the *Universal Jewish Encyclopedia* of forty years ago" (p. 417). An article on homosexuality by Chief Rabbi Immanuel Jacobovitz of London and two responses by a Reform Rabbi, Solomon Freehof, clearly supported negative Biblical and Talmudic attitudes on homosexuality, which regard biblical injunctions condemning homosexual relations in general without regard to any historical context. Another Rabbi, Walter Jacob, collected "Jewish Sources on Homosexuality" and found no texts that challenged the prohibition of homosexuality in Judaism.

On the other hand, Rabbi Allen Bennett has argued that biblical writers had no idea of what homosexuality was and would not have wasted their time legislating against it had they understood its true nature. Bennett based his assertions on the contention that among the Hebrews "the denunciations seem to be not so much against homosexuality as against idolatry associated with it, or they spring from fears of assimilation" (Soloff, 1983, p. 417). This explanation of biblical strictures against homogenital behavior has been taken up and used by a large number of Christian authors who argue against using certain biblical texts without utilizing some of the contemporary critical and exegetical tools available to biblical scholars to arrive at a more accurate understanding of the meaning of the text in its linguistic, cultural, political, social, and theological contexts.

Soloff believed that neither traditional nor antitraditional explanations of the condemnations of homosexuality provide a basis for a Reform response to homosexuality. Even if the authoritative body of Reform Judaism should adopt one or the other interpretation of the Levitical verses, it would still leave many unanswered questions. Many Reform Jewish leaders such as Rabbi Judith Lewis maintain that positions about homosexuality ought not to be made on the basis of tradition unless Jews are "prepared to take an equally traditional stand on family purity, *kashrut*, and other such matters" (Soloff, 1983, p. 419).

Because large numbers of Jewish men and women do and will

continue to identify themselves as gay and lesbian, the question that
some Jewish teachers are asking is how does Judaism respond legitimately as a liberal Jewish movement. While it is possible for the
reform tradition to adopt policies and norms that negate *halakhic*
teachings, as in the case of the new roles that women play in Reform Jewish life, and while a different response to homosexuality
may someday be accepted by Reform Judaism, Soloff admitted that
he has "not been personally confronted with evidence of any widespread shift of opinion among my colleagues away from the biblical
and talmudic prohibitions" (p. 420).

Rabbi Lionel Blue (1982), a lecturer at the Leo Bacek College in
England in charge of the religious court of the Reform Synagogue
of Great Britain, summarized the present position of Judaism with
regard to homosexuality:

> There is no direct unanimous Jewish answer for gays. For tra-
> ditionalists, homosexual behavior is forbidden. The compas-
> sionate see it as an illness and the rigorists as a sin. Neither
> permits it and the recommended therapy ranges from counsel-
> ing to stoning. If the will were there, there could be a develop-
> ment in Jewish law. Since interest is now allowed and capital
> punishment abolished, polygamy forbidden, and slavery obso-
> lete, then in theory a change in attitude could take place here
> too. But the will is not there. Like intermarriage and the food
> laws, and the sexual purity laws and the Sabbath observance
> laws, homosexuality is just another unresolved problem, set
> by an open and permissive society to a religious law which
> sought God's will in a closed and homogeneous one, drawn
> tight by external persecution and internal obedience. For the
> progressives and reformers in Judaism, there is a conflicting
> mixture of tradition, middle class attitudes, fears for the fam-
> ily, fears for their own image and a genuine sympathy with the
> minority, the underdog. They are struggling for an answer.
> They have not found one. (p. 4-5)

If final and definitive answers have not been found, then at least
some significant advances have been made. Saslow (1987) has recently chronicled these contemporary developments. In 1985, the

Reconstructionist Rabbinical College in Philadelphia voted to admit openly gay male and female seminarians. Presently, there are both gay and lesbian Rabbis working in the Jewish community. In the early 1970s individual temples catering to a predominantly gay membership sprang up in a dozen cities from Boston to Los Angeles. In 1973, the United Association of Hebrew Congregations accepted a Los Angeles temple for membership, and since then others have also been accepted, although the Conservative movement is still debating whether to follow suit. Apart from the Orthodox community, the Jewish support for civil rights has been strong and consistent, and there are major educational efforts underway in various branches of Judaism, including Hillel ministries on college and university campuses and among professional organizations of Jewish women, to address the issue of homosexuality.

We have discussed how major figures in both Christian and Jewish communities have voiced their concerns about traditional theological teachings and pastoral responses to homosexual members during the past several decades. These voices have moved churches and synagogues to undertake full-scale studies, sometimes resulting in policy statements and pastoral plans for ministry to homosexual people.

MAJOR STUDIES AND POLICY STATEMENTS IN CHRISTIAN DENOMINATIONS

During the past 10 years, many Christian denominations have devoted significant time and study to homosexuality and to related issues that surround its discussion in a religious context. Although individual issues are of special interest to particular denominations because of longstanding commitment to certain values and beliefs, most of the questions under discussion today cross denominational lines.

Batchelor (1980) showed how the various denominations approach the theological issues with slightly different emphases and attitudes stemming from their own moral and ethical traditions. Denominations and theologians utilize differently the classical sources for ethical reflection and moral decision making. Thus, for example, a tradition that places a high value on the natural law as the foundation of morality will stress certain philosophical and anthropological elements, while a more biblical-oriented group will draw primarily, or sometimes exclusively, on scriptural texts. The arguments favoring the acceptance of homosexuality in the churches and synagogues today find their strongest warrants in empirical studies of homosexuality and the contemporary experiences of religious gay and lesbian people. Spong (1988) acknowledged that scientific evidence, coupled with the witness of gay and lesbian people, made him aware that his prejudice grew out of ignorance. Yet, as Hays (1986) remarked, "Those who defend the morality of homosexual relationships within the church may do so only by conferring upon these warrants an authority greater than the direct authority of Scripture and tradition at least with respect to this question" (p. 211).

In their attempts to articulate particular beliefs about homosexuality and a more comprehensive and unified body of teaching on human sexuality, Christian moralists draw on the biblical data, church theologies and traditions, the social and empirical sciences, and Christian experience reflected on and critiqued in light of the gospel message. The Evangelical wing in the Protestant churches and the independent Bible churches rely almost entirely on biblical testimony, while the majority of Christian churches draw more substantially on theological traditions and data from the empirical and social sciences. Roman Catholic teachings on sexuality are developed from a natural law perspective interpreted by a teaching authority (magisterium) of the Pope and bishops. The role and function of professional theologians in this process has been a source of tension in recent years. This tension surfaced most prominently in the case of Charles Curran, a professor of theology at the Catholic University of America. In 1987, after several years of correspondence between Curran and the Vatican over his views on several issues including homosexuality, the Vatican declared that Curran was not fit to teach as a Catholic theologian at the University in Washington because his views differed from those of the Catholic hierarchy. Concerned bishops and theologians are seeking ways to promote a more balanced and healthy form of cooperation between theologians and the magisterium. While the exact role for theologians in contributing to the articulation and development of church teaching has been acknowledged by the Pope and bishops, U. S. lay Catholics are also asking for greater consultation and participation in the formulation of church beliefs and decision making (Fox, 1987). Cahill (1983) has pointed out that only through a balanced interaction and consideration of all of these sources and even others, as Maguire (1979) noted, can we come to a fuller expression of truth.

Krody (1979) and Blix (1979) have indicated many of the issues that confront the churches in studying homosexuality. Krody wrote:

> A central concern in the religious debate on human sexuality is the issue of biblical authority and interpretation. Persons who hold to an inerrant view of the Bible will not be likely to come to the same conclusions as those who accept biblical "higher criticism." Tradition holds a much more important place in some churches than others. For some, only the scripture and tradition are to be used as norms; for others empirical scientific data and personal experience take precedence over what are seen to be culturally bound interpretations of the Bible and church history. The moral absolutist's rules and regulations do not square with the situation ethicist's approach to individual decision making. These issues will not be resolved between those at the extremes, although there seems to be some consensus developing in the broad middle ground of the Christian faith. (p. 129)

It will be helpful for us to review briefly some of the major studies produced by various church bodies to see how this consensus might be developing and to exemplify some of the diversity evident among mainline Christian denominations.

In 1969, the United Church of Christ (UCC) published *The Same Sex* as the first church-related collection of essays on homosexuality that allowed gay and lesbian Christians to speak for themselves (Weltge, 1969). In 1972, the UCC became the first Christian denomination to ordain an openly gay candidate, William Johnson, for ministry. While only a small part of the UCC's (1977) study of human sexuality deals with homosexuality, Blix (1979) wrote that "as a survey of human sexuality, in light of the Christian faith, it is unsurpassed" (p. 4). In its study, the UCC moved beyond viewing homosexuality in isolation to consider it as part of the fabric of human sexuality, an approach that has in general been accepted and adopted by other studies. The UCC's treatment of the psychosexual development processes of the human person is one of the study's best summaries of contemporary research on the etiology of sexual identity.

In considering the principles of sexual morality, the study stated that love's justice requires a single standard for homosexual and heterosexual people alike. Farley (1983) more fully developed and applied this same point to homogenital expressions. The UCC principles include the beliefs that the physical expression of one's sexuality in relation to another ought to be appropriate to the level of loving commitment in the relationship, and that genital expression ought to be evaluated in terms of the basic elements of a moral decision informed by love, namely, the motive, the intention, the act, and the consequences. This is not unlike an approach which is embraced by a considerable number of revisionist theologians in the Roman Catholic community.

In 1978, the United Presbyterian Church, USA (UPC) published a report from a 19-member task force within the denomination that had been directed by the 1976 General Assembly to undertake a study of homosexuality. The issue that moved the denomination to study homosexuality was the question of ordaining homosexual candidates. The final report began with a review of current scientific findings on homosexuality in order to stress the view that the normative Scriptural teachings on any phenomenon cannot be applied unless the phenomenon itself is first identified. The biblical section of the report dealt extensively with various texts purportedly speaking of homosexuality and then offered one of the most exhaustive treatments of the problems and models of biblical authority alluded to above by Krody. The report concluded that scripture gives no clear and definitive guidance on homosexuality and suggested that all the biblical questions converge into one: "What is the relation between the ancient Israelite view of orders of creation and the Christian view of the creative, sanctifying work of the Holy Spirit?" (p. D-62).

The majority report of the UPC study included a policy statement and several recommendations urging (a) study of homosexuality throughout the denomination; (b) development of outreach programs to the gay and lesbian communities; (c) seminary admissions without regard for sexual orientation; and (d) dialogue, counseling, and support structures for gay and lesbian persons and support for civil rights. A five-member minority report included many of the same recommendations, but added a rejection of the "sin of homophobia" among Presbyterians and support for homosexual individuals who seek "reorientation" or celibacy. The General Assembly chose not to accept either report, but drafted its own compromise report that prohibited presbyteries from asking candidates for ordination about their sexual orientation. It also prohibited the ordination of an openly gay or lesbian candidate. There would be no bar to ordination in effect for celibate or closeted homosexual candidates. Glaser (1988) detailed his attempts at ordination in the Presbyterian church and his ongoing struggle to help the church respond to homosexuality.

In 1978, the Presbyterian Church US (Southern) reaffirmed their previous year's statement supporting civil rights, but also indicated their belief that homosexuality falls short of God's plan for sexual relationships. At the same time, they rejected another statement that would have labeled homosexuality a sin.

In 1977, the Disciples of Christ published a "Study Packet on Homosexuality and the Church." It began with a consideration of scripture and only later dealt with data from the sciences. In doing so, the study introduced a pronounced bias in which heterosexuality is treated as the only proper form of human sexual expression.

The Episcopal church in the United States undertook a lengthy study of sexuality and homosexuality in preparation for a 1979 General Convention and appointed a commission to study the question of ordaining homosexual candidates. One recommendation of the report stated that there should be "no barrier to ordaining those homosexual persons who are able and willing to conform their behavior to that which the Church affirms as wholesome" (Krody, 1979, p. 131). While such behavior is nowhere explicitly defined, it has generally come to mean celibacy in singleness and faithfulness or sexual exclusivity in marriage. Each year, the Episcopal General

Convention grapples with various lesbian and gay-related issues that come before it. After a resolution was adopted disallowing the ordination of self-affirming and noncelibate homosexual candidates, a minority of bishops issued a statement that they could not in conscience abide by such a regulation. In recent years several Episcopal dioceses, in task forces and mandated studies on sexuality, have raised and supported the issue of a church blessing or sanction for homosexual couples. Spong (1988) called for public and official sanction of same-sex committed relationships in the church, and Yale medievalist, John Boswell, is preparing a book for publication which reveals ancient Christian liturgies once used for the blessing of same-sex marriages and bonded friendships.

The American Lutheran Church in 1979 issued a position paper on homosexuality stating that homoerotic behavior was wrong, but that celibate homosexual people do not violate the Lutheran understanding of Christian behavior. The statement also urged local church support for gay and lesbian civil rights.

The Lutheran Church in America (LCA), in a 1970 statement titled "Sex, Marriage and Family," stated that "homosexuality is viewed biblically as a departure from the heterosexual structure of God's creation" (Lutheran Church in America, 1986, p. 1). In 1986, LCA published a study guide on homosexuality that was not intended to be a social statement, a church resolution, or any official Lutheran stance on the topic. Rather, the work was basically intended to promote dialogue in all segments of the Lutheran church family and to help the church engage in the same struggles that the committee itself had undertaken in drawing up the study. The committee concluded that it was convinced that "this church can neither condemn, nor ignore, nor praise and affirm homosexuality" (Lutheran Church in America, 1986, p. 38). According to the study, the church is in an interim situation relative to homosexuality and, far from being able to instruct the world about the meaning of homosexuality, finds itself with the world struggling to understand and to know where to praise and where to judge. At its 1987 convention, the LCA determined that the local synodal authorities should deal individually with the particular issue of ordaining homosexual candidates.

Recently, Lutherans Concerned, an unofficial Lutheran caucus for lesbian and gay issues, published "A Call for Dialogue," noting that homosexuality is often regarded as "one of the most divisive issues to face the church in this generation" (Lutherans Concerned, 1985, p. 1). The statement also expressed disappointment at the lack of pastoral and theological discussion of homosexuality among Lutherans, and pointed out that churches have issued authoritative statements about a significant minority of people in their midst "with little significant or intentional participation of the people whose lives are involved" (p. 1). The "Call for Dialogue" was intended to generate more lively interest and moral debate in the Lutheran family and outlined two essentially incompatible views of homosexuality. One view sees heterosexuality alone as divinely willed and homosexuality as a reflection of the flawed and broken nature of the world after the Fall. The second view unreservedly sees that the homosexual orientation has a causality totally apart from the willful disobedience of the human family or the choice of any individual; rather, the homosexual orientation is to be understood as still another facet of the complexity of God's created order.

American Baptists have urged their members to engage in fellowship, study, and action with homosexual people, but have denied, at least in one case, ordination to a gay candidate. American Baptists Concerned, a gay and lesbian caucus, has been denied official recognition, and a 1988 resolution of the Southern Baptist Convention, after ten minutes of debate, condemned homosexuality as an abomination in the eyes of God, a perversion of divine standards and a violation of nature. At the Baptist Church's 1987 Biennial convention, a right to life group within the church circulated a petition in an attempt to amend a convention AIDS statement. The amendment stated that the Scriptures repeatedly depict homosexuality as a social and moral evil, and affirmed the historic teaching of the Christian church that the unrepentant homosexual has no claim to full acceptance in the Christian community. The statement also expressed concern that those who hold such biblical views have not always succeeded in presenting them in a way that demonstrates the deeply sacrificial love of Christ. In the end, however, the statement on homosexuality failed to pass by a vote of 474 to 408, with 71 abstentions.

In 1976, the United Methodist Church adopted as official policy the statement that because the practice of homosexuality is incompatible with Christian teaching, self-avowed, practicing homosexual people are not to be accepted as candidates, ordained as ministers, or appointed to serve in the United Methodist Church. This decision was also reaffirmed in strong language at 1984 convention. In 1987, Rosemary Denman, a lesbian minister who came out publicly in 1985 while on leave from her parish, was asked to choose one of three alternatives: quietly withdraw from the ministry, allow church authorities to vote on whether or not she should remain, or face an ecclesiastical trial. She chose the third option as a way of educating others on the topic. After an official ecclesiastical trial, she was suspended from her ministry for less than a year, but subsequently she decided to transfer her church affiliation to the United Church of Christ. In 1988 delegates to the United Methodist Church's legislative General Conference reaffirmed their denomination's ban on ordaining self-avowed practicing homosexuals.

Other churches, such as the Moravian, the Friends, and the Unitarian Universalist Association, not only have voiced official and strong support for lesbian and gay people in the area of civil rights, but also have endorsed same-sex genital expression as fully compatible with Christian morality and human sexuality. Not surprisingly, many Evangelical, Pentecostal, and smaller, independent Bible churches remain adamantly and vociferously opposed both to homogenital behavior and to any support for societal or ecclesial recognition of what they see as a moral or psychological evil and a serious threat to family values.

The Greek Orthodox Church officially condemns homosexuality in all forms as sinful, a perversion of human sexuality, and an illness in need of medical attention.

The major Roman Catholic study on human sexuality came not from the U.S. Catholic hierarchy, but from a committee of the Catholic Theological Society of America (CTSA). The report, accepted by the CTSA's Board after spirited debate, was strongly criticized by both Vatican authorities and the Doctrinal Committee of the National Conference of Catholic Bishops. It was, however, overwhelmingly endorsed by the majority of mainstream Catholic theologians (Kosnik, Carroll, Cunningham, Modras, & Schulte, 1977). In its most innovative move, the study's authors replaced creative growth for integration as the chief purpose or basic finality of sexual intercourse, as opposed to the procreative and unitive dimension that classical Roman Catholic doctrine teaches. In discussing homosexuality, the authors delineated four possible approaches. Homogenital acts are (a) intrinsically evil, (b) essentially imperfect, (c) to be evaluated in terms of their relational significance, (d) essentially good and perfect. The study opted for the second and third stances as most compatible with the view of human sexuality the authors advanced in other sections of the work dealing with tradition, biblical data, historical developments, and scientific information.

A pastoral plan for lesbian and gay ministry in the Archdiocese of San Francisco broke new ground in official Catholic thinking (Senate of Priests, 1983). The document insisted that homosexuality can be adequately addressed not only by considering church teaching, but also by incorporating the results of the modern social sciences and the real lived experiences of homosexual people themselves. For the first time, official Catholic teaching denied that the homosexual orientation is necessarily a form of truncated sexual development. More importantly, the plan also described homosexuality as a building block rather than a stumbling block in a person's search for unity and harmony. Although it repeated in more nuanced terms the traditional prohibition of homogenital expression, it also recognized that many homosexual people experience their sexuality as right and good. It warned that an attempt to formulate a realistic plan of ministry for homosexual people cannot either deny or disregard those feelings, and that a sensitive minister will help gay and lesbian people respect their inner secret core.

Another major Catholic document also appeared in 1983. The Catholic bishops of the state of Washington issued a lengthy statement on prejudice and church ministry. This document, devoted primarily to a treatment of the moral evil of antihomosexual prejudice and discrimination, frankly argued that the church needs to rethink and redevelop its teachings on homosexuality. In suggesting various ways to combat discrimination and prejudice, the statement proposed that the church can foster "ongoing theological research and criticism, with regard to its own theological tradition on homosexuality, none of which is infallibly taught" (Washington State

Catholic Conference, 1986, p. 53). Nugent (1987) detailed some of the advances that have been made in Roman Catholic teaching over the past several years, and Gramick (1987) focused on the social discrimination experienced by lesbian women in the Catholic church.

The Vatican's Congregation for the Doctrine of the Faith (1986) issued a document on the pastoral care of homosexual persons. While not coming directly from the Pope and certainly in no way an infallible statement, the letter to the Catholic bishops of the world contained restatements of traditional Catholic teaching and other social and psychological comments that evoked serious criticisms from many quarters. The letter was seen by many as an attempt to halt more progressive developments on the issue of homosexuality in some Catholic circles, notably in the U.S. Not surprisingly, it reiterated the traditional condemnation of homogenital behavior as an "instinsic moral evil." The document also described the homosexual inclination or condition as an "objective disorder." Reaction to the letter was widespread and generally negative (Gramick & Nugent, 1988). Apologists for the letter attempted to put it into perspective by accenting its positive elements and distinguishing between theological and sociological judgments (Quinn, 1987; Williams, 1987). In responding to Williams, Coleman (1987) argued that the Genesis story of Sodom cannot be used alone to condemn *all* forms of homogenital behavior; that Paul condemns *pederasty* and not *all* forms of homogenital activity; and that, if the orientation is connatural for some people as Aquinas taught, we must ask whether it is authentically understandable to refer to a particular individual's orientation as "disordered."

Given this brief overview of contemporary church policies and statements, we will now delineate several stances that religious bodies might take toward homosexuality and offer some critiques. We will also attempt to articulate and clarify those common issues and questions that the religions face and will have to address in the coming years if any real consensus is to develop and if any substantial modification is to occur in official positions toward homosexuality and lesbian and gay people.

ISSUES AND QUESTIONS
FOR THE CONTINUING DIALOGUE

It is our basic assumption that the dialogue on homosexuality in and among the churches will perdure and intensify in the coming years. There will be inevitable setbacks, misunderstandings, and even occasional failures in this process, but the process itself will continue, and at times breakthroughs will occur. The churches will continue to build on the small advances already made in validating the topic for public theological discourse. At one time or another, a particular denomination or group will take the lead in the discussion, probing tradition and exploring new ground, thus challenge other church bodies, who will in turn embrace the new positions, carefully or critically, or else reject them outright. Ironically enough, the October 1986 letter from the Vatican on homosexuality has as one of its unintended effects the fostering of ongoing research and exploration of many of the issues raised by contemporary scholarship in biblical studies, pastoral theology, behavioral sciences, and other related disciplines.

Assertions by the churches of views that are inaccurate, unproved, or unconvincing, no matter how well-intentioned, will continue to be scrutinized closely and carefully by a growing number of individuals who are dissatisfied with the repetitions of past formulas that command little credibility among lesbian and gay people and other critical church members. This is not to say that both lesbian and gay church members and their supporters will not have to continue their own struggle to have their concerns included on the agendas of the church bodies. Sustained efforts will be necessary if a moral debate among the churches is to be part of the ecumenical enterprise and if the debate will be given the adequate resources and personnel that the topic requires. There is a danger even among liberal church groups that this will not happen.

McNeill (1987), for example, commented on the curious absence of serious debate on homosexuality among American churches. He ascribed it to a therapeutic mentality that is uncomfortable with moral arguments about rightness and wrongness and that prefers instead to embrace a pluralism that stresses the uniqueness of the individual. The therapeutic approach concludes that there is no common moral ground and no publicly relevant morality. Moral debate generally leads to conflicts or coercion. Many gay and lesbian people themselves warmly welcome the therapeutic approach, a live and let live mentality, that for them is more satisfying than the moralistic condemnations and inflexible ethical standards that have been their lot until recently. McNeill (1987) argued that:

> [the] mainline Protestant churches . . . share the therapeutic mentality. In the place of the moral question, Is this right or wrong? they pose the therapeutic question, Is this going to work? The liberal churches tend to assert individual autonomy and freedom, and the right to do your own thing. However, this therapeutic attitude is usually accompanied by an institutional search for compromise on moral issues. (p. 244)

The more conservative and fundamentalist groups are also reluctant to engage in a moral debate about homosexuality, but for much different reasons. These groups believe that they have direct, clear, and unambiguous revelation of God's will in scripture regarding homosexuality. This position is in turn supported by a conservative acceptance of cultural norms in the area of human sexuality. The magisterium or teaching authority in the Roman Catholic community, especially after the 1986 Vatican letter on homosexuality, seems much less willing to participate in any substantial discussion on homosexuality. But, as in the Protestant churches, there are various theological and pastoral positions within Roman Catholicism that are already engaged in a limited but vigorous debate on homosexuality, and the dissent that the Vatican faces in the U.S. Catholic community on several sexual issues does include homosexuality. That dissent seems unlikely to be terminated by the Vatican letter. Even after its publication, Genovesi (1987) continued to present cautiously, but persuasively, dissenting theological positions. Indeed, the letter itself provided some grounding for such developments when it suggested that the document was not an exhaustive treatment of the topic and that what is required of church ministers is "attentive study, active concern and honest, theologically well-balanced counsel'' (Congregation for the Doctrine of the Faith, 1986, par. 2).

In this final section, using Nelson's (1977) model, we shall attempt to outline several contemporary church positions on homosexuality that generally cross denominational lines. A critical approach to each of these positions is necessary if the public debate on homosexuality in the churches is to promote a discernible theological and pastoral consensus in the coming years. Some of these positions are spelled out rather clearly as the articulated official position or teaching of one denomination or another. Others reflect more a particular theologian or school of theology. Still others present more comprehensive and even radical challenges to traditional understandings of human sexuality.

Rejecting-Punitive View

The rejecting-punitive view sees both homogenital expression and the homosexual condition/orientation as sinful and prohibited by God. This judgment relies heavily on biblical texts that are traditionally understood as clearly and unequivocally condemning homosexuality. Extremist representatives of this position also cite the biblical sanctions that impose the death penalty for homosexuality, although mostly as proof of their conviction that it is a moral evil. Some extreme fundamentalists have been known to endorse publicly the death penalty for homosexual people, and the ''AIDS as God's punishment'' argument is a thinly disguised version of the same. The general pastoral approach of this stance is to urge individuals to acknowledge their sinfulness, renouncethe evil of homosexuality, experience a spiritual conversion, and change from homosexuality to heterosexuality by spiritual healing if not through psychological means. Refusal or inability to do one or the other can result in expulsion from the denomination, as is the case with Mormons.

Kelsey (1983) believed that although no living theologian publicly defends this extreme view, and the mainline churches have moved away from it in their formal statements, ''this probably is still the most common view, at least implicitly, in the actual practice of most church members'' (p. 9). Over the centuries this view has certainly received support from the policies and practices of religious groups, whose response to homosexual people has included stoning, burning, ostracism, imprisonment, banishment, and even torture or sexual mutilation as punishments or cures for homosexuality.

The primary challenge to this position concerns the use of the Bible as an authoritative source for moral and ethical norms. One can ask the historical questions "What exactly do the biblical passages condemn and what do the ancient texts say?" The theological question that follows is "How should what these texts say bear on contemporary Christian judgments on homosexuality?" Supposing that the biblical writers knew nothing of the distinction between homosexuality as a sexual identity/orientation and homosexual behavior, we might say that what is condemned are homogenital expressions and not the orientation. We can also ask the question whether homogenital acts are rejected precisely because they are homogenital, or because they are related to other prohibited behaviors such as rape, temple worship, or idolatry. Scroggs (1983) and Edwards (1984), for instance, argued that the Jewish scriptures are irrelevant to the contemporary discussion on homosexuality because they are not describing what is known today as constitutional homosexuality. It is not clear, then, that homosexuality *as such* is being declared intrinsically evil by all relevant texts of the Bible.

The Levitical judgment on homosexuality as an "abomination" means that homogenital acts rendered one unholy in relationship to cultic activities. Many acts rendered individuals defiled or stained and therefore unfit to take part in certain activities. Again, the context for the condemnation is cultic practices. The theological question that arises is, as Kelsey (1983) framed it, "Is what the Holiness Code means by 'unclean' in connection with the cult, the same as what we mean by 'sinful' in connection with discipleship?" (p. 10). Can contemporary Christians who do not relate to God through Israel's cultic practices still continue to hold fast to a judgment that condemns all homogenital acts as absolutely sinful in whatever context?

The rejecting-punitive stance argues that one must adopt and reassert what biblical texts say is God's command, namely, that homosexuality must be rejected and punished. Yet even its adherents adopt and reassert biblical texts selectively or based on certain criteria. They have discarded, for whatever reason, many of the prohibitions listed in Leviticus, such as the dietary laws. Some principle of selection is used by even the most fundamentalist interpreters to decide what is binding and what is not. It is simply not enough to quote the Bible to settle the question; one must argue theologically for this or that principle of selection that guides the decision to maintain, modify, or drop biblical commands.

Rejecting-Nonpunitive

The rejecting-nonpunitive position rejects homogenital *acts* but not homosexual *persons*. Homogenital acts are condemned as contrary to human nature. In Roman Catholic teaching, they are described as "intrinsically evil" because sexual intercourse (which can be morally good only in marriage) is ordained for the two purposes of union with the beloved and procreation. By their very nature, or "intrinsically," homogenital acts preclude the possibility of procreation, and are, therefore, an inordinate or wrongly ordered use of the sexual faculty conceived of basically as a biological reality. This view relies heavily on the physical or biological differences between men and women, especially genital differentiation, to discover the meaning and purpose of human sexuality. Its proponents claim this view is also supported in the Bible, in human experience, and in the theological traditions of particular denominations. A more contemporary and personalistic version of this argument builds on the physical differences to argue for an innate complementarity between male and female that extends into the psychological and spiritual realms (Durkin, 1983). Hannigan (1988) rejects both the intrinsic connection between sexual intercourse and procreation, which the magisterium holds, and the assumption of the revisionist theologians that homosexual people have an a priori right to sexual pleasure and intimacy. He holds that the ritual enacted in heterosexual intercourse is a two-in-one flesh unity that has its created basis in the physical and biological complementarity of male and female.

The pastoral response of this stance to homosexual persons includes reorientation where possible, or a life of complete sexual abstinence supported by prayer, self-discipline, spiritual counseling, and other religious aids. The sexual drive and energies are to be sublimated in a healthy way in pursuit of service to God and others. The formation of one to one stable relationships with other gay or lesbian individuals is possible provided there is no ongoing genital expression. Where this occurs periodically, provided the persons involved are genuinely but gradually striving to reach the ideal of a celibate relationship, there is no need to break off the relationship; such physical expression can be supported and nourished for its positive values to the human growth of the people involved.

Challenges to this position concern use of the biblical texts and a certain concept of human nature that the position seems to require if it is to be convincing. Methodologically this view evaluates the morality of homosexual genitality on the basis of a *biological* analysis of heterosexual intercourse. Noonan (1965) showed how Aquinas used the physical act of insemination to distinguish natural from unnatural sexual acts. The bottom line for this analysis is the possibility of insemination. Those acts that promote insemination are natural and, therefore, both moral and good; those acts that impede or eliminate insemination are unnatural and, therefore, both immoral and bad. The argument here rests on whether or not one is convinced that the possibility of insemination is or should be a requirement for the moral acceptability of sexual intercourse.

Hellwig (1987) characterizes the classical myth of sexuality as one which believes that "God has created people according to a blue-print which is written in their bodies, in their anatomy; they are made to operate in a certain way, and when they operate in that way, their mission and purpose is fulfilled" (pp. 12-13). In place of what she calls the anatomical toy-maker myth, a quite different myth is gradually shifting into place. In the new myth

God creates human persons in the divine image by awakening them into freedom, self-determination, and creativity, in which they discover that they are essentially relational and that their humanity is realized in the ways they shape the earth, themselves, one another, and their societies; in this they are fulfilling and realizing the creativity of God; when they shape communities which offer liberation, happiness and fulfilling relationships to all, they fulfill the purpose of creation. (p. 13)

More recently, an attempt has been made, in response to objections from moralists arguing that sexuality ought to be judged in the context of the person and not of biological acts, to condemn homogenital behavior on the grounds that it is always destructive of human personhood. This is especially evident in the Vatican letter, which states that homosexual activity thwarts the call to a life of self-giving and confirms a disordered sexual inclination that is essentially self-indulgent. Others object to homosexual behavior because it confirms and deepens what they assume is basically an immature or arrested development lacking permanent commitment, transcendent growth, and a complimentary fulfillment found in heterosexuality. These objections are refuted by a serious consideration of available empirical studies on the psychological health and durability of same-gender relationships. They are also based on a particular psychiatric position that views homosexuality as a psychological maladjustment, a position that, in light of the policy change by the American Psychiatric Association, is open to refutation. Likewise, the pastoral solution that demands total genital-sexual abstinence has not proven successful for the majority of gay and lesbian Christians. In those cases where a healthy and viable celibate lifestyle is evidenced, religious support structures such as religious orders and lay communities are also present. To impose total sexual abstinence on an entire class of people because of their sexual identity raises serious questions about justice, the natural human right to sexuality, and the right of individuals to develop their sexuality responsibly and within a religious context. While traditional Christian teaching requires single, unmarried heterosexual people to observe sexual abstinence, in many of these cases (e.g., divorced, widowed, single), there remains at least the possibility for future bonded relationships that include genital sexuality.

Support for this position, as indicated in the Vatican letter, is claimed to come from the constant tradition of the scriptures, especially the traditional texts appearing to condemn homosexuality. This appeal, however, is made at times without proper consideration of the fuller context and meaning of the passage that scripture scholars from a variety of denominations have pointed out over the past few years. The discussion of biblical words and concepts pertaining to homosexuality continues unabated among scholars today. In referring to a discussion on the proper translation of a word in Paul's letter to the Romans that remains contested among scholars, Hays (1986) put before us two basic choices:

> Those who follow the church's tradition by upholding the authority of Paul's teaching against the morality of homosexual acts must do so with due humility . . . those who decide that the authority of Paul's judgment against homosexuality is finally outweighed by other considerations [empirical investigations and contemporary experience] ought to do so with a due sense of the gravity of their choice. (p. 211)

The key theological issue this position raises is understanding or definition of human nature. In the Catholic tradition, some developments have occurred that seem to allow for a reconsideration of the classical concept of human nature from a Thomistic philosophical approach. Thus, for example, Vatican II, in its *Pastoral Constitution on the Church in the Modern World*, declared that the objective norms of Christian morality are based on the "nature of the human person and [his] acts" (Abbott, 1966, p. 256). In stating this the Council indicated that it is important to realize that human nature or human experience is historical, relational, and diverse. Cahill (1985) claimed support from Vatican II in saying that "The human race has passed from a rather static concept of reality to a more dynamic, evolutionary one" (p. 497). Kelsey (1983) summarized it by asking:

> Is there anything about Christian faith and life, or about the disclosures of God to which they are a response, that obliges us in all self-consistency to claim that heterosexuality is a timelessly unchanging structure of human nature which the Creator intends as part of human fulfillment? (p. 10)

Those who respond yes point to the Genesis accounts of creation and argue that God's plan for sexuality clearly only includes heterosexual marriage and procreation. Authentic humanity is cohumanity that is fulfilled only in relationship with the sexual other. Those who respond no ask whether the point of Genesis 2-3 is heterosexuality or, more generally, the importance to our humanity of relationships regardless of gender. Is Genesis to be interpreted literally or more poetically? What of the thousands of years of Jewish and Christian understanding of these texts? Related to the understanding of Genesis and human nature are important and still unanswered questions about human sexuality. One of these concerns the etiology of sexual orientations. For many denominations, a crucial element of the ethical and moral reflections on homosexuality is the question of whether or not individuals have any conscious role in the shaping of their sexual orientation, and whether or not orientations can be changed or even significantly modified. The empirical questions have an important role in moral judgments, as does the experience of individual gay men and lesbian women who communicate to churches their own appreciation and understanding of their sexuality.

There is also a theological issue at stake here. Kelsey (1983) asked:

> Does Christian faith have any stake in defending the view that human nature is an unchangeable essence, a structure given by the Creator and unchanging cross-culturally and in all historical periods? And, more particularly, has it any stake in claiming that heterosexuality is part of that structure? (p. 11)

Those who argue for full acceptance of homosexuality believe that our understanding of what is normative for human beings is not found in a doctrine of unchanging created nature, but rather in a Christian life to which we are summoned as a future promise and goal rather than a past accomplishment. In religious terms, some would say that God is doing something new; part of a new, ongoing creation is found in believing, faith- and Spirit-filled homosexual Christians whose experiences, values, and decisions about their lifestyles have something positive to say to the larger church.

Qualified Acceptance Position

The qualified acceptance position holds that although a homosexual orientation including, in some cases, genital expression, can be an acceptable way of living out the Christian life, it is still somehow inferior to heterosexuality. Theologians describe homosexuality variously as imperfect, essentially incomplete, non-normative, not an ideal, and not human sexual expression at full term. All revisionist theologians ultimately arrive at some justification for homogenital expression in certain limited contexts. While homogenital expression in these contexts is not immoral, sinful, or evil, it remains nevertheless inferior to heterosexual expression. Curran (1971; 1983) is a leading exponent of this stance. In his articles, he argued that the Christian tradition has constantly taught the view that homosexuality goes against the Christian understanding of the meaning of human sexuality. While he granted that at times the tradition has been wrong, he did not think it so in this instance. He recognized the shortcomings of the Thomistic natural law approach, but contended that "it still seems to correspond to a certain human connaturality condemning homosexuality as wrong" (Curran, 1971, p. 471). He also believed that the majority of the data from the human sciences seems to point to the fact that human sexuality has its proper meaning in terms of the love union of male and female.

The acceptance of homosexuality in this light is grounded in the judgment that people do not freely choose their sexual orientation and cannot change it. Pastorally, this position accepts homogenital behavior in some contexts as not absolutely immoral. A variety of approaches are employed in justifying homogenital expression in the context of a committed, monogamous relationship in which the partners are striving for permanency and in which there is mutual growth and positive human development. This position acknowledges the reality that not everyone is capable of reaching the ideal in many areas of human existence. Thus, it may be necessary at times reluctantly to accept homosexual unions and genital expression as the only way in which some individuals can find a satisfying degree of humanization of their sexual identity. Even Malloy (1981) and Barnhouse (1977), two of the most stringent critics of homosexuality who represent the rejecting-nonpunitive position, allow for such a possibility in some cases.

As a compromise position, this stance has found its way into many church statements and recommendations, including a document from the Roman Catholic Bishops of England and Wales (Catholic Social Welfare Commission, 1980). It has proved to be a workable position, especially on the pastoral level, for many clergy and counselors. Yet it remains unacceptable to increasing numbers of gay and lesbian people as not addressing adequately or forcefully the challenges that contemporary biblical studies, the empirical sciences, and their own experience present to this stance. It leaves unproven, for example, its basic assumption that heterosexuality is necessarily the human ideal. More importantly, if the ideal of heterosexuality is utterly incompatible with one's own unique personality structure, can it really be called an "ideal"? The negative evaluation of homosexuality as a non-ideal can be a substantial violation of the rights and dignity of gay and lesbian people if the presumed thesis is incorrect. At the very least, its proponents need to remain open and sensitive to new data from the sciences and ongoing biblical studies of the issues. Furthermore, and more importantly, they must be willing to address the hard theological questions regarding human nature, ongoing revelation, and living witness of homosexual people.

Full Acceptance Position

The full acceptance position holds that homosexuality is part of the divine plan of creation, that homosexual people are present as a sign of the rich diversity of creation, and that homosexual expression is as natural and good in every way as heterosexuality. It has been argued by McNeill (1987) that if lesbians and homosexuals were to disappear, society's development toward greater humanness could be seriously endangered. He is convinced that "there is a special providence in the emergence of visible gay communities within the Christian churches at this point in history" (p. 243).

For those who represent this stance, wholesome sexuality is not to be evaluated in terms of procreation, but by the nature and quality of the relationship of the persons involved, regardless of gender.

According to one view, homosexual expressions are neutral in themselves; they become moral or immoral to the extent that they are expressive of self-giving love, capable of grounding friendship and fostering mutuality, or generating friendship that enables the partners to grow and become more fully human. The pastoral approach in this case is the encouragement of full self-acceptance and acceptance by both society and the churches. Included in church acceptance would be some form of religious ceremony for couples who wish to commit themselves to each other in a bonded covenant with the support of the faith community. Baum (1974) wrote that it is the task of homosexual people "to acknowledge themselves as such before God, accept their sexual inclination as their calling, and explore the meaning of this inclination for the Christian life" (p. 481). And McNeill (1987) in stronger language claimed:

> that the love between two lesbians or two homosexuals, assuming that it is a constructive human love, is not sinful nor does it alienate the lovers from God's plan, but can be a holy love, mediating God's presence in the human community as effectively as heterosexual love. (p. 243)

This position presents human sexuality as totally relational; sexuality is viewed solely as a way of intercommunication. From a Christian viewpoint, sexuality has traditionally required responsibility and even self-sacrifice. It is in terms of human sexuality that the love of God for humanity is couched in the scriptures. The Song of Songs is primarily an erotic love poem between two human beings utilized by the author to hint of the intensity and passion of divine love for humanity. But the question remains: Are the criteria of mutual love, faithfulness, and caring for another sufficient of themselves and as interpreted by each individual, or are they too vague and too general to be of any real help in ethical and moral evaluations of sexual expression? To claim that love makes sexual expression good is to ask a further and far more difficult question. What is authentic love?

This position also fails to address the issue of how homosexuality can be procreative or life-serving, which for all religious traditions is an important component of human sexuality. One response has been to suggest that, while homosexual couples are not biologically procreative, there are other equally important ways to be life-giving. Same-sex couples need to be generative in their relationships so that they transcend themselves in new ways and avoid the danger of self-preoccupation. Guindon (1986) has suggested that the real issue for discussion in human sexuality is not procreation but fecundity, and that all authentic human sexuality, including even celibate sexuality, must be characterized by fecundity.

A further consideration relating to the question of generativity is the fact that many homosexual couples are already rearing children from previous marriages, adopting children of their own and, in the case of lesbian women, being naturally or artificially inseminated from known or unknown donors. While these examples of child-rearing might satisfy the need some have for considering the element of procreativity in human sexuality, for others, some of them raise serious ethical concerns involving the nature of parenthood, the definition of family, and even social, moral, and legal questions. Technological advances further complicate these issues.

The issue of "recreational sex" is one that, while not included as such in any of the four positions outlined, relates in some way to the fourth stance. If homosexuality is good and natural, proponents of recreational sex would argue that homogenital behavior, like eating and drinking, can at times be valid and acceptable for purely recreational purposes without any deeper personal commitment. This approach is sometimes adopted by counselors who are trying to assist a person to accept his or her homosexuality and to express it without regret, self-pity, or guilt. It is also experienced by many gay men whose coming out and socializing processes in the homosexual culture were delayed and who seem to be making up for lost time and opportunities. Genital sex, heterosexual as well as homosexual, can be used to express a variety of feelings and emotions, some healthy and mature, others not. It can also be used simply for the purpose of obtaining satisfying pleasure and tension release, as well as for intimacy and bonding. According to the sex-for-recreation viewpoint, there are no outside claims other than the free consent of the persons involved. An argument could be made that there is always some element of the personal bonding instinct that is present in every human interaction involving genitality, at least where there is mutual agreement of the persons engaged in the expression. Indeed, some would argue that if homogenital behavior is humanly good and natural, then logically it ought not be reserved to constitutionally homosexual persons; others should be free to choose this form of sexual expression as a legitimate variant or preference in sexual relationships.

The issue of recreational sex is not taken seriously by any mainline Christian denomination, at least not as a valuable or ideal means of sexual expression. Recreational sex is criticized for having little regard for Scripture; its sole foundation for moral or ethical evaluation is a totally subjective and personal experience. There are some ethicists, however, who would be willing to look at such an experience as a therapeutic step from severely repressed sexuality to a more holistic and integrated sexuality. Others would be willing to learn from such experiences a certain erotic playfulness that could enhance sexual expression in other forms of committed sexual relationships.

CONCLUSION

The theological issues that have emerged from our outline of these four positions are all interconnected. Yet it is not simply a matter of settling one issue so that others can, in turn, be resolved and some type of general agreement be reached. How the churches evaluate homosexuality as a sexual identity will strongly influence how they minister pastorally to people and how they respond to the questions and challenges of gay and lesbian people. There are no simple answers to these very complex issues. How the churches evaluate and utilize the various sources of ethical and moral reflection (the Bible, traditions, human knowledge, human experience) will vary from group to group.

The continuing growth of the lesbian and gay social movement will have an impact upon the churches, both positive and negative. Yet one thing is certain. The struggle for clearer knowledge about human sexuality in general, and homosexuality in particular, to which so many have contributed will continue to engage both society and the churches. Consequently, it is our hope that all the questions raised in this article will be explored and developed even further. The tensions raised in the churches between homosexuality and traditional Christian beliefs and values will not, however, be resolved quickly or effortlessly.

The fishbone remains caught in the churches' collective throat and will be neither swallowed nor ejected easily or soon. But there are strong and positive signs that serious attempts are underway in all of the mainline denominations to find answers to the questions confronting the believing community. The implications of this new-found knowledge and the tentative answers arrived at will continue to call the churches to an even greater trust in God. The challenging and questioning voice of lesbian and gay believers in all denominations can prove to be a liberating presence in the church whose founder came to free people from their fears, false securities, and idols. The struggle will not be without pain and disappointment, even anger and resentment. For many, the changes will not be either substantial enough or come soon enough.

From an historical perspective, the development of the churches' teaching on marriage and family took centuries of study and thought. The testimony of personal experience, and clashes between different schools of thought, with definitions and challenges to the received position, led, in turn, to new positions and continuing evolution. Resolution of the questions of usury, slavery, religious freedom, the divine right of kings, and other social issues likewise developed gradually. No one considering any major issue that the churches face can escape this historical fact. Some believing and church-affiliated gay and lesbian people today will content themselves with being a part of this process. McNeill (1988) outlines new directions for church-affiliated lesbian and gay people and urges that the accumulated wisdom of homosexual believing people be put at the service of the church. In this way, they can sustain their religious commitments by drawing on the best of their traditions from the past, nourish their faith lives by solidarity with like-minded people in the present, and offer a significant contribution to the shaping and moulding of their churches and faith communities especially in the area of human sexuality for future centuries. Others, perhaps, will chose to explore a spirituality for themselves outside of the more traditional church groups, classical symbols, and creeds of Judaism and Christianity. While human sexuality does not constitute or exhaust the fullness of human identity or existence in its entirety, it is, nonetheless, an integral element in human and divine relationships. If a paradigm shift is occurring in the churches and synagogues, then gay men and lesbian women will have an even more important part to play in helping explore, understand and embrace that shift. If war is too important to leave to the generals, then spirituality and sexuality are too important to leave to the theologians and hierarchical leaders.

REFERENCES

Abbott, W. (1966). *Documents of Vatican two.* New York: Guild Press.

Anderson, J. D. (1986, April). PLGC-PUBC dialogue. *More Light Update, 6*(9), 1-4.

Bailey, D. S. (1955). *Homosexuality and the western Christian tradition.* Hamden, CT: Shoe String Press.

Barnhouse, R. T. (1977). *Homosexuality: A symbolic confusion.* New York: Seabury Press.

Batchelor, E. (Ed.). (1980). *Homosexuality and ethics.* New York: Pilgrim Press.

Baum, G. (1974, February 15). Catholic homosexuals. *Commonweal,* 479-482.

Blix, D. S. (1979, May-June). Homosexuality and the American churches. *Integrity Forum,* pp. 2-7.

Blue, L. (1982). Godly and gay. *Integrity Forum, 8*(2), 1-7.

Boswell, J. (1980). *Christianity, social tolerance and homosexuality.* Chicago: University of Chicago Press.

Cahill, L. S. (1983). Moral methodology: A case study. In R. Nugent (Ed.), *A challenge to love: Gay and lesbian Catholics in the church* (pp. 78-92). New York: Crossroad.

Cahill, L. S. (1985, September 20). Morality: The deepening crisis. *Commonweal,* p. 497.

Catholic Social Welfare Commission. (1980). *An introduction to the pastoral care of homosexual people.* Mt. Rainier, MD: New Ways Ministry.

Chandler, R. (1987, August 23). Americans like Pope but challenge doctrine. *Los Angeles Times,* pp. 1, 20.

Coleman, G. (1987). The Vatican statement on homosexuality. *Theological Studies, 48,* pp. 727-734.

Congregation for the Doctrine of the Faith. (1986, October 1). *Letter to the bishops of the Catholic church on the pastoral care of homosexual persons.* Vatican City: Cardinal Joseph Ratzinger.

Curran, C. (1971). Homosexuality and moral theology: Methodological and substantive considerations. *The Thomist, 30,* 447-481.

Curran, C. (1983). Moral theology and homosexuality. In J. Gramick (Ed.), *Homosexuality and the Catholic church* (pp. 138-168). Chicago: Thomas More Press.

Durkin, M. G. (1983). *Feast of love: Pope John Paul II on human intimacy*. Chicago: Loyola University Press.

Edwards, G. R. (1984). *Gay/Lesbian liberation: A biblical perspective*. New York: Pilgrim Press.

Farley, M. (1983). An ethic for same sex relations. In R. Nugent (Ed.), *A challenge to love: Gay and lesbian Catholics in the church* (pp. 93-106). New York: Crossroad.

Fox, T. (1987, September 11). U.S. laity want much greater say, yet remain loyal, NCR poll finds. *National Catholic Reporter*, pp. 1, 7-8.

Genovesi, V. J. (1987). *In pursuit of love: Catholic morality and human sexuality*. Wilmington, DE: Michael Glazier.

Glaser, C. (1988). *Uncommon calling*. New York: Harper and Row.

Gramick, J. (1987). Social discrimination of lesbians and the church. *Concilium*, *194*, 72-78.

Gramick, J., & Nugent, R. (Eds.). (1988). *The Vatican and homosexuality*. New York: Crossroad.

Guindon, A. (1986). *The sexual creators*. Lanham, MD: University of America Press.

Hannigan, J. P. (1988). *Homosexuality: The test case for Christian sexual ethics*. New York: Paulist Press.

Hays, R. B. (1986). Relations natural and unnatural: A response to John Boswell's exegesis of Romans 1. *The Journal of Religious Ethics, 14*(1), 184-215.

Hellwig, M. (1987). *The role of the theologian*. Kansas City: Sheed and Ward.

Hiltner, S. (1980). Homosexuality and the churches. In J. Marmor (Ed.), *Homosexual behavior: A modern reappraisal* (pp. 219-231). New York: Basic Books.

Jones, H. K. (1966). *Toward a Christian understanding of the homosexual*. New York: Association Press.

Kelsey, D. (1983). Homosexuality and the church: Theological issues. *Reflection*, *80*(3), 9-12.

Kosnik, A., Carroll, W., Cunningham, A., Modras, R., & Schulte, J. (1977). *Human sexuality: New directions in American catholic thought*. New York: Paulist Press.

Krody, N. E. (1979, October). Human sexuality and the Christian churches. *Ecumenical Trends, 8*(9), 129-135.

Lutheran Church in America. (1986). *A study of issues concerning homosexuality*. Division for Mission in North America.

Lutherans Concerned. (1985). *A call for dialogue*. Chicago.

McNeill, J. (1970). The Christian male homosexual. *Homiletic and Pastoral Review, 70*, 667-677, 747-758, 828-836.

McNeill, J. (1976). *The church and the homosexual*. Kansas City, MO: Sheed, Andrews & McMeel.

McNeill, J. (1987, March 11). Homosexuality: Challenging the church to grow. *The Christian Century*, 242-246.

McNeill, J. (1988). *Taking a chance on God*. Boston: Beacon Press.

Maguire, D. (1979). *The moral choice*. New York: Doubleday.

Malloy, E. (1979, June). Homosexual way of life: Methodological considerations in the use of sociological considerations in Christian ethics. *Proceedings of the Catholic Theological Society of America*, *34*, 123-140.

Malloy, E. (1981). *Homosexuality and the Christian way of life.* Washington, DC: University Press of America.

Nelson, J. (1977, April 4). Homosexuality and the church. *Christianity and Crisis*, pp. 63-69.

Noonan, J. T. (1965). *Contraception.* New York: Mentor-Omega.

Nugent, R. (1987). Homosexuality and the magisterium. *Irish Theological Quarterly*, *53*(1), 66-74.

Oberholtzer, W. D. (Ed.). (1971). *Is gay good?* Philadelphia: Westminster Press.

Pittinger, N. (1976). *A time for consent: A Christian's approach to homosexuality* (3rd ed.). London: SCM Press.

Quinn, J. R. (1987, February 7). Toward an understanding of the letter on the pastoral care of homosexual persons. *America*, *156*(5), 92-95, 160.

Rashke, R. (1976, April 6). Dignity like a fishbone lodged in the church's throat. *National Catholic Reporter*, p. 28.

Salvatorian Gay Ministry Task Force. (1974). *Ministry/USA: A model for ministry to the homosexual community.* Milwaukee: National Center for Gay Ministry.

Saslow, J. M. (1987, February 3). Hear O Israel. *The Advocate*, pp. 38-41, 44-48, 108-111.

Scroggs, R. (1983). *The new testament and homosexuality.* Philadelphia: Fortress Press.

Secor, N. A. (1969). A brief for a new homosexual ethic. In R. Weltge (Ed.), *The Same sex: An appraisal of homosexuality* (pp. 67-79). Philadelphia: Pilgrim Press.

Senate of Priests. (1983). *Ministry and homosexuality in the archdiocese of San Francisco.* San Francisco: Senate of Priests.

Soloff, A. R. (1983). Is there a reform response to homosexuality? *Judaism*, *32*, 417-424.

Spong, J. S. (1988). *Living in sin?* San Francisco: Harper and Row.

United Church of Christ, Board of Homeland Ministries. (1977). *Human sexuality: A preliminary study.* Philadelphia: Pilgrim Press.

United Presbyterian Church. (1978). *The church and homosexuality.* San Diego: The General Assembly of the United Presbyterian Church in the United States of America.

Washington State Catholic Conference. (1986). The prejudice against homosexuals and the ministry of the church. In J. Gallagher, (Ed.), *Homosexuality and the magisterium* (pp. 46-54). Mt. Rainier, MD: New Ways Ministry.

Weltge, R. W. (1969). *The same sex: An appraisal of homosexuality.* Philadelphia: Pilgrim Press.

Williams, B. (1987). Homosexuality: The new Vatican statement. *Theological Studies*, *48*, 259-277.

Wood, R. (1960). *Christ and the homosexual.* New York: Vantage Press.

Judaism and Homosexuality:
The Traditionalist/Progressive Debate

Rabbi Yoel H. Kahn, MAHL

San Francisco

SUMMARY. This article critically reviews modern Jewish teaching on Judaism and homosexuality. The historical prohibition of homosexual acts is grounded in a world-view that views heterosexuality as natural and heterosexual marriage as the only route to religious and personal fulfillment. Progressive Jews have begun in recent years to question the underlying premises of traditional Jewish teaching on sexuality. Employing the categories of covenant theology and applying the interpretative methodology of liberal Judaism, the author argues for the valuation of the person as homosexual as a legitimate expression of human and Jewish covenantal obligation.

Any discussion of Judaism and homosexuality must begin with an acknowledgement of the unequivocal condemnation of homosexuality by the Jewish religious tradition. In fact, some authors view the very discussion of the topic as evidence of the influence of licentious Western values on the Jewish religious community (Spero, 1979). Relying on the Talmudic statement, "Jews are not suspect of such a practice" (Kiddushin 82a), they have attributed the paucity of Jewish commentary, both ancient and modern, to the allegedly low incidence of homosexuality among Jews.

Yoel H. Kahn was ordained at Hebrew Union College-Jewish Institute of Religion in 1985. He is rabbi of Congregation Sha'ar Zahav, 220 Danvers St., San Francisco, CA 94114.

Correspondence may be sent to the author at the above address.

47

The very scarcity of halakhic (i.e., Jewish legal) deliberations on homosexuality, and the quite explicit insistence of various halakhic authorities, provide sufficient evidence of the relative absence of this practice among Jews from ancient times down to the present. (Lamm, 1974, p. 381)

While a great deal has been written by gay and lesbian Jews about their personal experiences and the relationship between their gay and Jewish identities, formal discussion of Judaism and homosexuality by scholars and Jewish leaders has been isolated.[1] Three major periodicals have published symposia, beginning with the *CCAR Journal*, the major journal of the Reform movement, in 1973 (in conjunction with the first application of a gay-outreach synagogue for membership in the national synagogue body), the nonsectarian *Judaism* in 1983, and *Reconstructionist*, the publication of the Reconstructionist movement, in 1985. The most widely read and frequently quoted articles were written within close proximity: Solomon Freehof's (1973) responsum on a gay and lesbian synagogue (the lead article of the 1973 *CCAR Journal* symposium) and Norman Lamm's "Judaism and the Modern Attitude Towards Homosexuality" (1974). Both view the claim that homosexuality is a legitimate expression of human personhood as "a symbol of the whole contemporary ideological polemic against restraint and tradition" (Jakobovitz, 1973, p. 861).[2]

The majority of contemporary writers insist that homosexuality must remain, in Lamm's words, "Jewishly unacceptable." By and large, they differentiate between homosexuality and the proper stance the Jewish community should assume toward homosexuals. They would grant civil rights and legal protection to the homosexual *as person*. The homosexual person is welcome to worship in or become a member of the synagogue, they say. However, Orthodox and many Conservative and Reform thinkers—as well as secular Jews (Weiss-Rosmarin, 1986)—cannot accept the call for validation of the *person as homosexual* because of the apparently irreconcilable contradictions between being gay or lesbian and traditional Jewish teaching and expectations.[3] Equality and protection, therefore, are extended in all spheres that are regulated by the secular authorities, up to and including private, consenting sexual acts; in the religious sphere, any acknowledgement or legitimacy is denied. In Moshe Spero's (1979) words, homosexuality "destroys the individual's ability for ontological fulfillment in the halakhic world" (p. 59). Spero and others object to the establishment of synagogues with a special outreach to gay and lesbian people because such synagogues confer the affirmation and communal approval that they believe must be withheld. The sanctification of same-sex unions is considered to be the ultimate symbol of legitimacy and acceptance and, accordingly, is rejected. Only the most liberal authors will even entertain the question of such unions or the possibility of leadership roles for openly lesbian and gay Jews.

TRADITIONAL SOURCES AND INTERPRETATION

The prohibition on homosexual relations in halachah (traditional Jewish law) is based on the explicit prohibitions of Leviticus 18:22 and 20:13. Certain narrative passages are also associated by traditional Jewish commentators with homosexual acts, including Gen. 9:22, 19:5, 39:1 and Judges 19. While only male sexual relationships are identified biblically, later talmudic law extends the prohibition to women as well. The prohibitions are codified in Maimonides' authoritative 12th-century work, the *Mishneh Torah*.ᐟ Maimonides distinguishes between male homosexual acts, which are capital crimes, and female homosexual acts, which are merely "obscene." This distinction, I believe, reflects the biblical and rabbinic concern with *shefichat zerah* (the prohibition on spilling of semen). Although some modern scholars have suggested that the Levitical prohibitions refer to idolatrous cult prostitution, and the transgressions of Sodom and Gomorrah to a violation of the ancient Near Eastern code of hospitality (Umansky, 1985), the consistent interpretation of Jewish law since biblical time has been against such an understanding.

Detailed accounts of the historical development of Jewish teaching on homosexuality have appeared in English (Lamm, 1974; Spero, 1979; Gordis, 1978; Schwartz, 1979), and we will not review them here. Instead, we shall limit this essay to the recent discussion of these traditional sources and their contemporary application.

The most widely known article is "Judaism and the Contemporary Attitude Towards Homosexuality," by Norman Lamm (1974).[5] First published in the *Encyclopedia Judaica Yearbook* in 1974, it has since been widely reprinted and quoted. The article reflects an Orthodox Jewish perspective, especially in relation to the eternality and authority of traditional Jewish law. Lamm's firm rejection of homosexuality has been influential throughout the Jewish community.

After reviewing the historical sources, Lamm (1974) suggested three reasons why the condemnation of homosexuality is part of "immutable divine law": (a) it frustrates the divine intent of sexuality to promote procreation, (b) it undermines the family, and (c) it is anatomically and biologically unnatural (pp. 197-198).

After advancing these three rational possibilities for the prohibition, Lamm (1974) extended the source of the condemnation to a prior, transrational source. He claimed that the biblical text's use of "abomination" removed the act from the realm of human analysis and placed it in an absolute category that precedes our judgment:

> It may be . . . that an act characterized as an abomination is *prima facie* disgusting and cannot be further defined or explained. Certain acts are considered *to'evah* (abomination) by the Torah, and there the matter rests. It is, as it were, a visceral reaction, an intuitive disqualification of the act, and we run the risk of distorting the biblical judgment if we rationalize it. *To'evah* constitutes a category of objectionableness *sui generis*: it is a primary phenomenon. (p. 198)

This argument is intended to preclude the common practice in liberal Judaism of investigating the historical circumstances that produced the original law. Lamm's position on homosexuality is rooted in an Orthodox world-view that teaches that divine law, as understood through the halachah, is immutable and, ultimately, beyond our understanding. In contrast to liberal Jewish thinkers who hold that modern Western values should influence Jewish legal perspective (Borowitz, 1984a, 1984b), contemporary Orthodoxy stands firm in its insistence that halachah is the only source of value. Lamm would agree with Moshe H. Spero's (1979) claim that the halachah presents a view of "ontological fulfillment" within which homosexuality is untenable and unresolvable. Specifically, homosexuality conflicts with the primary religious duties of hetero-sexual marriage and bearing children.

Turning to contemporary social policy, Lamm (1974) reviewed four possible Jewish attitudes, which he characterized as repressive, practical, permissive, and psychological. The repressive position begins with the statement: "Pederasts (sic) are the vanguard of moral malaise . . . They are dangerous to children. . . ." Those who support this position call for imprisonment of all homosexuals. Lamm rejected this position on practical grounds, arguing that the law could never be fairly applied, that it would discriminate against one group of sexual offenders to the exclusion of others (e.g., adulterers), and that it is not reasonable and appropriate to apply biblical standards of punishment (e.g., the death penalty) to all violators of biblical law today. Nowhere did he disagree with the premises of this position; he only objected to the impracticality and inadvisability of its application.[6]

The second response Lamm called "practical." Because laws forbidding homosexuality are unenforceable, and imprisonment for homosexual acts alone causes people who enter prison mildly attracted to other men to exit as "confirmed criminals," all legal strictures should be abolished. Lamm objected to the "practical" solution because:

> Jewish law places us under clear moral imperatives over and above penological [considerations while the] very practicality of this position leaves it open to the charge of evading the very real moral issues, and for the Jew the halakhic principles, entailed in any discussion of homosexuality. (p. 198)

Lamm (1974) concluded that the laws prohibiting homosexual acts should remain on the books, as a statement of societal disapproval, but, by universal consent, be unenforced: "Since capital punishment is out of the question, and since incarceration is not an advisable substitute, we are left with one absolute minimum: strong disapproval of the proscribed act" (p. 204).

Lamm's strongest words were reserved for the permissive liberals. He rejected outright the suggestion that sexual freedom is a right derived from the individual's autonomy:

> If every individual's autonomy leads to lend moral legitimacy to any form of sexual expression he may desire, we must be ready to pull the blanket of this moral validity over almost the whole catalogue of perversions described by Krafft-Ebing, and then, by the *legerdemain* of granting civil rights to the morally non-objectionable, permit the advocates of buggery, fetishism or whatever to proselytize in public. In that case, why not in the school system? And if consent is obtained before the death of one partner, why not necrophilia or cannibalism? Surely, if we declare pederasty (sic) to be merely idiosyncratic and not an "abomination" what right have we to condemn sexually motivated cannibalism — merely because most people would react with revulsion and disgust? (p. 197)

Nor was he willing to acknowledge that societal oppression alone is sufficient basis for changing religious law:

> Homosexuality imposes on one an intolerable burden of differentness, of absurdity, and of loneliness, but the biblical commandment outlawing pederasty (sic) cannot be put aside solely on the basis of sympathy for the victim of these feelings. (p. 201)

Adopting a psychological view, Lamm concluded that homosexuality should be considered a form of illness. Although this attitude reflected the general popular understanding of homosexuality at the time the article was written, it was already being increasingly discredited by professionals. In support of his analysis of homosexuality as illness, Lamm quoted from sources that are now themselves considered homophobic and unreliable.[7] Ultimately, Lamm was perhaps willing to extend sympathy to those "genuine" homosexuals who are "addicted to this illness," but it remains a "perversion" and, he insisted "under no circumstances can Judaism suffer homosexuality to become respectable" (p. 204).

Moshe H. Spero agreed with Lamm, if in a calmer tone, in Spero's 1979 article, "Homosexuality: Clinical and Ethical Challenges." Written for an Orthodox journal, his article discussed psychotherapy for homosexuals from an Orthodox perspective. While exhibiting little of the homophobia and prejudice about homosexual practices so common in other sources, Spero relied upon outdated and discredited sources to advocate therapy to change a homosexual orientation. Spero, along with other Orthodox-identified thinkers (Lamm, 1973; Novak, 1978, 1986), posited a fundamental Jewish world-view, based on halachah, whose values are divinely inspired, unchangeable and unresolvably incompatible with homosexuality. According to Spero, homosexuality "destroys the individual's ability for ontological fulfillment in the halakhic world." Against the contemporary backdrop of changing sexual values, Spero, like Lamm, argued for the absolute and transcendent truth of the halachah. In those cases when modern psychology and Jewish tradition present different etiologies of human behavior, the halachic takes precedence. Spero explained: "Halakhah's obligations to society and the individual are not relativistic and must be understood as reflecting a higher understanding of human nature" (p. 69).

The sexually active homosexual is a sinner in the eyes of the halachah, explained Spero, and may feel guilty as a consequence. The experience of such "non-neurotic religious guilt" is appropriate under these circumstances, and, according to Spero, should in fact be encouraged by the therapist. Addressing himself to other observant therapists, Spero characterized any attempt to treat homosexuality as a normal sexual preference as a violation of the biblical commandment: "Do not place a stumbling block before the blind" (Lev. 19:14), that is, a deliberate act of leading people astray in a religious matter.[8]

Walter Wurzburger (1983) suggested that the halachah itself already recognizes homosexuality as an illness and incorporates this interpretation in its standards:

> [In] contrast with our permissive culture, Judaism categorically rejects the notion that homosexuality constitutes a "legitimate alternate life-style" . . . Judaism unequivocally proscribes homosexual *practices*, but does not blame individuals for being afflicted with pathological homosexual preferences. What is frowned upon by the halakhah is the indulgence in homosexual acts—not the experience of sexual preferences. (p. 425)

While sidestepping the etiology of sexual preference, Wurzburger argued that the situation of the "unchangeable" homosexual is already adequately accounted for in Jewish law:

> Individuals with homosexual preferences are encouraged by the *halakhah* to practice self-control and to restrain whatever urges cannot be legitimately satisfied . . . Since Judaism opposes sins rather than the sinner, even those who [engage in homosexual practices] . . . should be accorded the kind of sympathy and compassion which is due to all those who fail to live up to the stringent demands of Judaism. (p. 425)

For those whose ultimate arbiter is the halachah, no amount of modern scientific analysis can alter the explicit rejection of homosexual sex. Modern insights may alter our attitude toward the person who engages in the act, but the act itself is sinful:

> From the standpoint of Jewish law, this debate [about etiology] must be irrelevant; as with the Sabbath breaker or idolater, here, too, our judgment has nothing to do with the findings of psychology or medicine. Judaism does declare homosexual indulgence a sin, of which the most and the least healthy are capable. Having said so we can consider the circumstances and temper our judgment of the act with compassion for the actor. (p. 425)[9]

The earliest published discussion in the Reform movement assumes the traditional perspective.[10] In 1969, Solomon B. Freehof wrote a responsum (legal opinion) in reply to a question about what Jewish law says on the subject. Freehof quoted the well-known historical sources cited above. He concluded:

> All in all, considering how much detail there is in the law on every kind of forbidden sexual relationship, the very paucity of biblical and post-biblical law on the matter speaks well for the normalcy and the purity of the Jewish people. (p. 238)

CHANGE IN THE TRADITION

The possibility of change in the traditional Jewish attitude toward homosexuality is suggested in Herschel J. Matt's 1978 article, "Sin, Crime, Sickness or Alternative Life Style?: A Jewish Approach to Homosexuality." For many years this widely-quoted article was considered to be the liberal statement on Judaism and homosexuality.

Following a brief rehearsal of the traditional sources, Matt wrote: "It would, thus, appear absolutely clear that a Jewish approach to homosexuality must end where and as it starts: with utter condemnation and categorical prohibition" (p. 14).

Matt identified four reasons for the Jewish tradition's condemnation of homosexuality: (a) it is contrary to the "Order of Creation"; (b) homosexuality precludes reproduction; (c) it denies the possibility of a family because "only with the appearance of a second and third generation can there be a family in the full sense of the word"; and (d) "Homosexuality precludes history"—personal and social. This "denial of history" is considered detrimental to the survival of the Jewish people and therefore compromises the Covenant, God's promise of an ongoing relationship with the people of Israel (p. 15).

Reflecting the approach of the Conservative Jewish movement, with which he is most closely identified, Matt (1978) affirmed the authority of halachah but questioned

> the rationale and presuppositions of the traditional stand; and . . . whether there are now any changed circumstances or new data in the light of which the Torah's stand today—though based on the same divine and enduring concerns and purposes—might possibly involve changed formulations or different emphases. (p. 14)

Matt did not find a greater legitimacy for homosexuality because of any changed contemporary circumstances. Instead, he introduced the possibility that homosexuality is an unalterable feature of personality instead of a freely chosen sin or a mental illness." He used this information as the basis for interpreting homosexual behavior in a different halachic context from that of the received halachah.

The halachah recognizes the category of *me'ones* (constraint) as an excusing factor in circumstances beyond one's control. Though generally applied to individual actions (e.g., committing a crime under threat of punishment or temporary mental illness), Matt advocated applying this status to homosexuals as a permanent resolution of the halachic prohibition against homosexual acts. (This interpretation is also advanced by Mihaly, 1973.) Because there is no possibility of "change" to heterosexuality, the homosexual should be considered as acting *me'ones* and judged accordingly. This evaluation, explained Matt (1978), has the benefit of removing the stigma of illness without endorsing homosexuality as "equally acceptable with heterosexuality as simply an 'alternate life style'":

> The most truly Jewish stance would be one that takes with equal seriousness both the authority of traditional standards and the significance of modern knowledge. As already indicated, such a stance would maintain the traditional view of heterosexuality as the God-intended norm and yet would incorporate the contemporary recognition of homosexuality, as clinically speaking, a sexual deviance, malfunctioning, or abnormality—usually unavoidable and often irremediable.
>
> Such an approach . . . remains faithful to the Torah-teaching that heterosexuality is, in principle, not merely recommended but commanded, and that homosexuality is not merely discouraged but forbidden . . . It removes from those homosexuals who . . . find that they cannot change, all burden of blame and guilt, accepting them as they are. (p. 20)[12]

In addition to calling for an end to prejudice and discriminatory legislation, as well as full civil rights and social acceptance, Matt (1978) went further than any other writer in endorsing the possibility of sanctified homosexual unions. Traditionalists object to Matt's resolution of the matter. In their eyes, the immutability of sexual orientation (a point not necessarily conceded) does not license acting on the "sinful behavior."

Nine years later, in an article for *Conservative Judaism* entitled "Homosexual Rabbis?," Matt (1987) went even further by rejecting his own notion that homosexuality should be tolerated only because homosexuals are acting out of uncontrollable compulsion and instead affirmed homosexuality as part of creation and the possibility of homosexuals leading full Jewish lives. In conclusion, he expressed strong support for the rabbinic ordination of gay men and lesbians. This position is discussed in full in the final section of the present article.

CIVIL BUT NOT RELIGIOUS RIGHTS

By and large, the organized Jewish community has supported efforts to guarantee civil rights and equal treatment under the law for homosexuals. In 1972, the San Francisco Board of Rabbis, representing rabbis from all three movements, voted to support the legalization of any private sexual act between consenting adults. This vote reflected the conjunction of an American social value, the right to personal privacy, with the historical Jewish concern to keep the state from imposing laws based on religious doctrine. Having supported civil rights for various minority groups throughout the last two decades, politically liberal American Jews transferred their concern to another group. As a citizen, the American Jew easily came to defend the civil rights of individual homosexual citizens, especially in the face of police harassment and other forms of oppression. The homosexual's claim for those rights that derive from the personhood of the individual is supported by the Jewish community and its communal and religious leaders.

Thus, all of the articles reviewed for the present article call for an end to unjust discrimination against homosexuals. Although Lamm (1974) insisted that the laws against homosexual relations remain on the books, he proposed that "by mutual agreement of police and prosecutors they remain unenforced" (p. 398). Most of the authors went on to call for the decriminalization of private, homosexual acts. Even after condemning homosexuality as unnatural, Robert Gordis (1978) concluded:

> [Homosexual] activity, when carried on by adults in private and violating no one's wishes and desires, should be decriminalized on the statute books. . . . The homosexual in contemporary society has a just claim to be free from legal penalties and social disabilities. (p. 157)

Despite widespread Jewish support for civil rights, however, the Jewish community has been reluctant to grant religious or communal recognition to gay and lesbian Jews. Earl Raab, Director of San Francisco's Jewish Community Relations Council, asked in a 1972 op-ed article, "At what point do we cross the line—from supporting individual rights—to bestowing society's official approval to homosexuality as an alternative life style?" (p. 25). Many rabbis and communal leaders would prefer to avoid the topic completely. So long as the homosexual engages in private activities that can be ignored, homosexuality and homosexual rights can be treated as of no concern to the Jewish community. To these leaders, the homosexual is welcome within the organized Jewish community only so long as she or he remains invisible and refrains from asking for recognition and legitimacy. The establishment and support of synagogues with a particular outreach to gay and lesbian people is held by many to provide the very social and religious approval that they believe must be withheld. Although the right of the homosexual *as person* to enjoy civil rights is readily granted, the validation of the person—and Jew—*as homosexual* is withheld.

DEBATE WITHIN THE REFORM MOVEMENT

The earliest Reform Jewish statement on Judaism and homosexuality is Solomon Freehof's 1969 responsum which upholds the halachic view of homosexual behavior as sinful. Wider discussion within the movement began in 1972 with the application of Beth Chayim Chadashim, the gay and lesbian-outreach synagogue of Los Angeles, for membership in the UAHC. In conjunction with its application, the *CCAR Journal*, the periodical of the movement, published a symposium on "gay synagogues." At this time Solomon Freehof (1973) wrote a second responsum answering the question: "Is it in accordance with the spirit of Jewish tradition to encourage the establishment of a congregation of homosexuals"?[13] This somewhat lengthier essay was first published as part of the symposium in the *CCAR Journal* and independently in the *CCAR Yearbook* (1973). It has been widely quoted since.

Freehof's responsum was similar to Lamm's (1974) article. He focused on the biblical characterization of homosexuality as an abomination. "If scripture calls it an abomination, it means that it is more than violation of a mere legal enactment; it reveals a deep-rooted ethical attitude" (p. 50). Homosexuals "are to be deemed sinners" and homosexuality "runs counter to the *sancta* of Jewish life" (p. 50). Arguing that "sinners" of any stripe are welcomed unquestioningly into all synagogues, Freehof objected to a gay/lesbian congregation under any circumstances, declaring it "forbidden to force them into a separate congregation." Similarly, a 1974 CCAR *ad hoc* Committee on Homosexual Congregations urged "homosexuals (to) affiliate with existing family-oriented congregations" (p. 28) and that the UAHC not accept homosexual congregations to membership (Stern, 1974).[14]

> [The committee] drew a major distinction between the necessity to offer a place to every Jew, whatever his lifestyle, within the fellowship of a congregation, and the act of granting official recognition and sanction to a congregation which includes homosexuality as part of its congregational self-identification. (Stern, 1974, p. 27)

Others learn the responsibility to reach out towards homosexuals from the historical experiences of the Jewish people. Sanford Ragins (1973), rabbi of the synagogue that provided Beth Chayim Chadashim its first home, compared the Jewish experience of intolerance and oppression to the parallel homosexual experience. Ragins found through an ethical consideration a religious imperative for accepting homosexuality. Ragins (1973) calls for a response to contemporary oppression of gay people that is informed by the historical Jewish experience of discrimination, and insists that a heightened sensitivity to homosexuals' calls for justice and liberation must take precedence over the traditional Jewish teaching. "Our heritage is not limited to . . . the Book of Leviticus" (p. 45).[15]

Ragins (1973) went on to defend the foundation of a congregation of homosexuals so long as homosexual Jews are made to feel unwelcome in other synagogues. He was the first to affirm that homosexuality can be a legitimate expression of Jewish and human personhood:

In principle, such a synagogue should not exist, because all synagogues should be so open that all Jews may feel fully welcome and at home in them. . . . Until the temples we already have are able to accept Jewish homosexuals *in their homosexuality*, as they are and not as we would want them to be, homosexuals who want their own congregations should not only be allowed to have them, but encouraged and assisted. . . . (p. 45)

The General Assembly of the UAHC voted to accept Beth Chayim Chadashim's application for membership and since then three additional gay and lesbian outreach synagogues have joined the UAHC.

In 1975, the UAHC passed a resolution calling for full civil rights for homosexuals in the civic sphere. A proposed 1976 CCAR resolution calling for non-discrimination against homosexuals in society in general, and Reform Jewish religious organizations in particular, was referred to a newly appointed committee. The final version of the resolution, adopted the following year, deleted the proposed text's explicit call for non-discrimination within Jewish communal and Reform organizations. In addition, language calling for an end to "discrimination against (homosexuals) because of their sexual orientation" was replaced with a call to end "discrimination against them as persons" (CCAR, 1976; Kahan, 1977).

In November 1981, a group of Reform rabbis met for a Conference on Jewish Sexual Values with the purpose of developing position papers as a basis for an official policy of the Central Conference of American Rabbis. The working group on homosexuality prepared a statement declaring, "We reaffirm that sexual orientation is irrelevant to one's status as a Jew," and called for full acceptance of homosexual Jews in the community and as rabbis and religious and communal leaders (CCAR, 1983). The draft statement was widely criticized at the plenary session of the conference and, to date, the Reform rabbinate has not adopted any official policy on homosexuality beyond its 1977 resolution on civil rights.

Rav Soloff, a member of the 1981 working group, contributed the article "Is There a Reform Response to Homosexuality?" to a 1983 symposium in *Judaism*. He concluded his article with a draft version of a Reform responsum on homosexuality. The draft noted the earlier resolution, which called for full civil rights for homosexual persons and for decriminalizing legislation. It concluded:

> [While] earlier generations spoke out of their times and cultural settings, so too we must consider the lessons of contemporary scholarship. . . . [W]e must not practice any discrimination against homosexuals as persons.
>
> We do not discriminate against Jewish persons seeking membership in our congregations on the basis of race, sex, sexual orientation, disability or handicap. We do not discriminate against them in employment. We reject the unfounded fear that the healthy sexual development of children or young adults can be jeopardized by the presence of a qualified, well-behaved adult such as a teacher, administrator, cantor or rabbi who is of any specific race, sex, sexual orientation, stage of pregnancy or limited by a disability or handicap. (p. 424)

Soloff's proposed resolution was never endorsed. In 1981, the Responsa Committee published "Homosexuals in Leadership Positions" (Jacob, 1981). After a brief review of historical sources on standards for communal leadership, the responsum concluded:

> Overt heterosexual behavior or overt homosexual behavior which is considered objectionable by the community disqualifies the person involved from leadership positions in the Jewish community. We reject this type of individual as a role model within the Jewish community. We cannot accept such an individual as a role model nor should he/she be placed in a position of guidance for children of any age. (p. 54)

The committee effectively side-stepped the question through the careful phrasing of its response. What "is considered objectionable by the community" was the only standard of behavior used. One whose behavior is "objectionable" is strongly and firmly rejected from any leadership role in the community. No effort was made to define objectionable "overt heterosexual behavior," let alone "overt homosexual behavior." It would appear that the wish of the committee was that the homosexual be accepted so long as he or she does nothing to offend the community (i.e., remains closeted). The wider question of the legitimacy of homosexuality, though, was not addressed at all.

This avoidance of the underlying question is perhaps most clearly illustrated in Walter Jacob's (1987) responsum on "Lesbians and Their Children" (1976).[16] In contrast to the responsa cited above, those in *Contemporary Reform Responsa* are not published in the name of the CCAR Responsa Committee but are Walter Jacob's own. Three of the questions in this volume are about homosexuals. The issue in "Lesbians and Their Children" concerned the status of two women who have raised a child together. "[The] child is about to be *Bar Mitzvah* and the two women want to participate in the service as any parents. Should they be permitted to do so?" (p. 297).

After reviewing the historical Jewish sources on lesbianism, the responsum stated:

> Everything we do should strengthen the family. We should therefore, ignore the lesbian relationship and feel no need to deal with it unless the individuals involved are flagrant about their relationship and make an issue of it. If they do not, then their lesbian relationship is irrelevant; it should not be recognized. They should be permitted, along with other individuals both male and female, to participate in the Torah readings as well as other portions of the Friday-evening *Shabbat* service. (p. 297)

In most congregations, the parents of the *bar* or *bat mitzvah* are given a special role in the service. The implication of the question, it would seem, is whether they can "participate in the service as any parents," for example receiving a joint *aliyah* (public honor). It is clear from the question that both women are parents to the child. Does honoring the two lesbian parents of the child with an *aliyah* constitute "recognition" of the relationship? The author treats one woman as the mother and the second as a friend of the family with no relationship to the child. Lastly, Jacob did not explain what in his eyes constitutes "flagrancy." This responsum begs the question it set out to answer.

The other responsa in the volume are about the conversion of a homosexual (1982), which Jacob permits, and about *kiddushin* (Jewish marriage) for two homosexuals (1985), which he does not. Although permitting the conversion of an openly gay or lesbian person (1982), Jacob (1987) expressed concern about the formation of a *havurah* (group) within the synagogue:

> We must ask ourselves whether it is simply for the purpose of companionship or is it a group who will seek to attract others to a homosexual lifestyle. In the case of the latter, we could certainly not accept a convert who intends to influence others in that direction. (p. 89)

This passage echoed the language of Freehof's 1973 responsum and gave credence to the long disproved and inflammatory fear that homosexuals "recruit." In fact, the author based this part of his Jewish legal opinion on a position which conflicted with the overwhelming consensus of contemporary scientific research and teaching.

Many Reform rabbis disagree with the historical Jewish attitude on homosexuality which Jacob (1987) personally advocates and considers to be the official Reform position as well. The unequivocal rejection of the halachah's teaching on homosexuality (as reflected in Soloff's proposed but unendorsed 1983 resolution) has been advocated in debate within the movement and in the sermons of individual rabbis. The placement of a student rabbi at Beth Chayim Chadashim in Los Angeles in 1976 was an important step because it introduced a generation of young rabbis to identified homosexual Jews. Numerous sermons about homosexuality have been preached at the seminaries of the Reform movement. The four gay and lesbian outreach congregations of the UAHC, two of which are served by ordained rabbis, together with the 24 other member organizations of the World Congress of Gay and Lesbian Jewish Organizations, have created further contacts between the organized Jewish community and gay and lesbian Jews. The 1985 and 1987 UAHC Biennial Convention schedules included programs designed to increase the understanding and acceptance of gay and lesbian Jews. Many similar programs have taken place at the regional and congregational level. The November 1986 issue of *Keeping Posted* magazine for high school youth was devoted to a discussion of homosexuality. In 1986, a proposed CCAR resolution banning discrimination on the basis of sexual orientation within the rabbinate was referred to committee for discussion.

At its 1987 biennial convention in Chicago, the UAHC General Assembly endorsed a resolution proposed by the Stephen Wise Free Synagogue of New York which stated that "[sexual] orientation should not be a criterion for membership or participation in an activity of any synagogue." The background statement of the resolution began with Isaiah's prophecy: "Let My house be called a house of prayer for all people" and continued: "Each of us, created in God's image, has a unique talent which can contribute to that high moral purpose (*tikkun olam*); and to exclude any Jew from the community of Israel lessens our chances of achieving that goal." The resolution called on the member congregations of the Union to:

1. Encourage lesbian and gay Jews to share and participate in the worship, leadership and general congregational life,
2. Develop educational programs in the synagogue and community which promote understanding and respect for lesbians and gays,
3. Employ people without regard to sexual orientation,
4. Urge the Commission on Social Action to bring its recommendations to the next General Assembly after considering the report of the CCAR [Central Conference of American Rabbis] Committee [on Homosexuality and the Rabbinate] and any action of the CCAR pursuant to it,
5. Recommend to the CCAR Committee on Liturgy that it develop language that is liturgically inclusive.

DEBATE IN THE CONSERVATIVE
AND RECONSTRUCTIONIST MOVEMENTS

The Reconstructionist movement had an intensive debate about homosexuality over a two-year period, culminating in a 1985 vote by the faculty of the Reconstructionist Rabbinical College in favor of an admissions policy of non-discrimination on the basis of sexual orientation. The college has not made public any report of the deliberations which led to this decision.

The Rabbinical Assembly of the Conservative movement referred an inquiry about congregations for gay and lesbian Jews to its Committee on Jewish Law, which wrote in a 1976 opinion, "No separate congregations should be established" (Schwartz, 1977, p. 27). The Committee has not publicly explained the basis of its decision.[17] Barry D. Schwartz (1977) endorsed the establishment of separate congregations, arguing that the Jewish community can support such congregations without endorsing homosexuality.

> Separate gay synagogues have been formed precisely because the homosexual has not felt comfortable in existing religious institutions. It is the opinion of this writer that as long as this condition prevails, these synagogues perform a vital religious function. We need not alienate any Jew or group of Jews who wish to gather for study and prayer . . .
>
> The homosexual should be accepted without his homosexuality being sanctioned or condemned. Accepting is not tantamount to condoning or encouraging. In receiving homosexuals openly, we need not sacrifice our traditional standards and the Jewish ideal of heterosexuality. (p. 27)[18]

THE PROGRESSIVE POSITION

The denial of homosexuality as a legitimate expression of personhood in traditional Jewish teaching shapes the response of the traditionalist position. In contrast, the progressive position affirms that the homosexual Jew can fulfill her or his covenantal obligations. We have used "progressive" in this article in opposition to "traditionalist" to characterize individuals' positions on homosexuality in relation to received Jewish teaching. Both progressives and traditionalists are found among the ranks of Reform, Conservative and Reconstructionist Jews. The remainder of this article sets out one interpretation of the progressive position.

The progressive authors have been informed by the considerable body of research and psychological insight into homosexuality that was lacking in past years. Such research addresses fundamental questions about which Jewish scholars and teachers—historically lacking accurate information—have been forced to speculate. Many of the perspectives advocated by earlier Jewish writers are based on assumptions that have come to be recognized as erroneous in the light of current knowledge. Much of the progressive Jewish critique of historical teaching and its contemporary traditionalist viewpoints on homosexuality is based on the failure of those positions to incorporate the extensive knowledge which has developed about homosexuality in recent years, particularly since homosexuals have come forth publicly in large numbers, permitting closer scrutiny of their personal lives and psychological character. The progressive position rejects the premises which have shaped traditional Jewish teaching and modern social attitudes. Its supporters reexamine the entire history of Jewish teaching from biblical times through the present in the light of contemporary scientific and humanistic teaching about human sexuality and homophobia.

Janet Marder (1985), when rabbi of Beth Chayim Chadashim in Los Angeles, described her own increasing understanding as an

> evolution from tolerance to full acceptance. I see [homosexuality] now as a sexual orientation offering the same opportunities for love, fulfillment, spiritual growth and ethical action as heterosexuality. . . .
>
> I believe, and I teach my congregants, that Jewish law condemns their way of life. But I teach also that I cannot accept that law as authoritative. It belongs to me, it is part of my history, but it has no binding claim on me. . . .
>
> The Jewish values and principles I regard as eternal, transcendent and divinely ordained do *not* condemn homosexuality. The Judaism I cherish and affirm teaches love of humanity, respect for the spark of divinity in every person, and the human right to live with dignity. The God I worship endorses loving, responsible, and committed human relationships, regardless of the sex of the persons involved.

Marder (1985) correctly observed that there is no *legal* basis for her belief within Jewish law as it exists. But, as noted above, the underlying assumptions about homosexuality that shaped the traditional position are now widely believed to be erroneous. These assumptions include: (a) heterosexuality is "natural" and homosexuality is unnatural, (b) "naturally" heterosexual people can "become" homosexual, and (c) the public approval of homosexuality will endanger heterosexual family life.

Scientists now generally believe homosexuality to be as "natural" to the human condition as heterosexuality. Because sexual orientation is a deeply rooted dimension of personality, people who are heterosexual cannot become homosexual, any more than those who are homosexual can become heterosexual. Further, because people do not become homosexual or heterosexual based on societal approval, greater acceptance of homosexuality will only remove oppression and barriers from gay and lesbian people without in any way threatening traditional institutions.

This progressive position, then, rejects the assertion that homosexuality is "against nature." The meaning of this phrase, as intended by those who use it, is not entirely clear. The concept of "nature" in Western thought is reviewed in the first chapter of John Boswell's (1980) *Homosexuality, Christianity and Social Tolerance*. The following discussion summarizes several of his key points:

Homosexuality is perceived by some as being contrary to the ordinary behavior of humans and all other animals. This assertion is not true of animals; there has been wide observation of homosexual behavior, including same-sex bonding, in a variety of different species (Boswell, 1980). However, were it to be true, then the proponents of the "unnatural" argument must claim that a behavior which is uniquely human is unnatural. In fact, virtually every species exhibits species-specific behavior which distinguishes it from all others. We do not consider such behavior to be "unnatural"; rather

> it is regarded as part of the "nature" of the species in question . . . If man were the only species to demonstrate homosexual desires and behavior, this would hardly be grounds for categorizing them as "unnatural." Most of the behavior which human societies most admire is unique to humans; this is indeed the main reason it is respected. No one imagines that human

society "naturally" resists literacy because it is unknown among other animals. (p. 12).

Most significant perhaps is the concept of idealized nature, that regardless of behavior there is a "natural" standard which is good. This is the force behind the continuing claim that homosexuality must remain *to'evah*. If by definition nature is "good" then that which is inherently bad surely is "unnatural." Boswell (1980) comments:

> Concepts of "ideal nature" are strongly conditioned by observation of the real world, but they are ultimately determined by cultural values. This is particularly notable in the case of "unnatural" which becomes in such a system a vehement circumlocution for "bad" or "unacceptable." Behavior which is ideologically so alien or personally so objectionable to those affected by "ideal nature" that it appears to have no redeeming qualities whatever will be labeled "unnatural," regardless of whether it occurs in ["real"] nature never or often, or among humans or lower animals, because it will be assumed that a "good nature" could not under any circumstances have produced it. (p. 13)

Philosophical schools which used the concept of idealized nature helped shape the bias in Western thought that all nonprocreative sexuality is "unnatural."

> Although the idea that gay people are "violating nature" predates by as much as two millennia the rise of modern science and is based on concepts wholly alien to it, many people unthinkingly transfer the ancient prejudice to an imagined scientific frame of reference, without recognizing the extreme contradictions involved, and conclude that homosexual behavior violates the "nature" described by modern scientists rather than the "nature" idealized by ancient philosophers. (p. 15)

People of faith transform this scientific debate into religious categories by substituting the term "creation" for "nature." Contemporary Jews' idealized view of the world—i.e., of creation—is not always the same as that of the ancient rabbis. Thus, beyond all of the scientific and critical arguments made in this section, the progressive argument ultimately depends on an article of faith: God does not create in vain.

REREADING THE SOURCES

Progressive Jewish teaching about homosexuality considers the historical Jewish sources, beginning with the Torah, in light of new insights about human sexuality. Biblical teaching about many matters has been radically altered by later Jewish law. Today, though, many are still reluctant to dissent from what they perceive to be an absolute moral prohibition in the Torah that has remained unaltered in its force over the generations (Kahn, 1986).

One approach to the problem of deciding what biblical legislation remains binding on subsequent generations is the distinction between "ethical" and "ritual" laws. The 19th-century founders of the Reform movement drew a distinction between laws that were "cultic or ritual" in origin and those that were considered "ethical." They deemed the ritual laws time-bound and outdated, while ethical laws were valued as the repository of the great contribution of the Judaic tradition, ethical monotheism (Borowitz, 1983). Thus, Freehof (1973) argued that the biblical prohibition of homosexuality is part of the Torah's ethical teaching and remains binding today.

The distinction between ritual and ethical acts, however, is not made in the Torah's text. It increasingly appears to be a superimposed eisegetical technique, formulated to advance the interpretation of Judaism as the religion of ethical monotheism (Petuchowski, 1970). The alleged distinction between ritual and ethical laws is not a valid distinction. The special contribution of our generation of Reform Jews is the clear teaching that ritual is inexorably connected to the ethical; each encourages and nourishes the other. Contemporary Reform Jews are more open to the ritual dimension of the Jewish religious tradition than were the 19th-century founders of the movement, and less assured of the constancy of the ethical laws the founders held so dear. It would appear that the determination of the

binding nature of biblical or traditional Jewish law cannot be determined on the basis of ethics versus ritual.

The Jewish tradition on sexuality has been as varied and subject
to change as all other aspects of biblical legislation. Further, many
modern Jews who quite freely abrogate biblical teaching about
other aspects of sexual morality, equally significant in the eyes of
the tradition and unaltered over the centuries, become fundamentalists exclusively on the topic of homosexuality. For example, the
halachic regulations on menstrual impurity, which prohibit intercourse and contact during and after menstruation and which were of
critical importance to the ancient rabbis, are ignored and deemed
irrelevant by the vast majority of contemporary Jews. Modern Jews
have not hesitated to abrogate traditional Jewish teaching about
other aspects of sexual morality. Why, then, is homosexuality
treated differently?[19]

Reform Judaism teaches that the Torah is a divinely inspired
work but, nonetheless, the product of human labor. As such, it
reflects the world-view and human understanding of a particular
culture in a particular period. As Marder (1985) explained:

> The Jewish condemnation of homosexuality is the work of hu-
> man beings — limited, imperfect, fearful of what is different,
> and, above all, concerned with ensuring tribal survival. In
> short, I think our ancestors were wrong about a number of
> things, and homosexuality is one of them. (p. 24)

Some scholars believe that the Bible's ban on homosexual relations is due, in part, to its place in idolatrous worship in the Ancient
Near East. Seeking to separate themselves from all association with
idolatry, the Israelites banned any related practice (Umansky, 1985;
Soloff, 1983). The ban might then be understood in its origin not as
an absolute moral prohibition, but instead as part of the "fence"
erected to separate Israelite practices from those of neighboring societies. This surely ought not be a basis for Jewish law today (Matt,
1987).

Traditional Jewish teaching on homosexuality is rooted in the
belief that humanity is created heterosexual, and that therefore homosexual attraction must be either a freely chosen sinful act or a

manifestation of pathology. Present knowledge shows this to be patently untrue. Moreover, progressive thinkers argue that the presumption that humankind was created heterosexual is an arrogant imposition of limits upon the Creator:

> Those of us . . . who insist that it is God's "right" to prescribe standards for human behavior in general and for Jewish behavior in particular, and who teach that heterosexual behavior is God's intended norm, must not be so presumptuous as to deny God's "right" to create or permit the "homosexual exceptions." Indeed, with regard to such "exceptions" we must strive to echo and mediate God's full acceptance and approval. (Matt, 1978)

Ellen Umansky (1983), among others, has taught that sexual orientation is part of the divine act of creation:

> Who are we to declare that the way in which God has created certain people is an abomination, and who are we to deny other human beings the joys of companionship on the grounds that their needs are not identical to our own? (p. 15)

PROCREATION AND FAMILY

Bearing and raising children is a central Jewish religious obligation. The responsibility to have children in order to guarantee the continuation of the Jewish people assumed particular urgency after the Holocaust. In his 1978 *Judaism* article, Hershel Matt asserted that the homosexual who does not have children "denies history" and, by extension, denies the Jewish Covenant. Homosexual acts are forbidden in the tradition partly because they are perceived as a mockery of heterosexual—and presumably procreative—intercourse while *being* a homosexual (an idea unknown to the ancient writers) is considered inconsistent with the Jewish identification of maturity with parenting. The progressive position differs both with the traditional model of human sexuality and with the modern view that asserts that a homosexual cannot fulfill her/his responsibilities as a Jew.

The Jewish tradition has always affirmed love and companionship as dimensions of sexuality, in addition to the procreative function (Ketubot 61b-62b; Biale, 1984; Feldman, 1968). Nonetheless, the halachah forbids all forms of sexual relations that are not, at least theoretically, procreative (i.e., intercourse by a husband with his post-menopausal wife is permitted while oral sex between them is not).[20] The condemnation of homosexuality fits into this sexual ethic, in which heterosexual intercourse is the only licit form of sexual expression. The prohibitions of masturbation and oral sex, in addition to homosexual relations, are derived from the biblical commandment not to "waste" semen. The Torah's condemnation of homosexual relations probably stems from this prohibition as well and from what the ancient world perceived as a perversion of the "natural order." The "sin" of homosexual sex prohibited in the Bible is anal intercourse, described in Lev. 18:22 as sexual relations between two men "as one lies with a woman." Sexual relations between women are not mentioned in the Bible. They are condemned by the later Jewish legal tradition as "promiscuous," but are considered to be less serious precisely because they do not involve, in the eyes of the rabbis, an act of intercourse or spilling of seed.[21]

Contemporary liberal teachers, to the extent that they speak of sexuality, do not forbid masturbation (Jacob, 1983) or oral sex to heterosexuals, nor are those who engage in them considered to be "deniers of history"; modern religious leaders acknowledge that these sexual acts can complement procreative relationships and they affirm the activities themselves as legitimate means of sexual expression. Some defend masturbation and oral sex when practiced in heterosexual relationships which do not preclude procreation, condemn the homosexual for finding fulfillment in a relationship which cannot produce children.[22] This modernist position treats non-procreative sex (presumably including heterosexual intercourse with birth control) as neutral or, in an appropriate context, desirable (thus Borowitz, 1969). Although the particular moment is not possibly procreative, the relationship itself, it is argued, does not preclude the eventuality of procreation. But what if age, infertility or medical disability prevent procreation? This does not keep the heterosexual couple from creating a sanctified relationship. Accordingly, it is not the non-procreative aspect of homosexual sex that is objected to, but *being* homosexual.

The halachah permits couples to be married even if it is known that they will not be able to bear children. Liberal rabbis do not forbid people who, for biological or medical reasons are unable to bear children, to marry or deny them the other benefits of a union and sexual relationship (Jacob, 1983). Nor is a couple's inability to bear children considered to be a threat to other potential parents or an endorsement of this behavior as more desirable.

Further, it must be noted that many homosexuals do have children, whether natural or adopted. Many more homosexuals would have children if society were more supportive of their becoming parents. The ethical action, it would appear, would not be to encourage homosexuals to deny their nature and to try to become heterosexual and marry, but rather to encourage the Jewish and general communities to endorse and support homosexuals as parents. It is not the homosexual who is not interested in fulfilling the covenant responsibility, as much as it is the community that stands in her or his way.

There are many homosexuals who do not and will not have children. However, there are ways of contributing to the rearing of children other than as parents. Many gay and lesbian people, just like childless heterosexuals, are directly involved in the child rearing of nieces and nephews and as "adopted" parents of close friends. Others are teachers, communal leaders, counselors, youth advisors, or other parental figures. In the Jewish tradition, the teacher is considered more praiseworthy than the parent (Baba Metzia 33a). In other circumstances, the Jewish community understands and supports these roles as a way to channel parental instincts. Why should homosexuals not be accorded such treatment?

Many gay and lesbian Jews have been cast out of their own families, due to their homosexuality. To charge that gay and lesbian people are anti-family is to fail to see the role parents and others play in excluding the homosexual family member from the family group where he or she would otherwise belong.

UNIONS

Gay and lesbian people have always built loving relationships, despite the absence of societal reward. In fact, public acknowledgment of a loving relationship between two men or women defies the social pressure to remain invisible and, therefore, has been specifically condemned by society. Simultaneously, moralists and psychiatrists have often cited the inability of gay people to maintain long-term relationships as a sign of their illness. The strength, number, and duration of gay and lesbian partnerships—in the absence of societal, familial or religious endorsement, and often with their explicit condemnation—is testimony to the courage of lesbian and gay partners and their devotion to each other. In the years since the gay liberation movement began, many gay and lesbian people have decided to affirm and celebrate their commitment publicly.

The first mention of the topic in Jewish circles is in Freehof's 1973 responsum on homosexual congregations:

> It is hardly worth mentioning that to officiate at a so-called "marriage" of two homosexuals and to describe their mode of life as *kiddushin* (i.e., sacred in Judaism) is a contravention of all that is respected in Jewish life. (p. 33)

In a sharp rejoinder to Freehof, Arthur Green (1973) became the first Jewish leader to affirm publicly the desirability and sanctity of homosexual partnerships. In his 1978 article, Matt presented a fictional letter from homosexual Jews. Noting that there is probably no possibility of a halachically acceptable union, he nonetheless suggests that such a relationship is "blessed by God."[23]

Walter Jacob (1987), in his responsum on marriage (1985), wrote that the etiology of homosexuality is irrelevant because, he claimed, Reform Judaism does not understand it "to be an alternative lifestyle which is religiously condoned":

> Judaism places great emphasis on family, children and the future, which is assured by a family. However we may understand homosexuality, whether as an illness, as a genetically based dysfunction or as a sexual preference and lifestyle—we

cannot accommodate the relationship of two homosexuals as a "marriage" within the context of Judaism, for none of the elements of *qiddushin* normally associated with marriage can be invoked for this relationship.

A rabbi cannot, therefore, participate in the "marriage" of two homosexuals. (p. 298)

Other than the presumption of heterosexuality, what is missing from the "elements of *qiddushin*"? As noted above, many homosexual families have children and the absence of the capability to bear children biologically is not a bar to heterosexual marriage. The Jewish tradition has always recognized the place of companionship and love in marriage. In so far as a *kiddushin* is a model or reflection of the Covenant, the loving and stable relationship between two partners of the same sex who are committed to a Jewish home and the Jewish people surely strengthens the Covenant.

Those rabbis who do officiate at ceremonies between persons of the same sex generally discourage calling the ceremony a "marriage." Marriage is licensed by the state and no state will grant a license to two people of the same sex. The emphasis in these *kiddushin* ceremonies is on the "sanctified relationship" the couple has established before God and the community. Marder (1985) explained the policies of Beth Chayim Chadashim in Los Angeles:

> A marriage between persons of the same sex would almost certainly never be accepted by halakhic Jews. Even so, it seems only right that rabbis . . . make an effort to respond to the needs of those gay and lesbian Jews who feel that their religion ignores or denigrates their loving commitments, and the families they establish.
>
> At the very least, rabbis can publicly recognize a couple's union by offering our own blessings and the congratulations of the community. My congregation offers couples an "Affirmation" service structured along the lines of a traditional Jewish wedding. . . . We also call couples up to the *bimah* [pulpit] for a special blessing over the Torah on their anniversaries. (p. 23)

A couple who invited their families and friends for a Celebration of Commitment in New York in June of 1986 explained their motivation:

> Lesbians and gay men have rarely proclaimed their love or expressed their intimate commitments before friends, let alone before the families of their birth. On the contrary, for years gay people have lived in the closet, scorned alike by religion and state, suffering discrimination in the world of work, all too often rejected by family and community, or justifying fear of such discrimination and rejection.
>
> But in this century, and especially since the Stonewall riots of 1969 [when gay people fought back against police violence], lesbians and gay people have begun to say "no" to this oppression, to affirm their self-worth, to demand the respect and recognition due them as human beings.
>
> We believe our ceremony grows out of and contributes to this movement of self-affirmation and sexual liberation. Even traditional forms can take on new meaning in a new historical and social context. As two gay men, our declaration before family and friends of enduring love for each other and of our wish to share a life together, subverts the institution of marriage as it appropriates it for a new purpose. (Klein & Horowitz, 1986)

With the recognition of homosexuality as more than discrete acts, but rather "a profound inner condition and basic psychic orientation, involving the deepest levels of personality" (Matt, 1987) will come the understanding that the fulfillment of the person that is only possible in relationship with another can only be realized for some with a partner of the same sex (Perry-Marx, 1983). These relationships, characterized by mutual love, care, sharing responsibility and faithfulness, are surely deserving of religious blessing and communal endorsement. The position that holds that permitting or approving such unions will threaten the place of traditional marriage in Jewish life is founded on the mistaken idea that homosexuality is deliberately chosen, and upon the homophobic fear that homosexuals "recruit" others. Those people who are heterosexual are not going to become homosexual because of greater social acceptance of homosexuality. Obviously, not all homosexual relationships are successful and enduring. However, compared to the divorce rate among heterosexual couples, who enjoy all the societal privileges of marriage, gay men and lesbians surely fare no worse. The success of their relationships can only be enhanced through public support and affirmation of the legitimacy of their unions.

CONCLUSION

The increasing visibility of gay and lesbian Jews, combined with a better understanding of homosexuality, has led to discussion about and, to a limited extent, acceptance of homosexual Jews within the organized Jewish community. The continuing growth of gay- and lesbian-outreach synagogues, and their active membership in national synagogue bodies and the Jewish community, advance this trend. Public understanding and acceptance is also furthered when openly gay and lesbian Jews affiliate with mainstream synagogues, as increasing numbers are choosing to do. The resistance to homosexuality, and to extending a place to homosexuals, is likely to continue in coming years in the traditionalist segment of the Jewish community, where the claim for acceptance of homosexuality is perceived as creating an irreconcilable conflict between traditional Jewish law and modern culture. Within the more liberal Jewish religious community, however, the increasing tolerance of recent years will likely foster further acceptance and understanding.

NOTES

1. The major sources are Lamm, 1974; Freehof, 1974; Gordis, 1978; Spero, 1979; and Schwartz, 1979. Spero apologizes for opening discussion of a topic about which it is not considered even proper to speak.

2. Jakobovitz relies on an earlier article by Lamm (1968), The new dispensation on homosexuality, *Jewish Life*, *35* (3), 11-13.

3. On the distinction between "person as homosexual" and "homosexual as person," compare the original and final versions of the 1976 CCAR resolution on homosexuality (CCAR, 1976, 75, and Kahan, 1977, 50-51).

4. *Mishneh Torah*, *"Issurai Bi'ah"* (Laws of Forbidden Intercourse), 1:14, 21:8.

5. Confusing in this and other articles is the admixture of terms and definitions. Lamm uses "homosexuality," "sodomy," and "pederasty" interchangeably, contributing to the homophobic association of homosexuality with abuse. The sexism of traditional Jewish law, extends to the discussion of homosexuality as well. The ideal, and in traditional Jewish law the only, acceptable expression of sexuality, is heterosexual intercourse within marriage. Male homosexuality was condemned because it was perceived to be unnatural and involved the non-procreative use of semen. In the eyes of the tradition, women do not have intercourse, waste seed, or have a religious obligation to bear children — the three transgressions the male commits (compare Biale, 1984, 197).

6. At the end of this discussion, Lamm hinted that there is "some halakhic warrant for distinguishing between violent and victimless (or consensual and nonconsensual) crimes." While Lamm appeared to be acknowledging that homosexuality is "victimless," and therefore a less serious matter, he was unwilling to say as much in print (p. 198).

7. Throughout the article, "pederast" was used to refer to a gay male (e.g., "Pederasts and lesbians," p. 201). Citing Arno Karlen, Lamm claimed that "50% are borderline psychotics while lesbians are even more disturbed" (p. 390). He relied on the psychoanalytic model of illness, based on the "warped" family background.

8. There are, of course, homosexual Jews who do consider themselves as halachicly observant in all areas of their life but one. See Rabinowitz, 1983.

9. The boundaries of the traditional discussion were made explicitly clear by Rabbi David Novak:

> Jews have a theology and that theology regards the *mitzvot* [commandments] as the fundamental realia of Jewish life. Now . . . our commitment to *mitzvot* as acts commanded by God (not just "folkways," etc.) presupposes our affirmation of free choice; . . .
>
> Since Judaism is inconceivable without the *mitzvot*, so is it inconceivable without the affirmation of the free choice that they presuppose. And since the prohibition of homosexuality is a *mitzvah* [commandment] according to all halakhic authorities, I must regard a homosexual act as freely chosen, one for which I am fully responsible before God. (D. Novak, personal communication, February 19, 1986)

10. In fact, the earliest discussion was in 1965. A resolution opposing discrimination was prepared for the UAHC Convention but never presented. Anticipating the UAHC resolution, the National Federation of Temple Sisterhoods (NFTS) convention passed a parallel resolution. Because the UAHC did not pass its resolution, NFTS never implemented its own.

11. While Ragins and other earlier authors may have shared Matt's position, none used this argument to advance a religious perspective.

12. Spero explicitly rejected the application of Matt's analysis.

13. Because the Reform movement does not consider traditional Jewish law binding, the ambiguous phrase "the spirit of Jewish tradition" is used in place of "Jewish law."

14. None of the synagogues which are affiliated with the Reform movement identify themselves as "gay synagogues." None has an exclusively gay membership nor do they wish to convey the message that they are only open to homosexuals. The preferred nomenclature is "special outreach" congregation.

Many who object to the establishment of such congregations in any form argue that their existence constitutes an endorsement of unacceptable activity. Gerald Kollin (1974) asserted that the proper Jewish attitude towards homosexuals is to "officially ignore them. . . . We have not . . . reached the point where homosexuality is sanctioned as a proper Jewish life-style option" (p. 95). Lamm (1974) compared such a synagogue to a gathering of adulterers, idol worshipers, or Sabbath violators. Further, the establishment of such a synagogue encourages transgression by allowing the homosexual to "more easily choose his partners" (Lamm, 1974, p. 203). Jakob J. Petuchowski (1985) stated that such a synagogue has as much religious basis as a "synagogue of thieves" (p. 125).

15. The debate about homosexuality illustrates the contemporary process of Reform decision making. Mutually independent criteria include traditional Jewish teaching, contemporary values, repsonsibility to the Jewish people, and personal conscience. See Petuchowski, 1970, 1986; Borowitz, 1984b; Kahn, 1986; Marmur, 1986.

16. The responsa in this volume were first circulated privately and only published in 1987. The date of authorship is given with each reference; they are found in the bibliography as Jacob, 1977.

17. In a letter to the editor of *Conservative Judaism*, Mortimor Ostow (1987) wrote:

> As Sandrow Visiting Professor of Pastoral Psychiatry at the [Jewish Theological] Seminary, and Chairman of the Department, I recommended to Chancellor Cohen that only those homosexual applications be accepted for rabbinic training who abstain completely from homosexual indulgence, who agree that homosexual behavior is halakhically unacceptable, who acknowledge the perverse nature of their homosexual inclination, and who undertake intensive psychotherapy in the hope of overcoming it. (p. 103)

18. The article was published with a disclaimer from the editors noting that it did not reflect official Conservative movement policy.

19. *Niddah*, ritual immersion after menstruation, is but one example. See Gordon, 1983, and Kahn, 1986.

20. Although many rabbis may in fact have felt that it was not technically forbidden, it was a "source of embarrassment to the many moralists who could

not bring themselves to accept so liberal a ruling even in theory." (Feldman, 1968, 155 ff.)

21. See Maimonides, *Mishneh Torah*, *"Issurai Bi'ah"* (Laws of Forbidden Intercourse), 1:14, 21:8. The prohibition against wasting semen is not applicable to women (see Biale, 1984). Mehler (1977) was the first to point out the general inapplicability of halachic values about sex to contemporary behavior. Also, see Boswell (1980) on the "Alexandrian rule."

22. The halachic grounding turns on the statement in Nedarim 20b, "A man can do what he will with his wife." See Feldman, 1968, 155-157. Feldman concludes

> [S]uch coitus, though irregular, still appertains to acceptable conjugal relations and *hash-hatat zera* is just not applicable. Scandalous as this may seem at first glance, the act is *proper to heterosexual expression*. (p. 157, emphasis added)

23. This extra-halachic suggestion would be totally unacceptable to the Orthodox, who hold that all legitimate relationships are already sanctified within the bounds of *halachah* (also see Mihaly, 1973).

SOURCES

Biale, R. (1984). *Women and Jewish law*. New York: Schocken.

Borowitz, E. B. (1969). *Choosing a sex ethic*. New York: Schocken.

Borowitz, E. B. (1983). *Choices in modern Jewish thought*. New York: Behrman House.

Borowitz, E. B. (1984a). The autonomous Jewish self. In *Modern Judaism, 4*, 39-56.

Borowitz, E. B. (1984b). The autonomous Jewish self and the commanding community. *Theological Studies, 45*, 34-56.

Boswell, J. (1980). *Christianity, social tolerance, and homosexuality*. Chicago: University of Chicago Press.

Central Conference of American Rabbis (1976). Resolution on homosexuality. *CCAR Yearbook, 86*, 75.

Central Conference of American Rabbis (1981). Report of conference on Jewish sexual values task force. South Fallsburg, NY.

Feldman, D. (1968). *Marital relations, abortion and birth control in Jewish law*. New York: Schocken.

Freehof, S. B. (1969). Homosexuality. In *Current reform responsa* (pp. 236-238). Cincinnati: HUC Press.

Freehof, S. B. (1973). Homosexuality and Jewish tradition. *CCAR Journal, 20* (30) 29-31. [*CCAR Yearbook, 88* (1973), 115-119.]

Gordis, R. (1978). *Love and sex: a modern Jewish perspective*. New York: Farrar, Strauss, & Giroux.

Gordon, S. (1983). Homosexuality: a counseling perspective. *Judaism*, *32*, 405-409.

Green, A. (1974). Disappointed with responsum (Letter to the editor). *CCAR Journal*, *21*, 79-80.

Jacob, W. (1981). Homosexuals in leadership positions. *CCAR Yearbook*, *91*, 69. New York: CCAR.

Jacob, W. (Ed.). (1983). *American reform responsa*. New York: CCAR.

Jacob, W. (1987). *Contemporary American responsa*. New York: Central Conference of American Rabbis.

Jakobovitz, I. (1973). Homosexuality. In *Encyclopedia Judaica* (Vol. 8, pp. 861-862). Jerusalem: Keter.

Kahan, N. (Chair). (1977). Report of the *ad hoc* committee on homosexuality. *CCAR Yearbook*, *87*, 50-51.

Kahn, Y. H. (1986). Reform Judaism's diminishing boundaries: Responses. *Journal of Reform Judaism*, *33* (4), 28.

Klein, S. and Horowitz, P. (1986, June 7). *A celebration of commitment*. Brooklyn. (Privately printed.)

Kollin, G. (1974). Not a Jewish life-style option. *CCAR Journal*, *21* (3), 95. (Letter to the editor.)

Lamm, N. (1968). The new dispensation on homosexuality. *Jewish Life*, *35* (3), 11-16.

Lamm, N. (1974). Judaism and the modern attitude to homosexuality. In *Encyclopedia Judaica Yearbook 1974* (pp. 194-205). Jerusalem: Keter.

Marder, J. R. (1985). Getting to know the gay and lesbian shul. *Reconstructionist,* *51* (2), 23.

Marmur, D. (1986). Reform Judaism's diminishing boundaries: Responses. *Journal of Reform Judaism*, *33* (4), 29-32.

Matt, H. J. (1978). Sin, crime, sickness or alternative life-style?: A Jewish approach to homosexuality. *Judaism*, *27*, 13-24.

Matt, H. J. (1987). Homosexual rabbis? *Conservative Judaism*, *39* (3), 29-33.

Mehler, B. A. (1977, February/March). Gay Jews: One man's journey from closet to community. *Moment*, pp. 22-24.

Mihaly, E. (1973). Responsum on homosexuality. (Privately circulated.)

Ostow, M. (1987). (Letter to the editor). *Conservative Judaism*, *40* (1), 103-106.

Perry-Marx, J. P. (1983, February 10). *The strangers in our midst*. Sermon presented at Hebrew Union College-Jewish Institute of Religion, New York.

Petuchowski, J. J. (1970). Criteria for modern Jewish observance. In A. Jospe (Ed.), *Tradition and contemporary experience* (pp. 249-256). New York: Schocken.

Petuchowski, J. J. (1985). "Beth Geneva Chadasha." *Journal of Reform Judaism*, *32* (3), 125-127. (Letter to the editor.)

Petuchowski, J. J. (1986). Reform Judaism's diminishing boundaries: "The grin that remained." *Journal of Reform Judaism*, *33* (4), 15-24.

Raab, E. (1972, May 26). Homosexuals and the Jews. *San Francisco Jewish Bulletin*, p. 4.

Rabinowitz, H. (1983). Talmud study in a gay synagogue. *Judaism, 32*, 433-443.

Ragins, S. (1973). An echo of the pleas of our fathers. *CCAR Journal, 20* (3), 45.

Schwartz, B. D. (1977). Homosexuality: A Jewish perspective. *United Synagogue Review Quarterly, 30*, 27.

Schwartz, B. D. (1979). The Jewish view of homosexuality (Doctoral dissertation, Jewish Theological Seminary of America, 1979). *Dissertations Abstracts International, 40*, 4637A.

Soloff, R. A. (1983). Is there a reform response to homosexuality? *Judaism, 32*, 417-424.

Spero, M. H. (1979). Homosexuality: Clinical and ethical challenges. *Tradition, 17* (4), 53-73.

Stern, J. (Chair). (1974). Report of the *ad hoc* committee on homosexual congregations. *CCAR Yearbook, 84*, 28-29.

Umansky, E. (1985). Jewish attitudes towards homosexuality: A review of contemporary sources. *Reconstructionist, 51* (2), 9-15.

Weiss-Rosmarin, T. (1986). Please stay in the closet. *Jewish Spectator, 50* (3), 7 (editorial).

Wurzburger, W. S. (1983). Preferences are not practices. *Judaism, 32*, 425.

No Longer Invisible: Gay and Lesbian Jews Build a Movement

Aaron Cooper, PhD

San Francisco

SUMMARY. The organized movement of lesbian and gay Jews took root in the mid-1970s when groups of Jewish homosexuals in the United States, England, and Israel began gathering for religious, educational, and social purposes. After centuries of denial, the Jewish community was faced with the reality of this increasingly visible and vocal minority. By 1989, nearly 30 groups of Jewish gay men and women throughout the world were part of the World Congress of Gay and Lesbian Jewish Organizations, an international body devoted to community education about homophobia and support for both member and newly emerging gay Jewish groups.

The organized movement of gay and lesbian Jews took root during the period of radical social change that characterized the 1960s and early 1970s. When patrons of New York's Stonewall Inn aggressively resisted a routine police raid in 1969, the gay rights movement was born. Its energy derived partly from the feminist critique of traditional gender roles, partly from the antiestablishment feeling of the Viet Nam era, and partly from the trend toward ethnic and group pride, as exemplified in the slogan "Black is Beautiful." With the proliferation of gay and lesbian organizations during the early 1970s—political, social, educational, and reli-

Dr. Cooper is a clinical psychologist specializing in counseling gay and lesbian couples and individuals. He was the executive director of the World Congress of Gay and Lesbian Jewish Organizations from 1982-1987.

For further information about the World Congress, write to P.O. Box 18961, Washington, DC 20036.

gious—Jewish gay men and lesbians came forth to stake their claim.

Groups of Jewish gay men and women had always gathered informally—in homes, at bars and dance clubs, and at gay Christian organizations—to share friendship and support in the face of a society and a religion opposed to their existence as homosexuals. Because of the homophobia of Jewish institutions, these Jews rarely looked to agencies of the Jewish community for affiliation and opportunity. The synagogue, the community center, and the charitable organizations were usually avoided. Jewish homosexuals were well aware of the heterosexual bias that characterized Jewish community life. Those who attended synagogues or joined organizations sacrificed a great measure of openness or comfort. They could not bring a same-sex date or lover to temple; if they did, they consciously refrained from some of the behaviors common to and natural among nongay couples or friends; for example, extending Sabbath or Yom Tov (holiday) greetings in the form of a hug or kiss. Nongays, of course, never faced such restrictions within the Jewish community. The recognition awarded only to heterosexual couples on the occasion of an engagement, anniversary, or sanctification of a new home further heightened the alienation for the Jewish lesbian or gay man, for whom these ritual observances were unavailable. As a result, in Jewish settings most gay and lesbian Jews chose to identify as single, reluctantly tolerating offers of social introductions or invitations to "singles" events. Surely their need for same-sex companionship was never addressed.

Many Jewish gay men and women during the seventies who felt attached to their religion, but unwelcome as gays in the synagogue, were inspired by the existence of the Metropolitan Community Church (MCC), the national gay and lesbian Protestant denomination. In different cities throughout the country, MCC had become a spiritual home for Jews seeking camaraderie and support for religiosity without having to deny their sexual orientation. It wasn't long before a group of Jews attending MCC/Los Angeles recognized that the time was ripe to create a gay and lesbian Jewish alternative.

It was in 1972, 3 years after the Stonewall Riot and the birth of the gay rights movement, that Beth Chayim Chadashim (BCC) was founded in Los Angeles. It was a place where Jewish lesbians and gay men could shape their own ritual life and social environment and thereby step out of the shadows of second-class status as Jews. It was the first synagogue of its kind in history.

Following its founding, advertisements were placed in the local gay and lesbian press announcing the existence of a new option for Jewish homosexuals. BCC's founders approached the local office of the Union of American Hebrew Congregations (UAHC), the Reform synagogue movement, to seek advice and assistance. With a measure of support that has always characterized the Pacific Southwest Council of the UAHC, arrangements were made quickly for prayerbooks to be donated by Los Angeles' prominent Wilshire Boulevard Temple. A regular schedule of worship services was begun and BCC was on its way.

From its rented space within the Metropolitan Community Church, BCC began to cultivate relationships with mainstream Jewish organizations, always striving to raise consciousness about homosexuality within the Jewish (and secular) communities. In 1973, BCC began discussions with the UAHC about attaining membership in that body. The existence of a "gay-outreach" synagogue, and the debate resulting from BCC's application into the Reform movement, stimulated discussion and controversy on a national level. (See Rabbi Kahn's article in this collection.) With the strong support of the UAHC regional office, BCC was voted into UAHC membership in 1973 in an historic action that opened the door of mainstream Judaism to gay and lesbian Jews.

Once a member of the Reform movement, BCC found many opportunities to become involved in the Jewish community, as well as to educate and raise Jewish consciousness about homosexuality. Congregants spoke to synagogues throughout southern California, conducted Sabbath services for Jewish elderly in local nursing homes, and raised money for the variety of charitable causes that dot the Jewish fundraising calendar. Unbeknown to those men and women in Los Angeles, gay and lesbian Jews in other parts of the world were engaged in a similar process of "coming out" as Jews in the gay community, and as gay men and women in the Jewish community. Outside the United States, London saw the creation of the first European gay Jewish group. Between 1972 and 1975, at least 10 lesbian and gay Jewish groups were established in the United States and abroad.

The Metropolitan Community Church (MCC) remained an important vehicle during the mid-seventies for this new Jewish movement. In 1974, and then again in 1975, a handful of gay Jews attended the annual MCC convention, using the opportunity to share experiences, offer one another moral support in their efforts to sustain their fledgling groups or synagogues, and plant the seeds of the network that would result, several years later, in a formal gay and lesbian Jewish organization.

The growth of the movement was further stimulated in 1975 as a result of a "crisis" precipitated by the United Nations. The Arab world, together with many Third World nations falling under increasing Arab influence, succeeded in pushing through the U.N. a resolution that equated Zionism with racism. This action cut to the heart of Jewish self-esteem and demanded an immediate response from Jewish circles. As the mainstream Jewish community loudly condemned the U.N. action, gay and lesbian Jews responded as well. Congregation Beth Simchat Torah (CBST) of New York City, a young gay-outreach synagogue, convened an "Emergency Conference on Anti-semitism" for Jewish lesbian and gay organizations. Representatives from Beth Chayim Chadashim (Los Angeles), Beth Ahavah (Philadelphia), B'nai Haskalah (Boston), and Temple Mishpucheh (Washington, D.C.) came together with CBST in what was the first organized meeting of gay and lesbian Jewish organizations. In addition to passing a resolution condemning the United Nations action, the conference also put forth the desire of the participants to maintain closer contact and extend mutual assistance to each other and to new organizations in their formative stages.

Eight months later, in 1976, representatives from Montreal (Naches), Toronto (Ha Mishpacha), and London (Jewish Gay Group) joined the United States groups in Washington, D.C., for the First International Conference of Gay and Lesbian Jews. Through resolutions establishing membership standards and the concept of rotating host cities for annual gatherings, the international organization was born. Spirits were high as these Jewishly committed people perceived the beginnings of an international movement that would give voice to their concerns and validate their existence as a legitimate segment of Am Yisroel (the People of Israel).

In 1977, Beth Chayim Chadashim (BCC), still the sole gay-out-reach congregation in the national UAHC, faced one of the greatest challenges in its then short history. On that year's agenda at the UAHC 54th Biennial Assembly (the national convention) was a gay rights resolution. BCC knew it had made many friends within the Los Angeles Reform Jewish community, and so looked with hopeful anticipation to the passage of this resolution.

Entitled "The Human Rights of Homosexuals," the resolution was not expected to be controversial by its authors and supporters. One of those authors, Rabbi Irv Herman, UAHC regional director in Los Angeles at the time, saw in the national landscape the rising tide of antigay bigotry in the forms of Anita Bryant, California's Briggs Initiative, and voter referenda seeking to overturn existing gay rights ordinances in several cities. Rabbi Herman hoped that a UAHC resolution would lend support to the progressive, antiprejudicial position in this national debate. Yet when the resolution came before the UAHC delegates, it received a mere 20% vote of support and was returned to committee for rewriting. The floor debate made clear that few delegates to the Assembly knew of BCC's existence, let alone its membership as a UAHC congregation. BCC recognized that the resolution would pass only through immediate intensive lobbying on its part—in effect, a crash course to demystify homosexuality.

As a result of a heroic 24-hour effort by BCC delegates, and several speakers who addressed the Assembly about the substantial role that BCC played within the Los Angeles Jewish community, the following resolution passed with nearly 80% vote of support:

> WHEREAS the UAHC has consistently supported civil rights and civil liberties for all persons, and
> WHEREAS the Constitution guarantees the civil rights of all individuals,
> BE IT THEREFORE RESOLVED that homosexual persons are entitled to equal protection of the law. We oppose discrimination against homosexuals in areas of opportunity, including

employment and housing. We call upon our society to see that
such protection is provided in actuality.
BE IT FURTHER RESOLVED that we affirm our belief that
private sexual acts between consenting adults are not the
proper province of government and law enforcement agencies.
BE IT FURTHER RESOLVED that we urge congregations to
conduct appropriate educational programs for youth and
adults, so as to provide greater understanding of Jewish values
as they relate to the spectrum of human sexuality.

The Union of American Hebrew Congregations thus became the
first major Jewish organization to go on record in support of gay
and lesbian rights.

One year later, when the Third International Conference of Gay
and Lesbian Jews convened in Los Angeles in 1978, the conferees
decided it was time to affirm their worldwide commitment. Israel
was selected as the site of the Fourth International Conference. But
the process of preparing for the Israel conference was not easy. In
its planning stages, the Fourth International Conference faced
strong opposition from the Israeli Rabbinate, which threatened to
cancel the *kashrut* (kosher) certificate of any kibbutz or hotel that
agreed to host the meetings. A warmer welcome was extended by
the Ministry of Tourism, however, and the conference went ahead
as planned. To circumvent the Rabbinate's ruling, conferees stayed
in different locations and no single hotel or facility served as an
official convention host. Israel's gay and lesbian group, the Society
for the Protection of Personal Rights, welcomed registrants from
Paris, London, Australia, Bermuda, Canada, West Germany, Hol-
land, Mexico, Portugal, South Africa, and the United States.

The Israeli conference presented an additional unexpected challenge. Two years earlier, in 1977, members of gay and lesbian Jewish organizations had voted to undertake a joint tree project through
the Jewish National Fund (JNF). Their goal was to dedicate a woodland in Israel as a memorial to gay and lesbian Jews through the
ages. Almost $9,000 was raised and sent to the JNF in Israel. The
1979 conference seemed like a fitting occasion during which to dedicate the woodland formally. When conference participants gathered in the city of Lahav, where the dedication ceremony was to

occur, they were shocked to learn that the JNF had cancelled the program. The JNF decided it would not inscribe the words "gay and lesbian" on the customary dedication plaque, and it offered to return the money. The conference leadership knew it would be impossible to return the money to the mostly anonymous donors and so refused to take back the $9,000. After several years of unsuccessful efforts to resolve this dilemma, conference leaders chose to accept a blank plaque and wait for the time when antigay prejudice is less prevalent within the Jewish National Fund.

By the final days of that 1979 conference in Israel, conferees were filled with frustration and anger at the JNF. At the same time, they were filled with pride for, and felt solidarity with, their Israeli brothers and sisters. En masse, they descended on Tel Aviv's Independence Park for Israel's first gay rights demonstration. Many curious onlookers engaged in animated discussion with the demonstrators, hungry to question and to learn about gay and lesbian Jews. Television cameras and reporters recorded the event for posterity, and later that night Israel's first television program on gay/lesbian rights filled the airwaves.

The year 1979 marked another historic first for the Jewish gay and lesbian movement: Congregation Sha'ar Zahav in San Francisco, with a primarily gay and lesbian membership, engaged Allen B. Bennett, an openly gay man, as its first rabbi. Although Rabbi Bennett had lived and worked in San Francisco, prior to his position with Sha'ar Zahav he had not "come out" as gay in most professional Jewish circles. When Sha'ar Zahav elected him its spiritual leader, it was apparently the first time in Jewish history that a homosexual rabbi could openly and honestly integrate his personal and professional identities.

Perhaps no more exciting event occurred during Rabbi Bennett's tenure than on the Sabbath evening in 1980 when he sermonized to over 300 Jewish gay men and lesbians in the impressive sanctuary of Congregation Sherith Israel, one of San Francisco's premiere Reform synagogues. The service was part of the Fifth International Conference of Gay and Lesbian Jews. Sherith Israel had opened its doors to the Jewish gay and lesbian community and set a precedent that has since been followed by major Reform congregations throughout the United States.

By the time of the Fifth International Conference in 1980, there was a strongly felt need for a formal organization of Jewish gay and lesbian groups. An international umbrella association would serve as a link for all the groups worldwide, enabling them to exchange news, support, and the wisdom of experience. A Committee on Structure had been established in 1978 to draft bylaws for such an organization. The 16 groups attending the Fifth International Conference in 1980 expanded upon the framework of that committee's efforts and officially founded the World Congress of Gay and Lesbian Jewish Organizations (WCGLJO).

The mere existence of the WCGLJO was of immeasurable value, particularly to those more isolated gay men and women in smaller cities who often questioned on a personal level their own "legitimacy" and, in turn, the feasibility of gathering in an organized fashion with other gay Jews. Through the WCGLJO, individuals and groups both could feel connected to an entity that spanned the physical and psychological distances that were roadblocks in the struggle for a positive gay/lesbian Jewish identity. Individuals could know that they were not alone as they challenged the pervasive homophobia of Western culture and Jewish history. The victories of one group — overcoming the prejudice of a local Jewish press that refused to print worship schedules for the gay-outreach synagogue, receiving acknowledgment for participation in federation fundraising following several years of invisibility, finding rental space in a Jewish setting after numerous rejections by other Jewish agencies — these were shared victories that gave hope and inspiration to those facing similar struggles in other parts of the world.

Throughout the late seventies and early eighties, more and more communities became aware of the existence of Jewish gay people. Local Jewish newspapers began printing articles about Jewish gay and lesbian organizations. Jewish leaders were called upon for assistance in locating meeting space or planning educational programs and invited openly gay and lesbian Jews to participate in Jewish community events and charitable activities. This growing recognition of gay and lesbian Jews within the mainstream Jewish community was reflected in 1980 with the adoption at the national biennial convention of the American Jewish Congress (AJC) of a nondiscrimination resolution: "The American Jewish Congress opposes all discrimination against homosexuals—in employment, housing, military service, and other areas." While less far-ranging than the resolution passed 3 years earlier by the Union of American Hebrew Congregations, this action put the American Jewish Congress on record as the first nonsynagogal mainstream Jewish group to recognize and support the civil rights of gay people.

The number of gay and lesbian Jewish organizations has increased significantly since 1980, standing now at between 35 and 40 groups throughout the world. Unlike the gay-outreach synagogues in some cities (e.g., Miami, New York, Los Angeles), several of these groups define themselves primarily as political (e.g., Sjalhomo in Amsterdam), others as social-cultural (e.g., Am Tikva in Boston). Still others are smaller *havurot* (friendship groups) organized informally to provide camaraderie and support without the institutional trappings. All of these groups promote the integration of Judaism and homosexuality as two central and natural aspects of personal identity. Regardless of group size or purpose, they all serve as a source of strength and positive self-esteem for their members, providing a support base for Jewishly identified men and women that no other community institution can match.

Unlike traditional havurot or synagogues, these groups acknowledge and celebrate through Jewish ritual and observance essential aspects of what it means to be gay or lesbian. For example, most of the congregations have created rituals to bless gay or lesbian couples celebrating their anniversaries. Some groups perform sanctification ceremonies following the birth or adoption of children, ceremonies that, in the case of couples, acknowledge and affirm the parenting role of both partners. A commitment to gender equality pervades the movement, as reflected both in the ongoing development of a fully degenderized liturgy and in equal participation in ritual life. Some synagogues have developed prayers and even entire liturgies that blend the traditional with the new; for example, readings that call to memory the gay and lesbian Jews murdered through the ages. Because many gay men and lesbians never had children to recite the *kaddish* (mourners' prayers) in their memory, some congregations remember these ancestors through the recitation of prayers such as this one from Sha'ar Zahav's High Holy Days prayerbook:

Sister that I never held near
Comrade that I never embraced
Your memory is almost lost.

The one we don't talk about
The loving one who never married.
The one for whom no Kaddish was said.

Your loneliness calls out to me:
I know of your struggles; we are not strangers.
And if my path is easier, I will not forget who walked it first.

We call you to mind, but did you not sometimes think of us,
Your children, lovers across the years,
Those who would follow and would think of you
And bless your memory, and call you to mind?

With David and Jonathan, we will not forget you.
With Ruth and Naomi, we will not forget you.
In the name of God you are our sisters and our brothers, and
we ask that you be remembered in peace.

Public education about homosexuality has remained an important task for most of the groups belonging to the World Congress of Gay and Lesbian Jewish Organizations (WCGLJO). In 1981 Congregation Sha'ar Zahav, together with San Francisco's Bureau of Jewish Education and Jewish Family and Children's Services, sponsored a full-day program on Judaism and Homosexuality for Jewish communal service workers, rabbis, teachers, and agency professionals. Over 400 people attended a similar program in early 1986 at the Stephen Wise Free Synagogue in New York. A 1985 joint conference of Seattle's Jewish Family Service and gay-outreach Congregation Tikvah Chadashah focused on the special needs of families of gays, continuing a dialogue that received its greatest support when in 1982 the Jewish Community Federation of San Francisco awarded funds to its regional Jewish Family and Children's Services to develop a counseling program to help families of lesbians and gay men cope more successfully with homosexuality. This was apparently the first time any Jewish federation had extended financial support to a project addressing the needs of gay people and their families.

An additional sign of the growth and viability of this movement has been the hiring of ordained rabbis by WCGLJO member synagogues. After many years of enjoying the services of rabbinic interns from the Reform movement's Hebrew Union College, Beth Chayim Chadashim in Los Angeles decided in 1982 to convene a rabbi search committee. This was the first time that a synagogue with a primarily gay and lesbian membership sought to hire a rabbi through an open search process. (Because Allen Bennett had been a member of Congregation Sha'ar Zahav when he was elected rabbi in 1979, no search process was undertaken at that time.) BCC's endeavor demonstrated that the Jewish gay and lesbian synagogue was more than a temporary phenomenon on the landscape of Jewish life. Suddenly, rabbinic training centers and placement offices found themselves scrutinizing "the gay and lesbian synagogue" as a potential job placement for their graduates. In 1983, Rabbi Janet Ross Marder was selected to be the rabbi of BCC. Two years later, Sha'ar Zahav engaged Rabbi Yoel Kahn. Toward the end of 1986, Or Chadash in Chicago engaged Rabbi Roy Furman. Rabbis Marder, Kahn, and Furman were each ordained by the Reform movement's Hebrew Union College. When Sha'ar Zahav's rabbinic search committee in 1984 ran "position available" announcements in Jewish publications throughout the world, nearly 20 applications were received from groups as diverse as nongay Reform to closeted gay Orthodox rabbis.

Also in 1985, Congregation Beth Ahavah of Philadelphia engaged Rabbi Linda Holtzman, a graduate of and faculty member at the Reconstructionist Rabbinical College. Years of recognition of gay and lesbian Jews by the Reconstructionist movement were powerfully underscored in 1984 when the Reconstructionist Rabbinical College voted to incorporate into its admissions policy an official statement of nondiscrimination on the basis of sexual orientation. Although through the decades each branch of Judaism has unwittingly ordained closeted gay and lesbian rabbis, the Reconstructionist movement became the first to formalize a nonprejudicial policy.

By 1985, three gay-outreach synagogues had joined Beth Chayim Chadashim within the ranks of the Union of American Hebrew Congregations: Or Chadash (Chicago), Metropolitan Community Synagogue (Miami), and Sha'ar Zahav (San Francisco). At the

58th General Assembly of the UAHC in 1985, these synagogues presented the first workshop on homosexuality ever offered at a UAHC national biennial. Entitled "Towards a Better Understanding of Our Gay and Lesbian Brothers and Sisters," the program drew a standing-room only crowd of convention delegates.

The gay and lesbian Jewish movement continues to grow, and as it does, the task of educating the heterosexual Jewish world remains vitally important. While substantial inroads have been made within the Reform and Reconstructionist movements, Conservative and Orthodox synagogues and their associated communal organizations remain largely closed to the needs and concerns of gay and lesbian Jews. The myths and fear surrounding the AIDS epidemic in recent years have not made this work easier, either for gay people or those they seek to educate. But the movement for lesbian and gay rights—now over 15 years old—shows few signs of retreating. In early 1987, the World Congress of Gay and Lesbian Jewish Organizations launched a major educational project targeted for the Jewish community worldwide. Under the leadership of this author, the Public Education Project's goal was to reach out to every synagogue and major Jewish organization and challenge the prejudicial stereotypes that keep alive the fear, shame, and misunderstanding that have surrounded homosexuality for centuries.

A Critique
of Creationist Homophobia

George R. Edwards, PhD

Louisville Presbyterian Theological Seminary

SUMMARY. In 1978, the United Presbyterian Church in the United States of America prohibited the ordination of "practicing homosexuals" to the church's ministry. In this prohibition, by providing a pivotal role for homophobic interpretation of Genesis 1-3, Presbyterians linked up with the exclusionist policies of both the Roman Catholic and fundamentalist communions. The following article submits this use of the biblical narratives of creation to critical examination and provides an alternative liberationist perspective.

The term "creationist homophobia" refers to the uses of Genesis 1-3 that link those chapters with Genesis 19 (the destruction of Sodom and Gomorrah) and other passages of scripture conveniently employed for the moral and religious condemnation of homosexual persons. Creationist homophobia is most frequently evidenced in "Bible" churches following an evangelical-conservative theology, but it is by no means confined to such churches. Appeals to "nature" in theologies not characterized by biblical fundamentalism, for example, argue from the creation narratives to establish a sexual orthodoxy that claims cosmological sanctions and condemns those who do not conform to it.

The article has four parts. In the first, the somewhat recent and

George Edwards, Professor Emeritus of New Testament at Louisville Presbyterian Theological Seminary (1958-85), began his professional career as a parish minister. He is the author of *Jesus and the Politics of Violence* (1972) and *Gay/Lesbian Liberation: A Biblical Perspective* (1984).

Correspondence may be addressed to the author, 2317 Strathmoor Boulevard, Louisville, KY 40205.

qualitative work by Walter Brueggemann on Genesis 1 is briefly examined as a means of both commending and criticizing Brueggemann's use of sociological criticism. Part two provides examples of writing on Genesis 1-3 that demonstrate creationist homophobia in my own (Presbyterian) religious denomination. The third part shows how a determined, intelligent approach to creationist misogyny suggests what is then elaborated in part four as a liberation alternative to creationist homophobia.

SOCIOLOGICAL PARAMETERS OF A COMMENTARY ON GENESIS 1

In treating Genesis 1:1-2:4a, Walter Brueggemann (1982) correctly attacked the assumption that scientific history is conveyed by these familiar verses. It is clear that Brueggemann had in this case lined up against present-day creationists who wish to revive in one way or another the struggle against biological evolution associated with the work of Charles Darwin. Brueggemann worked on a dialectical pattern. Against the scientific history approach to the biblical creation narratives, he placed a rationalist one that emphasizes the mythological roots of these stories as found in the cosmogonies of Egypt and Mesopotamia and imported into Genesis by the authors and editors of Genesis 1.

But why do "mythology and rationalism" come off no better than literalism in his commentary? The reason is that for Brueggemann the older mythologies are transformed in Genesis to serve a "new purpose intimately related to Israel's covenantal experience" (p. 26). This new purpose is spelled out in terms of the sociological setting of the 6th century B.C. Jewish exile in Babylon when the Priestly stratum of the Pentateuch came into being. Due to the devastating fall of Jerusalem and the people's loss of confidence in divine providence, it was necessary to show that the God of Israel still governed over the cosmic destiny and overruled even the divinities of the Babylonian conquerors. That is, the theological and pastoral aims of the creation accounts in the 6th century B.C. replaced the earlier aims of the literature and transcended thereby, in the present use of Genesis 1, the religious barrenness of literalism on the one hand and rationalism on the other.

It is not difficult to see, however, that Brueggemann's solution to the literalist/rationalist dilemma was achieved by the placement of the text in still another sociological setting for which the Babylonian exile was simply a stepping stone to the present. The literature is now invested with a new aim: to facilitate the work of pastors, and more specifically pastors as preachers or teachers. Contemporary preaching, given a Barthian nuance by the term "proclamation," becomes the social act in which the pitfalls of fundamentalism and skepticism are averted. This proclamation, moreover, is a spoken word that "transforms reality" (p. 26). The point was carried even further, and quite beyond the bounds of any setting in the Babylonian exile, when Brueggemann added, "the text is none other than the voice of the evangel proclaiming good news" (p. 26).

Turning Genesis 1 into a pulpit for the Christian evangel is an evident example of "kerygmatic exegesis" criticized by Brevard Childs (1979). That is, the interpreter combines "historical critical analysis with a type of theological interpretation" (p. 74). A theme of the passage is linked up with a historical situation (viz., the exile), so it can serve a pastoral function in the repertory of contemporary preachers comprising the readership, located somewhere between the mythological and the literal perspectives, to whom the commentary is directed.

Even those who listen to the proclamation from the inside of the church can justly question how the sermon or teaching transforms reality. If one concedes the assumed context of the Babylonian exile, did it mean to the exiles a restoration of the Davidic monarchy? If the answer is yes, history belies this and compels us to read a putative transformation of reality rather than an actual one, because the restoration under Ezra and Nehemiah in the 5th century B.C. was no more enduring even if a little less glorious than the Maccabean one of the 2nd century B.C. Further, if, despite all the intrinsic features of Genesis 1 to the contrary, one allows an enlistment of the passage in the service of the Christian evangel, what does the evangel become in this second case but a psychological sense of well being, a candle on the glacier of global, national or (what is the more customary preoccupation of preaching) personal tragedy? Brueggemann's resistance of the creationist interpretation is commendable, but it leaves too many sexological abuses of the creation stories untouched if one seeks to move Christian preaching beyond its silence on, or contribution to, creationist homophobia.

It is sobering to realize that "be fruitful and multiply, and fill the earth" (Genesis 1:28) should in our time still be part of a dogma that condemns artificial contraception as intrinsically wrong, because "every marital act must remain open to the transmission of life."[1] Refusing to retract his moderate approval of artificial contraception that accords with "responsible parenthood and stewardship," Father Charles Curran was deprived on August 18, 1986, of his tenured teaching post at the Catholic University of America by the Vatican Congregation for the Doctrine of the Faith. Curran's heresy, however, was not confined to revisions of Vatican dogmas on contraception that, he insisted, have not been promulgated as "infallible" and are, hence, subject to critical, responsible evaluation.

The issue of homosexuality was a definite ingredient in Curran's dismissal. Among his other errors, Curran modestly and conservatively affirmed that "for an irreversible, constitutional or genuine homosexual, homosexual acts in the context of a loving relationship striving for permanency can in a certain sense be objectively morally acceptable."[2]

Though it is a standard element of Catholic teaching that appeal is made to creation texts of Genesis, along with other traditional and contemporary guidelines, to determine what nature commends or condemns, it is noteworthy that major Protestant bodies, not usually characterized as fundamentalist, also follow this pattern. At the conclusion of a 2-year study of the ordination of homosexual persons by a task force of 19 members, the 1978 General Assembly of the United Presbyterian Church voted down by an overwhelming majority the positive recommendation of this task force that "practicing" homosexuals meeting the denomination's ordination requirements should be accepted.

It cannot be doubted that arguments from Genesis 1-3 informed the negative position embraced by the Assembly majority in 1978 and reaffirmed by subsequent judicial action in 1985. In the prevailing position, barring the ordination of practicing homosexuals, the natural biological development of gender identity is linked to the

"Genesis account of the creation." Further, heterosexual expression of maleness and femaleness thus indicates "God's wise and beautiful pattern," while homosexuality is a "deviation" and a result of the fall (cf. Genesis 3). [See *Minutes of the General Assembly* (1978), pp. 261-262.]

INSTANCES OF PRESBYTERIAN CREATIONIST HOMOPHOBIA

Richard Lovelace, a Presbyterian professor of Church History at Gordon-Conwell Seminary, was a member of the United Presbyterian task force reporting to the church Assembly in 1978. His negative position on the ordination question was expressed, along with four other members of the task force, in a Minority Report opposing the position of the 15-member majority.

In his *Homosexuality and the Church* (1978), Lovelace laid out the centrality of creation texts for discussing homosexuality. "The starting point for understanding both human sexuality in general and homosexuality should be the account of the creation of man and woman in Genesis 1 and 2" (p. 103). Lovelace's sentence falters. Rhetorically, the sentence should read, ". . . human sexuality in general and homosexuality in particular . . ." Adding "in particular" would, however, make conspicuous his eisegetical (i.e., reading in what is not actually there) use of these primeval traditions.

As a matter of fact, Lovelace's discussion did not start with the Genesis stories of creation. Chapter 4 of his book, in which he interpreted "The Biblical Evidence," began with Leviticus 18:22 and 20:13, followed by conventional expositions of Romans 1:26f, 1 Corinthians 6:9f, various other New Testament texts, then back to Genesis 19, Judges 19, and so on before reaching a subheading called "The Broader Context of Biblical Teaching on Human Sexuality," where the above quoted statement on "The starting point" is found. It is obvious from this procedure that Lovelace was reading back into Genesis 1 and 2 the conclusions he had already reached by what he assumed to be "a central, pervasive, and consistent body of doctrine [on human sexuality] running through the whole structure of biblical ethics" (p. 103, bracketed words added from Lovelace's own context).

The notion of a "consistent body of doctrine" on human sexuality in the Bible is a remarkable overstatement, especially in the way Lovelace used it. Sarah fulfills her maternal duty to Abraham (Genesis 16) by providing him her maid slave as wife. Rachel acts similarly in the case of Jacob (Genesis 30), though he is already married to Leah (Genesis 29). Concubinage was regulated, but not prohibited in Mosaic law (Exodus 21:7-11; Deuteronomy 21:11-14). Polygamy was practiced by Gideon, Elkanah, Saul, David, Solomon, Rehoboam, and others. Prostitution is usually disapproved in scripture but winked at in the case of Rahab (Joshua 2), because she aids in the conquest of Jericho and thus is counted as a heroine of faith in Hebrews 11:31, a maker of liberation history according to Matthew 1:5 and James 2:25.

In a discerning essay on Proverbs 7, Brevard Childs (1970) did not contest the negation of prostitution in this chapter, but showed how the Song of Songs opposes, by its panegyric on erotic love between man and woman, without mention of marriage and family, the tendency in Proverbs to view the value of sex chiefly in its function as antidote to sexual incontinence. Childs appropriately warned us of the inclination of the New Testament to regard sexual passion as a mark of heathen immorality or a fire to be extinguished (1 Corinthians 7:9).

Though not discussed by Childs, Matthew 5:27-30 belongs to this context as well:

> You have heard that it was said, "You shall not commit adultery." But I say to you that every one who looks at a woman lustfully has already committed adultery with her in his heart. If your right eye causes you to sin, pluck it out and throw it away; it is better that you lose one of your members than that your whole body be thrown into hell. And if your right hand causes you to sin, cut it off and throw it away; it is better that you lose one of your members than that your whole body go into hell. (Revised Standard Version)

Helmut Koester (1978) has well argued that the passage is a Matthean construction that adapts and rearranges Mark 9:43-48. This tears it loose from its Markan setting of church discipline or excommunication (sustained, however, in the Matthean doublet at Matthew 18:8-9) and gives it, in the new Sermon on the Mount setting,[3] a specifically encratic content.

Defending the integrity of Old Testament teaching on sexuality (like that of the Song of Songs), Childs (1970) showed how Paul's views expressed in 1 Corinthians 7 are "balanced and criticized" by the Old Testament. Child's discussion was a healthy correction to simplistic generalizations that characterize uses of the Bible in evangelical conservatism.

Biblical theology and biblical ethics are many-faceted, and in many instances plainly heterogeneous. The truth at which one seeks to arrive in the study of scripture is not found by a facile compilation of prooftexts that sweeps counterbalancing evidence under the rug. The reappropriation of biblical guidance required by the moral and theological needs of succeeding generations means that evidence subdued or disregarded in the time-worn generalizations about a consistent body of doctrine may become decisive in the epochal shifts history imposes upon human responsibility.

Lovelace did concede that "new scientific knowledge" recasts the terms of moral judgment based on scripture. He then repudiated, however, the decisions of the American Psychiatric Association in 1973 and 1974 to remove homosexuality from the index of psychological pathology,[4] by appealing to "a recent poll of psychiatrists" reported in *Medical Aspects of Human Sexuality*[5] that showed that 69% of those polled believed that homosexuality is "usually a pathological adaptation." Lovelace did not disclose how many of the psychiatrists of this persuasion were members of the APA. He continued:

> Even if scientific opinion were to shift to support more fully the original APA vote, however, this should not necessarily occasion a shift in the church's opinion. The scientific community is often simply part of the fallen society the church confronts, and not the church's infallible mentor. (p. 115)

"Infallible mentor" is strongly suggestive of a Calvinistic view of scripture that does not in fact represent the present confessional position of the Presbyterian Church (U.S.A.).[6] Further, a 1980 poll of the Presbyterian Panel, as reported by Mount and Bos (1981), revealed that slightly less than 15% of a cross-section of 3,694 Presbyterians (clergy and nonclergy) held an inerrancy view of the Bible, including its statements about science, history, morality, and theology.

And yet, the United Presbyterian General Assembly of 1978, refusing the ordination of practicing homosexuals, adopted a position on creation sexuality patterned after that of Lovelace. That Assembly, commenting on Romans 1:26-27, defined "unnatural" as follows:

> By "unnatural" the Scripture does not mean contrary to custom or to the preference of a particular person, but rather *contrary to that order of universal human sexual nature that God intended in Genesis 1 and 2*. [*Minutes of the General Assembly* (1978), p. 263, emphasis added]

Evangelical conservatives seldom mention the fact that the mythic[7] creation account of the Elohist ends at Genesis 2:4a, followed by a second account of the Jahwist beginning at 2:4b. It is true that Genesis 19 also belongs to the Jahwist stratum of the tradition, though Lovelace chose to disregard the issue of sources in his discussion. It is logical to ask whether Genesis 19 and the second creation myth in Genesis 2, on the premise of a common source, share a polemic against homoeroticism. The Genesis commentary of Herman Gunkel (1910), despite its age, is useful in this connection. After canvassing various attempts to update or overthrow the work of Gunkel, Childs (1979) concluded:

> It is ironical that the revisions have not as yet resulted in any great measure of illumination and have certainly produced no close rival to Gunkel's initial analysis of Genesis. (p. 141)

Particularly incisive in Gunkel's study was his placement of Genesis 19 in a genre of ancient folklore centering upon the theme of hospitality/inhospitality. He found a prime example of this in the tale of Philemon and Baucis in Ovid's *Metamorphoses* (VIII, 610-715) (Ovid, 1971). Philemon and Baucis are an ancient Phrygian couple who welcome to their humble abode the weary gods, Zeus and Hermes, after they have been turned away from a thousand other doors. After sharing what little they have, it is disclosed to the elderly hosts who these divine visitors are. Then a calamitous flood destroys the whole area, wiping out the inhospitable neighbors, while Philemon and Baucis, unscathed, witness the disaster from a high place of refuge.

Moving from Gunkel's discussion, the theme of hospitality/inhospitality is confirmed in the prophetic view of Ezekiel 16:49: "This was the guilt of your sister Sodom: she and her daughters had pride, surfeit of food, and prosperous ease, but did not aid the poor and needy." Genesis 18 contextually reinforces the underlying motif of hospitality and its opposite in the succeeding chapter.

Singularly at odds with Lovelace's characterization of that view of sexuality he propounded as "a central, pervasive, and consistent body of doctrine running through the whole structure of biblical ethics" are New Testament references to Sodom that also underline the sin of inhospitality. Matthew 10:15, Luke 10:12, and the Majority text of Mark 6:11 demonstrate this, in face of an unreceptive attitude toward the apostolic emissaries. Similarly, at Matthew 11:23f and Luke 17:28f (cf. 17:25), an impenitent attitude toward the works and presence of Christ is assured of an apocalyptic doom. Most commentators, furthermore, see the Lot story behind Hebrews 13:2, and hospitality to unrecognized angel visitants is certainly a plausible ingredient at Matthew 25:37-40 as well as Luke 24:13-35 (particularly verses 28-31), though Sodom is not mentioned.

Gunkel's work shifted the moral weight of Genesis 19 in the direction already confirmed in Ezekiel 16:49, though he did not recognize the full import of it for the following reason: what Lovelace called "homosexuality" Gunkel called "pederasty" (German: *Knabenschändung, Knabenschänderei*). As a result of the traditional liberal arts education in Greco-Roman studies standard in Gunkel's day, pederasty was the cultural lens through which same-sex acts among males were seen. In Gunkel's (1910) commentary, as a result, the two angels of Genesis 19:1 were understood as pretty boys who kindle the lust of the men[8] of Sodom. Despite his solid contribution to the historical[9] understanding of Genesis 19, this one example is enough to show how prone all interpretations are to reflect the preunderstanding brought by the interpreter to the text.

Thorkil Vangaard (1972) has aided us in getting to the heart of the Sodom story as one of gang rape not to be identified correctly in our time either with homosexuality or pederasty. "The aggressive element, void of all eroticism, is precisely what is operating in such scenes of collective violence as that described in the biblical tale of Sodom" (102). As the parallel in Judges 19 should disclose to us, the xenophobic aggression of Genesis 19 exemplifies the kind of brutal humiliation not infrequently attested in literature of the ancient Mediterranean world, wherein the conquered was subjected by the conqueror to anal penetration as the consummate sign of domination. This means, in sum, that a connection of Genesis 19 with the doctrine of sexuality implicit in either Genesis 1 or Genesis 2-3 is fanciful.

One can also note at this point that Richard J. Hoffman (1983/84), following Edward Leach (1969), piled one imaginary conjecture upon another in trying to show that Cain's sin (Genesis 4:8) was not just murder but incestuous homosexuality. The notion that Cain (in Hebrew, *qayin*) goes back to Hebrew *qanah*, a homophone of "Canaan," a virtual synonym in Hoffman-Leach for same-sex vice among the Canaanites as seen from the standpoint of monotheism, is about as credible as the claim by Constantin Daniel (1966) that the reed given to Jesus in Matthew 27:29 discloses Jesus' affinity to the Zealots, because the Aramaic *qana* ("reed") is a homophone for *qannaya*, Aramaic for "Zealot."

It is not surprising that the use of Genesis 1-3 as illustrated from the work of Richard Lovelace is found also in Jerry Kirk, pastor of the College Hill Presbyterian Church in Cincinnati, in his book, *The Homosexual Crisis in the Mainline Church* (1978). Like Lovelace, Kirk affirmed that "a proper discussion of the theological understanding of homosexuality must begin with the Creation and Fall narratives in Genesis 1:26-31, 2:18-25, and 3:1-24" (p. 50). From these stories, according to Kirk, human beings are established as "persons who possess aspecific sexual identity," and the male/female differentiation of Genesis 1:27 is "essential to understanding what is fully human." From Genesis 1, Kirk continued, we learn "that to be human is to share humanity with the opposite sex," and Genesis 2 makes it clear that "in sexual intercourse a man and a woman become one flesh again as they enter into their physical union." (p. 51).

When Kirk moved to Genesis 3, "We find the goodness of God's creation distorted by sin and the divine pattern for male-female relationships is marred" (p. 51). "Rebellion and pride" distort "God's good gift to male and female" with resultant "strain between the sexes." "Homosexuality," he concluded, "is one result of this disjointedness" (p. 52).

Kirk's logic required, of course, that the "fall" (Genesis 3) express itself directly, without interruption, in the fallenness of homosexuality, because the whole of his discussion rested on the juxtaposition of God-ordained-heterosexual-man/wife-in-the-family on the one hand, and same-sex aberrancy on the other. Recognizing, however, that Genesis 3 says absolutely nothing about homosexuality, the reader must wait *15* chapters before the main point about human fallenness comes to light, namely at Genesis 18-19, where the judgment on Sodom enters the picture.

The next passage for demonstrating that fallenness really means (among other things) homosexuality is the familiar prohibition in Leviticus 18:22 and 20:13. These verses derive from what has since 1877 been called the "holiness code," according to the designation given to Leviticus 17-26 by August Klostermann. It must be kept in mind that even if Fohrer (1972) correctly dated the Holiness Code before the formation of the Priestly Code, it is still centuries subsequent to the Jahwist material underlying Genesis 3. Kirk was aware of the term "Holiness Code," but did not provide any rationale, literary or theological, for its connection with Genesis 3.

Christians and Jews alike recognize the hazards of importing into contemporary ethics selections from the Holiness Code or kindred legislation elsewhere in the Pentateuch.[10] At Mark 10:5 (also Matthew 19:8), Jesus annuls a Deuteronomic regulation on divorce, presumably because it was accommodated to male disregard of the rights of women. The tension between gospel and law reaches an acute level in Paul. Rudolf Bultmann (1955), in expounding the statement in Romans 10:4 that Christ is the end of the law, has correctly construed "end" (Greek, *telos*) in the sense of termination rather than complementarity.

In Christian belief, mainly deriving from the theology of Paul in texts like Romans 5:12-21, 1 Corinthians 15:20-25, 42-50, and 2 Corinthians 5:17, Christ, not Adam, constitutes the prototypical human being (*anthropos*). "Son of Man," an awkward expression in Greek, frequently used as a New Testament title of Christ, means in Aramaic and Hebrew, "human One." This presents for the doctrine of sexuality maintained by Lovelace, Kirk, Williams, and other evangelical conservatives an insurmountable barrier. If, as Kirk (1978), citing Williams, wrote, "to be human means to share humanity with the opposite sex" (p. 53), one is obliged to exclude Jesus, as The World's Most Famous Bachelor, from his status as the *anthropos* par excellence of the new creation.

The statement, "to share humanity with the opposite sex," is, therefore, an ambiguous expression. Is the real meaning to share (i.e., have) sex with the opposite sex? Again, Jesus seems to be left out of a humanity so described. If, on the other hand, humanity is supposed to mean "humanity," gay and lesbian persons would seem to qualify.

Regarding the heterosexual Christian family tradition, it must also be said that all earthly human values suffer transvaluation in the presence of the Kingdom of God. This underlies the pericope on the "true family" of Jesus in Mark 3:31-35 (see also Matthew 12:36-50, Luke 8: 19-21"): "Whoever does the will of God is my brother, and sister, and Mother."

Homosexual people are particularly capable of grasping the meaning of the "sword" of Matthew 10:34 (cf. Luke 12:51) — that is, the sword of family division — that also rests on the transvaluation of cultural norms found in early apocalypse from Micah 7:6 onward.

Homosexual inclusion presents a distinctive challenge to the churches not at all dissimilar to Paul's courageous advocacy of Gentile inclusion in face of a Jerusalem fundamentalism that insisted on cultural criteria alongside the faith righteousness advocated by Paul. Lovelace's "solution" (1978) to homosexual inclusion and ordination in the church — gays and lesbians should convert to heterosexuality "when this is possible" and adopt "a celibate lifestyle when it is not" (p. 125) — is comparable to the inclusion of slaves on church rolls during the Confederacy: separate and unequal.

Once again, the presupposition that both creation and nature condemn homosexual orientation and practice per se necessarily means that one repent thereof and abstain therefrom.

Daniel Maguire (1985) lamented a situation in the Republic of Ireland where "too many of the prominent Catholic bishops . . . are scandalously absorbed in issues of pelvic orthodoxy" (p. 512), by which he meant "contraception, sterilization, divorce, and abortion." His grief over this emerged from its effect on the apportionment of the moral energy and influence of the church in face of other pressing social concerns begging for more adequate understanding and implementation. Presbyterians are not strangers to Maguire's complaint. Reviewing the General Assembly of 1985 in Indianapolis, Vic Jameson (1985) reported in the *Presbyterian Survey* that "no other issue received as much attention" as the abortion issue. Even in 1978, Kirk wrote of *The Homosexual Crisis* in the church, and Don Williams (1978) one of the five signatories of the Minority Report opposing homosexual ordination by the United Presbyterian in 1978, asked, *Will Homosexuality Split the Church?* It is certain from action taken by the Presbyterian Permanent Judicial Commission in 1985 squelching a church in Buffalo, New York; when it announced its intention to ordain a gay or lesbian elder; from the presence of gay and lesbian students in Presbyterian seminaries; from the continuing vigor of the organization called Presbyterians for Lesbian/Gay Concerns; and from dozens of "More Light" Presbyterian Churches that receive members without discrimination as to sexual orientation; it is certain, in light of all these considerations, that the denomination's decision against homosexual ordination in 1978 is not settled. But there is also evidence that a continuing pubic preoccupation will preempt the church's social ministry.

A FRESH APPROACH TO CREATION SEXUALITY

Phyllis Trible (1978) has probed Genesis 1-3 in a manner instructive for the discussion of creation sexuality. In Kirk's (1978) approach to Genesis 1:27 he was quite content to place the male/female differentiation at the top of the agenda. This differentiation did not proceed from a primal androgynous, bisexual, or unisexual anthropos. The necessity of eliminating any preliminary stage antecedent to sexual differentiation is obvious: the male/female distinction constitutes humanness. That is, the "one flesh" associated by Kirk with Genesis 2:21-23 (N.B., the phrase does not appear until verse 24) refers to woman's being "taken from man," as it also connotes what happens in sexual intercourse, meaning, of course, only heterosexual intercourse.

Trible's agenda was altogether different from that of Kirk. Her concern was female rights. The common ground between her defense against misogyny and the present critique of creationist homophobia is a single liberationist objective which makes possible a new approach to the text.

Trible (1978) drew up a list of specifics characterizing the misogynous reading of Genesis 2-3 that has, in the history of interpretation, "acquired a status of canonicity":

- A male God creates first man (2:7) and last woman (2:22); first means superior and last means inferior or subordinate.
- Woman is created for the sake of man: a helpmate to cure his loneliness (2:18-23).
- Contrary to nature, woman comes out of man; she is denied even her natural function of birthing and that function is given to man (2:21-22).
- Woman is the rib of man, dependent upon him for life (2:21-22).
- Taken out of man (2:23), woman has a derivative, not autonomous existence.
- Man names woman (2:23) and thus has power over her.
- Man leaves his father's family in order to set up through his wife another patriarchal unit (2:24).
- Woman tempted man to disobey and thus she is responsible for sin in the world (3:6); she is untrustworthy, gullible, and simpleminded.
- Woman is cursed by pain in childbirth (3:16); pain in childbirth is a more severe punishment than man's struggle with the soil; it signifies that woman's sin is greater than man's.

- Woman's desire for man (3:16) is God's way of keeping her faithful and submissive to her husband.
- God gives man the right to rule over woman (3:16). (Trible, p. 73)

Trible (1978) probed in a fresh way the literary quality of the creation passages and reconstituted their aesthetic depth, teaching thereby that biblical texts are multifaceted and should not be constricted by a prescribed range of opinion closed to more light that may break forth from them. Because Genesis 1:27 serves as the clue to the whole scope of Trible's enterprise in this book, it is set forth here in parallel lines that mark it as a piece of Hebrew poetry:

> And God created humankind in his image;
> in the image of God created he him;
> male and female created he them.
> (Trible, p. 12)

A symmetrical design constitutes the arrangement of the 6-day creation account, each episode beginning, "And God said, . . ." and each concluding with a "refrain that identifies its particular day." The first 3 days are the skeleton — light/darkness, firmament/waters, earth/vegetation — while the last 3 days fill the skeleton out (1:14-19; 1:20-23; 1:24-30), the sixth day being the one in which land animals appear and humankind is created (1:24-30).

The distinctiveness of humanity's creation is not indicated only by the greater extent (verses 26-30) of the liturgy that expresses it, nor in the unique phrase of divine deliberation ("let us make humankind in our image," 1:26) that distinguishes this episode from the ones in 1:3, 6, 9, 14, and 24. Only for the human creatures, and not for the animals, do we find sexuality called "male and female." Further, and this is central to Trible's exegesis, the male/female sexuality "pertains not to procreation but to the image of God. Procreation is shared by humankind with the animal world (1:22, 28); sexuality is not" (p. 15). To humanity alone does God give dominion; only humanity is addressed in the first person (1:29-30).

Genesis 1:27 exhibits a parallelism in 3 lines. Line two ("in the image of God created he him") is an inverted parallel to line one,

built on a chiastic pattern. Using the Hebrew word sequence, Trible
(1978) showed this as follows:

a   b   c

And created God   humankind in his image;

c′   b′   a′

in the image of God   created he him.

(p. 16)

Lines two and three (male and female created he them") comprise a
formal or complementary parallelism in which "male and female"
explain "image of God" in line two, which is the fulcrum of the
three liturgical lines. It is clear from this that "male and female"
provide the clue for understanding "image of God" without sacrificing "the difference between Creator and created" (p. 15).

An essential benefit of Trible's (1978) primary association of the
sexual differentiation, male and female, with the image of God,
placing it first in a theological framework before exploiting its anthropological side, is to open the door for a recognition of the partiality of scriptural metaphors for God masculine (Father, King, Husband, Warrior, and so on) and the need for recovering scriptural
metaphors for God feminine. Despite the pessimism of some who
find the correction of biblical and ecclesiastical patriarchy a hope-
less labor, with the faith of the importunate woman in Luke 18:1-8,
Trible relentlessly and insightfully pursued the demise of androcen-
tric misuses of creation texts.

Genesis 2 and 3 are, again, developed under auspices of an extensive rhetorical structure with the fate of eros as the underlying
theme set forth in three developments: eros created (2:4b-24), eros
contaminated (2:25-3:7), eros condemned (3:8-24). These moments
in the primeval history of eros are sensitively subdivided by attention to numerous aesthetic devices in the construction of the narrative: (a) underlying parallel patterns, (b) word plays, and (c) a link-
ing of introduction and conclusion (Trible: "aftermath") by the
repetition of key words and phrases. Through patient probing of the
text by such devices as these, Trible followed already the clue established in respect to 1:27.

In spite of the imponderable strength of traditional social forces that have built up the misogynist interpretation, Trible's viewpoint has nevertheless made itself felt. It is noted in Brueggemann's commentary (1982), even if without elaboration. In Norman Gottwald's (1985) important introduction to the Old Testament, written with pioneering attention to sociological and literary canons, Trible's concern was both acknowledged and elaborated in his discussion of Genesis 2-3:

> The imposition of man's "rule" over woman (3:16) is presented as a lapsed condition that is reprehensible and might be overcome through a restored relation of the pair with Jahweh. Nevertheless, later Jewish and Christian exegesis has tended to read the story through male chauvinist eyes that blame woman disproportionately for the disobedience, even associating the eating of the fruit with sexuality itself and playing on the misogynist theme of "woman as temptress." (p. 239)

A LIBERATION ALTERNATIVE TO CREATIONIST HOMOPHOBIA

Phyllis Trible (1978) has significantly enriched the understanding of Genesis 1:27 in the theological direction by her insightful development of "the image of God male and female" (p. 23). She proceeded intrepidly from this clue with "a critique of culture in the light of misogyny" (p. 7) in order to establish in biblical theology not "a narrow focus upon women" but a greatly needed correction of entrenched patriarchy.

In earlier writing on Genesis 2, Trible (1978) defended the androgynous interpretation of *hā'ādām* (humankind). (Also see Powers, 1977). Her abandonment of this position in *God and the Rhetoric of Sexuality* led to the anomaly that the "earth creature" (*hā'ādām*) remains sexless until the creation of human sexuality in Genesis 2:21-24. While she admittedly proceeded in this regard on the basis of a literary or rhetorical analysis of the text without reference to its scientific verifiability, the modern reader instinctively questions the conceivability of an earth creature evolving from a process of natural selection without the vital element of sexuality.

Without attempting to argue that Genesis provides a scientific description of the earliest form of human sexuality, it is nevertheless possible, on the basis of Trible's earlier hypothesis on the androgynous God who creates the androgynous human being, to link the creation story with a significant body of both mythological and scientific material that can meaningfully reinforce contemporary disenchantment with theological and cultural patriarchy and dissolve, as well, the foundations of creationist homophobia.

In 1920, Freud (1920/1955) lamented the absence of scientific knowledge about the beginnings of human eroticism when he wrote: "Science has so little to tell us about the origin of sexuality that we can liken the problem to a darkness into which not so much as a ray of a hypothesis has penetrated" (p. 57). Straightforwardly after this statement, Freud adduced the creation myth (an antonym of "science" for Freud) that Aristophanes recounts in Plato's *Symposium* 189D-190A (Plato, 1946). According to this myth, there were at first three kinds of human beings: male, female, and androgynous. This classical text obscures whether the first two humans existed independently of or derived from the final one in Plato's idea, because the androgynous person was double in all respects, i.e., having four hands, two faces, four legs, two sexual organs, and so on, and then was split in two, male and female. Out of this division arose the erotic instinct, representing what Freud called "a need to restore an earlier state of things."

Freud (1905/1953) also observed the same androgynous beginning of humankind in the Hindu *Brihâdaranyka-upanishad*. Similarly Joseph Campbell (1968) emphasized the phenomenon of the androgynous deity in the Hindu Bodhisattva, the Pueblo Zuni, the Great Original of the *Chinese Chronicles*, the Greek Hermaphrodite and Eros, and the Elohist of Genesis 1:27.

George F. Moore (1927) also found in Genesis 1:27 androgynous humanity, characterizing this as "a bit of foreign lore adapted to the first pair in Genesis" (p. 453), citing *Midrash Rabbah* 8:1, where the 3rd century Rabbi Samuel bar Nahman said, "When God created Adam he created him facing both ways (d^eyo $partsuphin$) then he sawed him in two and made two backs, one for each figure" (p. 453). Just before this is the statement of Rabbi Jeremiah bar Leazar, "When God created Adam he created him androgynous (*andro-*

gynos) this is what is written, 'Male and female he created them'"
(p. 453). Harry Freedman's (1938) translation of this same passage,
however, renders the Greek loan word *androgynos* as "hermaphrodite [bi-sexual]" (p. 54).

The scientific evidence for human bisexuality is large. In Greco-
Roman culture, pederasty was a widespread form of erotic expression practiced in conjunction with honored social occupations such
as education, philosophical reflection, and the training for, or making of, war. Speaking of the creativity of Periclean Athens, its
gifted poets, philosophers, artists, and architects, William Cole
(1959) opposed the notion that it was *because* of *paiderastia*, as
some homophiles might argue, that such genius abounded:

> These creators, including Socrates, were for the most part
> married men with families! They loved boys, it is true, but
> they were by no means repelled by heterosexual relations, nor
> did they regard women with disgust. The Greeks found beauty
> magnetic without respect to sex. (p. 199)

Sappho, the illustrious poet of Lesbos, was the author of "the
strongest expression of female homosexual emotion in Greek literature" (Dover, 1978, p. 173), and was also a wife and a mother
(Durant, 1939, pp. 153, 302). Dover warned against the assumption, however, that her "finishing school" for girls was a place for
teaching sexual techniques.

Modern sexological research, which has broken the silence im-
posed by religious and legislative taboos on the subject of homosexuality, has strengthened awareness of the variety of stimuli to which
sexuality is responsive. In place of the "either homosexual or heterosexual" categorization to which public thinking has been accus-
tomed, the Kinsey group (1948, 1953) set up the now familiar graduated scale from zero (completely heterosexual) to six (completely
homosexual), with emphasis on the number of people who do not
fall in either absolute category but range at different periods of their
lives from one level of graduation to another. For example, Kinsey,
Pomeroy, and Martin (1948) reported:

Eighteen percent of the males have at least as much of the homosexual as the heterosexual in their histories (i.e., rate 3-6) for at least 3 years between the ages of 16 and 55. This is more than one in six of the white male population. (p. 650)

Freud (1905/1953) emphasized that a degree of hermaphroditism occurs in normal physiology, for "in every normal male or female individual, traces are found of the apparatus of the opposite sex" (p. 141). This point is underlined by Shafer (1978), who drew from Money and Tucker (1977). Despite Kinsey's (1948, 1953) need to formulate, outside the scale from zero to six, a category "X" of persons not responding to either heterosexual or homosexual stimuli, the notion that human beings are polymorphously sexual beings is descriptively valid. Freud's (1904/1953) discussion of the "polymorphously perverse disposition" to which children are subject under the influence of seduction correctly accents the malleability of the sexual disposition in early years. One does not have to adopt along with this Freud's larger theory on homoeroticism as a form of arrested sexual development. Bell, Weinberg, and Hammersmith (1981) tested the parental background and relationships of gay/lesbian people in San Francisco and found Freud's theory unsupportable. On the old question of nature versus nurture in the etiology of homosexuality, the Bell team emphasized nurture in line with the Kinsey-Freud tradition, but they did not disparage the possibilities emerging from ongoing biological research for modification of their traditional emphasis.

In sum, the creation stories do not provide explicit moral or theological evidence on homosexual practice. Homophobic interpretations of subsequent passages, such as Genesis 19, read back into Genesis 1-3 sexual ideas extraneous to those chapters. The important differences between homosexual practice and orientation are modern empirical distinctions of which we cannot expect Genesis 1-3 to be aware.

We do find, however, in the image of God male and female, as well as in the image of humankind male and female, a primordial androgyny that substantiates liberationist opposition to both misogynist and homophobic abuses of creation texts. It does not follow from this that heterosexuality, bisexuality, or homosexuality, are, in themselves, good or evil. From the biblical standpoint, a liberated sexuality can only be content to seek those forms of neighbor love that are based on equal regard for the rights of others and find their reason for being in the love of a God who does not show partiality toward Jew or Greek, slave or free, male or female, heterosexual or homosexual.

NOTES

1. The quoted phrases (aside from Genesis 1:28) are taken from the Louisville, Kentucky, archdiocesan newspaper, *The Record*, April 11, 1986, reporting on Curran.

2. *The Record*, March 20, 1986. It is also certain that his inclusiveness toward gay and lesbian Catholics was a factor in the censure of Archbishop Raymond Hunthausen of Seattle, Washington, resulting in extensive abridgement of his episcopal portfolio. See *National Catholic Reporter*, September 12 and 19, 1986.

3. No serious student of source and redaction criticism in Matthew can confidently pontificate about how much of Matthew 5-7 consists of the very words of Jesus. Georg Strecker (1988) for example, holds that the Sermon on the Mount is not a speech of Jesus but a literary composition of Matthew.

4. The action of The American Psychiatric Association was followed in 1975 by that of The American Psychological Association.

5. The article is entitled "Sexual survey no. 4: Current thinking on homosexuality" (November, 1977).

6. The Presbyterian Church in the U.S. and the United Presbyterian Church in the U.S.A. merged in 1983, becoming the Presbyterian Church (U.S.A.).

7. I use "mythic" in the simple *religionsgeschictliche* sense, *Gottesgeschichte*, or "narration about the activity of a divine being." As Bultmann (1958) said, "Myths give worldly objectivity to that which is unworldly" (p. 19).

8. The phrase "both young and old" at 19:4 (cf. verse 11) is a serious impediment to both Lovelace's and Gunkel's viewpoint. "Young" (Hebrew *na'ar*) can reach down even to infancy (e.g., Exodus 2:6; I Samuel 1:24). See my discussion (Edwards, 1984, pp. 27-32) of Gunkel.

9. In this setting, "historical" denotes the meaning of a text in its own time as opposed to what it means or should mean now, to borrow the significant distinction underlined by Krister Stendahl (1984).

10. This matter is seriously at issue in modern Israel. Orthodox Judaism is the only form of Judaism recognized there by law. Domestic law (marriage, divorce, and so on) is administered by religious courts. Sabbath ordinances and the right of conscientious objection are similarly determined by orthodox preference. This situation has provoked the formation of the American-Israeli Civil Liberties Coalition promoted by Professor Philippa Strum, Rabbi Balfour Brickner, and others.

11. Conzelmann (1960) correctly underlined how Luke intensified the conflict already present in Mark by putting the story in conjunction with Luke 8:18. Fitzmyer (1981), perhaps to sustain Mary's solidarity with Jesus, dulled Conzelmann's point.

REFERENCES

Bell, A. P., Weinberg, M. S., & Hammersmith, S. K. (1981). *Sexual preference: Its development in men and women* (2 vols.). Bloomington, IN: Indiana University Press.

Brueggemann, W. (1982). Genesis: A Bible commentary for teaching and preaching. *Interpretation*. Atlanta: John Knox.

Bultmann, R. (1955). Christ the end of the law. In J. C. G. Greig (Trans.). *Essays philosophical and theological* (pp. 36-66). London: SCM.

Bultmann, R. (1958). *Jesus Christ and mythology*. New York: Charles Scribner's Sons.

Campbell, J. (1968). *The hero with a thousand faces* (2nd ed.). Princeton, NJ: Princeton University Press.

Childs, B. (1970). *Biblical theology in crisis*. Philadelphia: Westminster.

Childs, B. (1979). *Introduction to the Old Testament as scripture*. Philadelphia: Fortress.

Cole, W. G. (1959). *Sex and love in the Bible*. New York: Association.

Conzelmann, H. (1960). *The theology of St. Luke* (G. Buswell, Trans.). New York: Harper & Brothers.

Daniel, C. (1966). Esséiens, zelotes, et sicaires et leur mention par paronymie dans le Nouveau Testament. *Numen, 13*, 88-115.

Dover, K. J. (1978). *Greek homosexuality*. Cambridge, MA: Harvard University Press.

Durant, W. (1939). *The life of Greece*. New York: Simon & Schuster.

Edwards, G. R. (1984). *Gay/lesbian liberation: A biblical perspective*. New York: Pilgrim.

Fitzmyer, J. A. (1981). The gospel according to Luke (I-IX). *Anchor Bible*. Garden City, NY: Doubleday.

Fohrer, G. (1972). *The history of Israelite religion* (D. E. Green, Trans.). Nashville: Abingdon.

Freedman, H., & Simon, M. (1939). (Trans. & Eds.). *Midrash Rabbah* (Vol. 1). London: Soncino.

Freud, S. (1953). Three essays on the theory of sexuality. In J. Strachey (Trans. & Ed.), *The standard edition of the complete psychological works of Sigmund Freud* (Vol. 7, pp. 125-245). London: Hogarth Press. (Original work published 1905)

Freud, S. (1955). Beyond the pleasure principle. In J. Strachey (Trans. & Ed.),

The standard edition of the complete psychological works of Sigmund Freud (Vol. *18*, pp. 7-64). London: Hogarth Press. (Original work published 1920)

Gottwald, N. (1985). *The Hebrew Bible – A socio-literary introduction*. Philadelphia: Fortress.

Gunkel, H. (1910). Genesis (3rd ed.). *Göttinger Handkommentar zum Alten Testament*. Göttingen: Vandenhoeck u. Ruprecht.

Hoffman, R. J. (1983/84). Vices, gods, and virtues: Cosmology as a mediating factor in attitudes toward male homosexuality. *Journal of Homosexuality*, *9* (2/3), 27-44.

Jameson, V. (1985, July/August). One hundred and ninety-seventh General Assembly Indianapolis. *Presbyterian Survey*, pp. 42-54.

Kinsey, A. C., Pomeroy, W. E., & Martin, C. E. (1948). *Sexual behavior in the human male*. Philadelphia: W. B. Saunders.

Kinsey, A. C., Pomeroy, W. B., Martin, C. E., & Gebhard, P. H. (1953). *Sexual behavior in the human female*. Philadelphia: W. B. Saunders.

Kirk, J. R. (1978). *The homosexual crisis in the mainline church*. New York: Thomas Nelson.

Koester, H. (1978). Mark 9:43-47 and Quintilian 8.3.75. *Harvard Theological Review*, *71*, 151-153.

Leach, E. R. (1969). *Genesis as myth and other essays*. London: Jonathan Cape.

Lovelace, R. (1978). *Homosexuality and the church*. Old Tappan, NJ: Revell.

Maguire, D.C. (1985). Ireland's other troubles. *Christianity and Crisis*, *45*, 511-512.

Minutes of the General Assembly of the United Presbyterian Church in the U.S.A. (Part 1). (1978). New York: Offices of the General Assembly.

Money, J., & Tucker, P. (1977). *Sexual signatures: On being a man or a woman*. London: Sphere. (Abacus ed.).

Moore, G. F. (1927). *Judaism* (Vol. 1). Cambridge, MA: Harvard University Press.

Mount, E. C., Jr., & Bos, J. W. H. (1981). Scripture on sexuality: Shifting authority. *Journal of Presbyterian History*, *59*, 219-243.

Ovid. *Metamorphoses* (Vol. 1). (1971). (F. J. Miller, Trans.) Loeb Classical Library. Cambridge, MA: Harvard University Press.

Plato. *Symposium* (Vol. 5 of Plato). (1946). (W. J. Miller, Trans.). Loeb Classical Library. Cambridge, MA: Harvard University Press.

Powers, E. A. (Ed.). (1977). *Human sexuality: A preliminary study*. New York: United Church Press.

Sexual survey no. 4: current thinking on homosexuality. (1977). *Medical Aspects of Human Sexuality*, *11*, 110-111.

Shafer, B. (1978). The church and homosexuality. *Minutes of the General Assembly of the United Presbyterian Church in the U.S.A.* (Part 1, pp. 213-260). New York: Offices of the General Assembly.

Stendahl, K. (1984). *Meanings: The Bible as document and as guide*. Philadelphia: Fortress.

Strecker, G. (1988). *The sermon on the mount: An exegetical commentary.* Nashville, TN: Abingdon.

Trible, P. (1978). *God and the rhetoric of sexuality.* Philadelphia: Fortress.

Vanggaard, T. (1972). *Phallós: A symbol of its history in the male world.* London: Jonathan Cape.

Williams, D. (1978). *The bond that breaks: Will homosexuality split the church?* Los Angeles: BIM.

Discourses of Desire:
Sexuality and Christian Women's
Visionary Narratives

E. Ann Matter, PhD

University of Pennsylvania

SUMMARY. This article compares and contrasts two autobiographical accounts by seventeenth-century Italian religious women: Benedetta Carlini of Pescia, and Maria Domitilla Galluzzi of Pavia. Both were visionaries, highly regarded by their communities, but subject to suspicion and close scrutiny by ecclesiastical authorities. The trial records of Benedetta Carlini relate a series of sexual contacts with her young assistant, while no overt sexual expression is evident in the life of Maria Domitilla Galluzzi. This article questions the relationship between the categories of scholars and the sexual self-understanding of figures in their own historical context. It suggests that "lesbian nun" is too simplistic a dichotomy, and that in comparison to the life of Maria Domitilla, Benedetta Carlini's sexuality revolved around an elaborate organic connection between the spiritual and the sensual.

Judith Brown's recent studies of the life of Benedetta Carlini, "a lesbian nun in Renaissance Italy," have raised many important issues in the historical study of lesbian sexuality.[1] Brown (1984) brought to light the story of a woman in the early 17th century who is documented as having had sexual relations with another woman; this is among the earliest explicit references to sex between women in the western European tradition.[2] In a field of historical inquiry for which there is little evidence, this discovery is in itself of great

---

E. Ann Matter is Associate Professor of Religious Studies at the University of Pennsylvania. She has written on medieval spirituality and biblical interpretation, and is currently at work on a study of Maria Domitilla Galluzzi.

importance. Further, the questions raised by Brown's analysis of Benedetta Carlini as lesbian raise very important issues about the relationship between the categories or labels of scholars and the self-understanding of the historical figures we study. This article is intended as a contribution to this theoretical and methodological problem.

This article examines the evidence Brown presented about Benedetta Carlini in the light of the autobiographical testimony of a contemporary Italian religious woman, Maria Domitilla Galluzzi, a nun in the Cappuccine house dedicated to the Blessed Sacrament in Pavia.[3] The documents regarding the life of this woman give no evidence of any sexual activity at all. Yet the parallels between her life and the life of Benedetta Carlini suggest a context of attitudes about the body and about love that can be instructive in our interpretation of even the most immodest acts of medieval and Renaissance women.

BENEDETTA CARLINI

Born in the Tuscan village of Vellano in 1590, Benedetta Carlini was immediately dedicated to religious life. When it seemed that both Benedetta and her mother would die in the birthing bed, the prayers of her father saved them; he promised that the "blessed child" ("Benedetta") would spend her life in the service of God. With such a beginning, it is not surprising that Benedetta's childhood was full of piety and miraculous events (Brown, 1986). At the age of 9, she was taken to Pescia, where she entered a newly founded community of women living under the Augustinian rule, known locally as the Theatines.[4] Benedetta apparently thrived in this struggling community, for some 20 years later, when the convent was finally recognized as a fully enclosed house and granted its own chapel, she was named abbess (Brown, 1986).

Evidently, a good part of the spiritual authority of Benedetta Carlini was the result of her fame as a visionary. Both within her community and in the town of Pescia she was revered for her spiritual powers. Her confessor, Paolo Ricordati, encouraged her in developing them. Benedetta's visions were often delivered by one of a number of angels who bore names and personalities otherwise unknown in Christian spirituality: Tesauriello Fiorito, Virtudioello, Radicello, and the most important to her story, Splenditello. Sometimes she found herself transported to direct communication with Christ.

Of course, the theme of women's religious life as a marriage to the "Heavenly Bridegroom" was a commonplace of medieval and Renaissance Christian spirituality, and many other women were known to bear the stigmata (the wounds of Christ's passion) as Benedetta Carlini did. But the length to which she carried this theme was unusual. In May of 1619, Benedetta announced, first to her confessor and then to her community, that Jesus had appeared to her with instructions for a wedding ceremony to be solemnly celebrated in the chapel of the convent (Brown, 1986). As the nuns began to prepare for the ceremony, gifts of altarcloths, candles, flowers, and tapestries poured in from other religious communities and from the laypeople of Pescia. The ceremony was celebrated with procession, hymns, and litanies; Benedetta, in a trance, spoke to the Virgin Mary, to various saints, and to Jesus, from whom she received a gold ring.

This mystical wedding was both the high point and the beginning of the end of Benedetta Carlini's fame as a mystic. The stir caused by the ceremony, her growing fame outside of the convent, and the amount of attention she called to herself all aroused the suspicions of the ecclesiastical hierarchy. There were questions, for example, about the veracity of these visions. After all, no one else present saw any of the heavenly visitors, nor could the ring given to Benedetta by her divine spouse be seen by anyone but herself. A climate of suspicion surrounded her from that time on and led directly to the two official investigations, whose documents have provided us with the story of her life.

The first investigation was carried out by Stefano Cecchi, the provost of Pescia, directly following the sensational public marriage of Benedetta Carlini and Christ (Brown, 1986). Cecchi visited the house 14 times in 2 months; each round began with an examination of the wounds on Benedetta's hands and head, and repeated questioning as to how she came to have these stigmata. The content of her revelations was scrutinized for orthodoxy and for signs of diabolical influence. Finally, the impact of Benedetta's visions on the other nuns of the community was considered. Here, a star witness was Bartolomea Crivelli, a young nun who had been serving Benedetta for 2 years as special companion to help her through the periods of ecstasy. Bartolomea had seen Benedetta receive the stigmata and a mystical exchange of hearts with Christ, and she had also heard the voices of saints who came to visit. Partly on the strength of Bartolomea's testimony, the provostial investigation judged Benedetta Carlini a true visionary.

Bartolomea Crivelli played quite a different role in the second investigation, which took place between August 1622 and March 1623, for it is by her testimony that the issue of "immodest acts" of a sexual nature was raised. Like the first investigation, this inquiry was launched to determine the truth and origin of Benedetta's mystical claims, which had taken a new turn with Benedetta's dramatic death and resurrection in March of 1621, an event prophesied by the angel Tesauriello Fiorito and attended by many of the community (Brown, 1986). This new miracle aroused the curiosity of the papal nunzio, Alfonso Giglioli, who was well aware of the earlier inquiry into Benedetta's reported miracles and visions. The attitude of the community toward their abbess seemed to have undergone a striking change, for the testimony of this second investigation was full of evidence of Benedetta's fakery and pretension. But the true surprise of Giglioli's investigation was the charge of Bartolomea Crivelli that Benedetta had, over the course of 2 years, forced her into sexual acts on a regular basis. These sexual exchanges, however, were perceived by Bartolomea within the context of Benedetta's power as a visionary, for it was always the angel Splenditello, or even Jesus himself, who was the lover, operating through the vehicle of Benedetta.[5] These acts were all the evidence the nunzio needed to determine that Benedetta had been deceived all along by the devil, but the commission he led took their time to determine her guilt. In November 1623, Benedetta Carlini was officially declared in error through the misleading of the devil. Her punishment was set by the nunzio himself: imprisonment in the convent until her death.

I would like to stress several aspects of this sad story before turning to the life of the Cappuccina of Pavia. First, the nature of Benedetta Carlini's sexual encounters with her sister nun is so bizarre as to defy our modern categories of "sexual identity." Certainly, this poses the large question of the use of the term "lesbian" in this case, but it also raises issues of less taxonomic description. For example, when Brown (1986) referred to the ecclesiastic's shock "that two women should seek sexual gratification with each other," related their "love story" to that of Heloise and Abelard, and described Bartolomea as Benedetta's "young lover" (pp. 118, 121, 125) she invited misinterpretation. It is clear in the overall context of the life of Benedetta Carlini that the primary object of erotic devotion was her heavenly bridegroom, Jesus Christ. Any human love story in such a life, especially one acted out in persistent metaphors of angelic visits, has to be seen in that spiritual context. Secondly, even though this sexual immodesty was an important element in Benedetta Carlini's condemnation, it was not the reason why she was investigated in the first (or, indeed, the second) place. The sexual life of this unfortunate woman was a complete surprise to her investigators, who were instead on the track of her claims to a special spiritual marriage with Christ.

MARIA DOMITILLA GALLUZZI

The life of this important figure of Lombard piety is told in an autobiography preserved in at least six manuscripts.[6] Even though the context and voice are thus strikingly different from the judicial narratives that tell the story of Benedetta Carlini, there are remarkable congruences in the significant events of these two lives. Maria Domitilla was born Severetta Galluzzi in the city of Acqui, Piemonte, in 1595. Her mother was from Genova, a city in which the young girl spent a good part of her childhood in the care of her Aunt Domitilla, the wife of a member of the important Beccaria family.[7] The miracles started before her birth. When Maria Domitilla's mother was pregnant, she fell down with such force that she feared she had killed the child. In desperation, after feeling no movement for 3 days and nights, the mother promised before a crucifix that the child would be raised and exhorted to the service of God. Immediately, Maria Domitilla gave a great kick. As Maria Domitilla later related it, "before I was born, she heard my voice."[8] At the age of 6, Maria Domitilla already wanted to serve "il dolcissimo mio Giesù" (my sweetest Jesus), and preferred to listen to the stories of the life and passion of Jesus than eat or sleep. When her mother tried to pierce her ears, the little Maria Domitilla refused, insisting that nuns did not wear jewels. When her younger sister died, the soul of the dead child visited Maria Domitilla to regale her with stories about paradise. And, in a proof of piety that fairly begs for a Freudian interpretation, the child saved a "most delicate glass" especially loved by her father, which she accidentally knocked off a window sill onto a pile of sharp stones. When Maria Domitilla prayed, the fragile object landed "without any spot," as among balls of cotton.[9]

For all this early piety, Maria Domitilla did not enter the religious life until the age of majority, joining the Cappuccine nuns of Pavia in 1616. Only 3 years later, she began to have frequent, intense, and erotic visions of Christ, particularly on Fridays and during Lent. In one instance, while praying before a crucifix:

> With such a great sweetness and gentleness, by his divine and holy goodness, he [Christ] descended to me so that he united his most holy head to my unworthy one, his most holy face to mine, his most holy breast to mine, his most holy hands to mine, and his most holy feet to mine, and thus all united to me, he bore me strongly with him onto the cross, so that I felt myself to be crucified, and all the stains of his most holy body stained my unworthy body, and feeling so much pain from him, I felt myself totally aflame with the most sweet love of such a most beloved Lord.[10]

In a later vision, Maria Domitilla related an image "to move a heart of stone: the good Jesus, in the guise of a sweet swan . . . saying 'little ones, I am with you'."[11]

Given the nature of these visions, it is not surprising that Maria Domitilla, like Benedetta Carlini, came under the close supervision of her confessor, Giovanni Batista Capponi, who became an important figure in her story. Capponi assigned Suor Beatrice Avita, the daughter of a doctor in the village of Lomello, to assist Maria Domitilla in her spiritual raptures. As a local and a non-aristocrat, Beatrice had little standing in the community. Maria Domitilla described her as "to the eyes of all covered with ashes," but testified that this younger woman:

> was to me a very real and confidential sister, who stayed close to me in every need . . . and she asked questions of me very sweetly, and assured me that she was most faithful to me, as I have always found her to be, and I can testify that only she witnessed, and she noted everything, and she shared with the confessor, who asked her then to always attend closely to me in all the extraordinary happenings which happened to me.[12]

Just how close might this attendance have been? In a letter written after the death of Maria Domitilla, Beatrice testified:

> I affirm that through obedience to my most worthy confessor the Very Reverend Giovanni Battista Capponi, I was always close and helpful to Suor Maria Domitilla in all those times which followed the sorrows of the Most Holy Passion and the sprinkling of blood in such a way that she, it would seem, could not breathe nor move; if I could not hear or see because her cell was shut . . . I made large holes through which I could see very well and I made the other mothers [the nuns] see her to better reassure myself.[13]

Even if most of the assistance given was not so voyeuristic, there is no hint that the relationship between Maria Domitilla and Beatrice ever was expressed in the overt carnality for which Benedetta and Bartolomea have left evidence.

Of course, it is important to remember that the lives of the two nuns of Pavia are reconstructed through sources that are more similar to hagiography than to inquisition. Any analysis of these lives must bear in mind that Maria Domitilla's story was told by herself and the most sympathetic of friends, while Benedetta Carlini's was the product of a legal process. Documents pertaining to Maria Domitilla were collected by Capponi after her death and sent to the Biblioteca Ambrosiana in Milan, where they awaited scrutiny by ecclesiastical authorities as part of a canonization process initiated by the confessor. At the same time, a fair copy of her major writings was gathered by the community in Pavia and bound together in a series of three volumes now in the Biblioteca Universitaria of Pavia. This collection includes over 80 letters written to Maria Domitilla by a variety of secular and church leaders in the Italo-Franco-Austrian world. The process of canonization seems to have been stopped cold by the same suspicion of the fervent religious devotion of women that led to the investigations of Benedetta Carlini and culminated in the condemnation of Quietism in 1678 (Romano, 1893). Even if never judged a saint, Maria Domitilla was always revered as pious and holy. An investigation into her miracles undertaken in 1633 by the important Cappuccine leader Fra Valeriano of Milan ended with the words, "I dissolve in tears not only when I read, but even when I think of Suor Domitilla."[14] In this life there was not even a whiff of immodest acts.

COMPARISON, CATEGORIES, AND TRANSLATION

Still, it is important to remember that the lives of Maria Domitilla Galluzzi and Benedetta Carlini bear striking similarities. Both the nun of Pavia and the nun of Pescia followed a pattern of sanctity marked by the same signs: miraculous events at or before birth and scattered through childhoods expressly committed to preparation for religious life; devotion to the crucified Christ (on the cross or in the eucharist) that took the form of a sacred marriage, replete with vivid sensual imagery; bodily states of rapture of such intensity that the assistance of a younger nun was required; the supervision of a father confessor who was closely involved in the spiritual life of his charge. As Caroline Bynum pointed out, these are all characteristics of the *vitae* of women saints of late medieval Italy (Bynum, 1987, 1985). Bynum was characteristically insightful in interpreting this intense carnal spirituality in its own social and religious context:

> Women saw themselves not as flesh opposed to spirit, female as opposed to male, nurture as opposed to authority; they saw themselves as human beings — fully spirit and fully flesh. And they saw all humanity as created in God's image, as capable of *imitatio Christi* through body as well as soul. Thus they gloried in the pain, the exudings, the somatic distortions that

made their bodies parallel to the consecrated wafer on the altar and the man on the cross. In the blinding light of the ultimate dichotomy between God and humanity, all other dichotomies faded. (Bynum, 1987, p. 296)

It is, perhaps, difficult for modern women, even those of a decidedly religious bent, to imagine such a close connection between one's own body and that of the crucified Christ; terms like masochism and hysteria leap to mind, and yet they do not describe conditions that would be recognizable to the medieval women under investigation. It is perhaps more difficult still for a modern researcher to interpret the trial of Benedetta Carlini without following Brown's lead in using "the terms 'lesbian sexuality' and 'lesbian nun' for reasons of convenience to describe acts and persons called 'lesbian' in our own time" (Brown, 1986, p. 171, note 54). But, whatever the difficulty, it is important to remember that Benedetta Carlini is not of our time, and that her life was far more similar to that of Maria Domitilla than to ours. If in the course of Benedetta's spiritual marriage to the bridegroom of the wafer and the cross, an angel (or Jesus himself) directed her to use her body, in his place, to make love to another woman, it is possibly a sign of something more complicated than a repressed lesbian love story.

Two theorists of women's experience have indicated some guidelines for the interpretation of such confusing data. Over a decade ago, Carroll Smith-Rosenberg suggested that:

rather than seeing a gulf between the normal and the abnormal, we view sexual and emotional impulses as part of a continuum or spectrum of affect gradations strongly affected by cultural norms and arrangements, a continuum influenced in part by observed and thus learned behavior. At one end of the continuum lies committed heterosexuality, at the other uncompromising homosexuality; between, a wide latitude of emotions and sexual feelings. Certain cultures and environments permit individuals a great deal of freedom in moving across this spectrum. (pp. 75-76)

Other cultures and environments, such as that of the monasteries of 17th-century Italy, present matters of sexuality in a code that must be translated before it can be analyzed. The broader the spectrum, the more flexible our taxonomic categories, the better our chances of understanding such events in context, without gross distortion.

Adrienne Rich's famous 1980 essay "Compulsory Heterosexuality and Lesbian Existence," which works off of the ideas formulated by Smith-Rosenberg, is often cited in historical inquiries such as this for its more developed vision of the "lesbian continuum":

> As we deepen and broaden the range of what we define as lesbian existence, as we delineate a lesbian continuum, we begin to discover the erotic in female terms, as that which is unconfined to any single part of the body, or solely to the body itself . . . We can see ourselves moving in and out of this continuum, whether we identify ourselves as lesbian or not. It allows us to connect aspects of woman-identification as diverse as the impudent, intimate girl-friendships of eight- or nine-year olds and the banding together of those women of the twelfth and fifteenth centuries known as the Beguines . . . who 'practiced Christian virtue on their own, dressing and living simply and not associating with men,' and who managed — until the Church forced them to disperse — to live independent both of marriage and of conventual restrictions. (pp. 650-651)

Brown (1986) dismisses this as "fundamentally ahistorical in its inclusiveness," (p. 172, n. 54), although by no means did she make it clear why "lesbian continuum" is ahistorical while "lesbian" is not. Rich's vision was certainly romantic in its description of women from many times and cultures making a stand against identification with patriarchy. From this perspective, Benedetta Carlini and Maria Domitilla seem disappointing, because they were not only cloistered but firmly and without complaint under the control of their (male) confessors. Still, Rich's approach was intriguing in just the area I have described as most difficult, namely, understanding the motives, passions, and true expressions beneath the formalized passions of spiritual narratives. Rich: "The lesbian continuum, I suggest, needs delineation in light of the 'double-life' of women . . . We need a far more exhaustive account of the forms the double-life has assumed" (p. 659).

The "double-life" of Benedetta Carlini, I suggest, did not revolve around the dichotomy of "lesbian/nun," but around more a complicated understanding of the interrelation of body and food, the organic connection between the spiritual and the sensual, and the deep philological identification of the passion of pain and the passion of pleasure. Her imitation of Christ's passion, in both of these senses, poured out in a narrative form strange and suspicious to us, but native to her monastic culture and respected in the lay world of her time. Male ecclesiastics found this form of passionate expression potentially dangerous and monitored it closely. Feminist analysis helps us to understand that these very personal relations of spiritual gifts were seen as exceptionally powerful. Although they arose naturally from the context of 17th-century Italian Christianity, the hierarchical structures of church and society felt it imperative to keep this personal affective spirituality of women under strict control.

Much about these narratives may seem self-denying and even deeply humiliating to modern readers, but the contemporary responses to Benedetta Carlini and Maria Domitilla suggest that they reflect and celebrate an imaginative and spiritual autonomy of considerable importance. The autobiographical writings of Maria Domitilla show that this form of ardent spiritual discourse was not peculiar to Benedetta Carlini and is not easily related to modern conceptions of sexual self-definition. The sexuality in such writings can be approached from many levels, ranging from the intense spiritual individualism of devotion to the heavenly bridegroom, to the daily corporeal life of cloistered women in community. For, surely, these discourses of desire are one aspect of the double life of traditional Christian women.

NOTES

1. Judith C. Brown first announced the discovery of the documents pertaining to this case in an article published in 1984 in the journal *Signs*. The book that developed out of this research was printed in 1986 and was advertised by Oxford University Press as "the earliest documentation of lesbianism in modern Western history."

2. Other important information about lesbianism in medieval and early modern Europe is found in the two collections edited by Licata and Petersen (1980/

81), and Freedman et al. (1985), in which Brown's 1984 article is reprinted. See also Matter (1986), for a discussion of these studies.

3. Manuscript documents for the life of Suor Maria Domitilla Galluzzi d'Acqui include a spiritual autobiography, preserved in at least six manuscripts; a collection of visions excerpted from this life; a Commentary on the Rule of Saint Clare of Assisi, extant in at least four manuscripts; a Forty Hours Devotion, and a collection of over 80 letters, some from very famous secular and ecclesiastical figures, written to her over the course of her lifetime. These manuscripts are found in the Biblioteca Ambrosiana and the Biblioteca Trivulziana, both in Milano, and the Biblioteca Universitaria and the Biblioteca Civica "Bonetta" in Pavia. The only published secondary studies I have found are by Romano (1893) and Bianchi (1968-69).

4. For a discussion of the community, see Brown (1986), pp. 31-41.

5. See Brown (1984), pp. 277-278, for a selection from the documents. I discussed the significance of this "male disguise" in Matter (1986), pp. 91-92.

6. "Sua vita," Milano, Biblioteca Ambrosiana A. 276 sussidio, I. 41 sussidio, H. 91 sussidio; "Vita scritta da lei medesima," Milano, Biblioteca Ambrosiana D. 77 sussidio, G. 97 sussidio; "Memorie a lei spettanti," Milano, Biblioteca Ambrosiana H. 47 sussidio. These titles date from Capponi's donation of the manuscripts to the Ambrosiana after Maria Domitilla's death in 1671. The text was written as short chapters to her confessor, Capponi, over a period of years, and thus appears in varying redactions. D. 77 may be an autograph, see Bianchi (1968-69), p. 26, n. 4.

7. Upon entering the religious life, Domitilla related "I changed my name from Severata [sic] to Domitilla out of respect for my aunt." "Vita," Milano, Biblioteca Ambrosiana G. 97 sussidio fol. 54v.

8. "Soleva anco dire che prima ch'io nascessi ella udì la mia voce." "Vita," Milano, Biblioteca Ambrosiana A. 276 sussidio, fol. 5v.

9. "E la trovai in terra senza alcuna macula posta tra quei sassi vivi come se fossa stata tra bambace." "Vita," Milano, Biblioteca Ambrosiana A. 276 sussidio fol. 15v, also G. 97 fol. 14v.

10. "Visiones," Pavia, Biblioteca Universitaria Ms. Aldini 306, vol. 1, fol. 3v.

11. "Visiones," Pavia, Biblioteca Universitaria Ms. Aldini 306, vol. 1, fol. 13v.

12. "Vita," Milano, Biblioteca Ambrosiana H. 47 sussidio fol. 7r-v

13. "Attestationi della Madre Suor Beatrice," "Vita," Milano, Biblioteca Ambrosiana G. 97 sussidio fols. 372v-373r. More details of Maria Domitilla's ecstasies are given in "Relatione di Suor Beatrice Avite Cappuccina" fols. 364v-372r.

14. "Mi risolvo in lagrime non solo al leggere, ma a pensare a Suor Domitilla," letter of Fra Valeriano da Milano, dated June 1633. Pavia, Biblioteca Universitaria Ms. Aldini 206, vol. 3 fol. 3v.

REFERENCES

Bianchi, M. G. (1968-69), Una 'Illuminata' del Secolo XVII: SuorM. Domitilla Galluzzi, Cappuccina a Pavia. *Bollettino della Società Pavese di Storia Patria*, new series *20-21*, 3-69.

Brown, J. C. (1984), "Lesbian sexuality in Renaissance Italy: The case of Sister Benedetta Carlini. *Signs: Journal of Women in Culture and Society*, 9, 751-758.

Brown, J. C. (1986), *Immodest acts: The life of a lesbian nun in Renaissance Italy*. New York: Oxford University Press.

Bynum, C. W. (1985), Fast, feast, and flesh: The religious significance of food to medieval women. *Representations*, *11*, 1-25.

Bynum, C. W. (1987), *Holy feast and holy fast: The religious significance of food to medieval women*. Berkeley: University of California Press.

Freedman, E. B., Gelpi, B. C., Johnson, S. L., & Weston, K. M. (eds.). (1985). *The lesbian issue: Essays from Signs*. Chicago: University of Chicago Press.

Licata, S. J. & Petersen, R. P. (eds). (1980/81). Historical Perspectives on Homosexuality [special issue] *Journal of Homosexuality, 6*.

Matter, E. A. (1986). My sister, my spouse: Woman-identified women in medieval Christianity. *Journal of Feminist Studies in Religion*, 2(2), 81-93.

Rich, A. (1980). Compulsory heterosexuality and lesbian existence. *Signs: Journal of Women in Culture and Society*, *5*, 631-660.

Romano, G. (1893). Suor Maria Domitilla d'Acqui: Cappuccina in Pavia. *Bollettino Storico Pavese*, *1*, 9-40, 119-150, 197-238.

Smith-Rosenberg, C. (1985), "The female world of love and ritual: Relations between women in nineteenth-century America. *Disorderly conduct: Visions of gender in Victorian America* (pp. 53-76). New York: Oxford University Press.

Aliens in the Promised Land?: Keynote Address for the 1986 National Gathering of the United Church of Christ's Coalition for Lesbian/Gay Concerns

Gary David Comstock, PhD

Marist College
Poughkeepsie, New York

SUMMARY. The following article is a condensed version of the keynote address given at the 1986 National Gathering of the Lesbian/Gay Coalition of the United Church of Christ (UCC). Problems encountered by lesbians and gay men in organized religion, especially within the liberal tradition, are identified by a method of inquiry developed by Christian educator John Westerhoff for assessing egalitarianism within institutions. The story of Queen Vashti from the Book of Esther in Hebrew scripture, and the emerging tradition of coming-out experiences by lesbians and gay men, provide the norm and model for declaring independence from denominations that neglect the concerns of lesbians and gay men and for constructing religious alternatives.

I must be very candid. I feel that I am nearing the end of what seems to have been a long process of trying to find a place for myself and other gay men and lesbians in the United Church of Christ (UCC). From the beginning I was realistic in expecting that

Gary David Comstock received his PhD in ethics from Union Theological Seminary in New York City. He is the Protestant chaplain and an adjunct instructor in philosophy and religion at Marist College in Poughkeepsie, NY. He has lectured and conducted workshops in the areas of sexual ethics, social justice, theology, and lesbian/gay concerns.

Correspondence may be addressed to the author, Box 29, Willow, NY 12495.

the effort would not be easy nor the outcome exactly as I would want it to be. But I am, quite frankly, discouraged at this time about going on in the denomination and excited about seeking alternatives. I am hoping that we can discuss our relationship with our denomination and redirect ourselves and perhaps our denomination.

I begin with the realization that I am in trouble in three important areas of my life as a member of the United Church of Christ. These three areas are (a) my personal happiness, (b) my faith commitment, and (c) opportunities for my professional life.

First, I find that the Church remains the place, or certainly a prominent place, where I am least comfortable as a gay man, the place where I still feel defensive and least encouraged to share the most meaningful and intimate parts of my life. The Church remains for me the place where the lump still tightens in my throat, where my stomach still knots in anticipation of rejection and difficulty.

The following example reflects that which runs deeply in our denomination. Last year I sent notices to the alumni/ae magazines of the college from which I had received my B.A., the UCC-affiliated seminary from which I graduated with a master's of divinity degree, and the newsletter of my hometown church. Wanting to be included in the announcements of interesting and important events happening in the lives of my classmates and fellow parishioners, I sent to all three publications a note about my lover and me—news that we had recently moved to Woodstock, New York, a word about his new job, and an update on my progress in the doctoral program in ethics at Union Theological Seminary in Manhattan.

The college alumni/ae magazine printed it in its entirety without question. My local church newsletter edited out the reference to my lover and printed the remaining parts.

The president of my seminary, however, wrote to me saying that my note would not be printed because referring to anyone's sexual orientation in seminary publications was improper. He, of course, overlooked the endless announcements of weddings and references to husbands and wives in seminary publications that leave little question about the sexual orientation of the people mentioned.

I would have to be very naive not to realize that something that is essential to me is more of a problem for the church than it is for other institutions with which I am affiliated.

The second area in which I find myself in trouble with my denomination has to do with the focus of my faith. The call to make justice by the prophets Amos and Micah in Hebrew scripture and by Jesus in the Gospel of Matthew 25:31-46 is central to my understanding of myself as a religious person. Besides seeing myself as one who fights with others against oppression related to differences in gender, race, class, age, and ability, much of my effort focuses on the concerns of lesbians and gay men.

Our denomination should be a community of people joining together to seek justice, but we lesbians and gay men have had to wage our most serious battles against and within our own denomination. Instead of being part of a denomination that collectively works to right the wrongs of a heterosexist world, we have had to try to get the denomination to take seriously our very existence.

I find it an annoying waste of our time to have to focus on our denomination when we need the denomination to work with us on such critical issues as the State of Massachusetts' prohibition of gay and lesbian foster parenting, the violation of our rights in negotiating for the custody of our children, the loss and sorrow of the AIDS epidemic, the threat of quarantine by the religious and political right, the rise of violence directed against lesbians and gay men, the Supreme Court's upholding of state laws that prohibit our making love, the fights in various municipalities for basic rights to housing and employment, and the entrenchment in our society of a socialization process that raises and teaches children to be yet another heterosexist generation.

That we have had to bother ourselves with fighting for the ordination of lesbians and gay men and the affirmation of lesbians and gay men in our denomination has drained our justice-making energy and potential for confronting and changing the injustices that face us in the world. Quite simply, we have needed the denomination to be our helpmate and not our opponent in these struggles.

To the concerns for my personal happiness and my commitment to making justice, I add a third: my concern for my professional life. More and more, I have to admit to myself that, even though I have the credentials, degrees, experience, and references, as a gay man I can neither be ordained nor employed by my denomination. I do not draw my conclusion hastily. I have tended to hang on, working and hoping for change. But it is necessary to learn from and speak out of my experience: the experience with supervisors of my field work during my seminary preparation who advised me to keep my affectional orientation secret because it would only interfere with my ministry; experience with search committees while looking for a position as a parish minister—those that said they would call back but did not after I had told them I am gay, and those that met with me and unanimously voted to hire me, but revoted and reversed their decision after I told them I am gay; experiences as a member of a well-known liberal urban congregation, whose good intentions to welcome lesbians and gay men proved specious when it vetoed a worship service proposed and planned by lesbians and gay men to celebrate Gay Pride Day; the experience of having my ordination blocked by the deacons of my hometown church solely because of my affectional orientation.

And I have felt deserted by leaders on various levels of the denomination who privately supported my integrity and effort to be openly gay in the church, but who would make no public statements against the discrimination I experienced. Although my ability and gifts for ministry have never been criticized, my affectional orientation has been an issue in every endeavor to become employed by my denomination.

My telling you this has little meaning if we do not share the commonality of our individual experiences and look at our denomination broadly. In discussing the ways in which children learn about equality from adults, John Westerhoff, a professor of religious education, wrote the following:

> We can teach about equality in our church schools, but if our language in worship excludes women, if positions of influence and importance are held only by men or those from upper socioeconomic classes, or if particular races are either implicitly or explicitly excluded from membership, a different lesson is learned. (Westerhoff, 1976, p. 18)

Westerhoff's comment, while not referring directly to lesbians and gay men, is helpful for assessing the degree to which our denomination has actually welcomed and involved us. How can we really tell when the UCC is working as an integrated body of equals? Westerhoff wrote that it is not in what the church says it is doing, but rather in what is actually happening, that its real statement on equality is made.

The UCC has a very good national statement on lesbians and gay men. The two resolutions passed at the two preceding national synods are excellent statements calling for the inclusion of lesbians and gay men in the life and leadership of the denomination. People outside of the denomination reading these two statements frequently conclude that the UCC, especially when compared to other denominations, has integrated lesbians and gay men as equals into the range of roles and positions performed by its members. To be a lesbian or gay man within the UCC, observing and experiencing the practice of the denomination on all levels, is to see its reputed inclusivity diminish significantly. In short, we are a denomination that promises more than what we deliver.

Let us briefly consider the reason for this. First of all, we know that synod resolutions in the UCC are not legislatively binding. They recommend, but they do not mandate. While they may be expressions of intention or indicators of what may someday be, they can neither promise nor deliver change.

The UCC's polity is bottom-up; the local church is an autonomous decision-making body. National agencies, state and regional bodies can advise and make recommendations to local churches, but they cannot make decisions for the churches. The legislative strength in the denomination lies therefore in the local church.

By comparison, for example, the polity of the Presbyterian Church-USA denomination is top-down. The national level makes decisions that are binding and legislative, while local churches make recommendations and provide delegates to the national decision-making bodies.

If we consider the lesbian/gay issue in each of these denominations, we will find that the efforts to integrate us into the life of the church occur at the level where legislative power is absent. In the Presbyterian, where the decision-making power rests on the national level, a ruling has been made prohibiting ordination of lesbians and gay men. However, considerable discussion and programs around our issues occur in local churches. In the UCC, by contrast, where decision-making power rests at the local church level, there has been a very liberal response on the national level, but few programs and little discussion about lesbian/gay issues occur on the local level. While national synods have passed resolutions to include us in leadership positions, local churches have not ordained us, hired us as clergy, or elected us to top leadership positions.

By inserting the words "lesbians and gay men" into Westerhoff's statement, we may ask the following questions. Are the words "lesbian" and "gay" still difficult for or avoided within our churches? Does the language used by our denomination reflect and acknowledge the meaningful events in our lives? Are lesbians and gay men visible or invisible in our churches? Are we and our lovers, companions, and partners accepted as being among the various relationships and familial groupings that make up the church community? Do we occupy positions of influence and importance? Are our gifts and contributions recognized? Are we called on to perform all functions and operations within the life of the local churches on through to the national offices? Are our interests and concerns proportionately represented in the publications of the denomination? Are we included as if the church could not do without us, as a gift from God, as important members of the religious community; or are we treated and viewed as an annoying problem?

We also need to ask why heterosexism is the only justice issue that our denomination does not attend to with either paid staff or national office space? Why does the UCC national president issue an immediate denunciation of Reagan's bombing of Libya, but does not make a public statement about the U.S. Supreme Court's decision to uphold Georgia's sodomy law until 6 weeks have passed and the story has dropped out of the press?

We need to face the dismal statistic that in the 20-year, post-Stonewall history of the lesbian/gay movement, the UCC has ordained only two open lesbians and one openly gay man. And since ordination none has found employment as a local church pastor.

Some of you, like me, may have thought or are thinking that it will be different for you—that you will go through all the procedures properly and that, unlike other lesbians and gay men before us, you will get a job, you will be ordained, and you will be an example and symbol of hope for others. My own understanding, after having been this route, is that the hurdle to our ordination is not procedural, but the selective use of procedures against us. For example, my being denied the necessary recommendation for ordination by my hometown church had nothing to do with the particular requirement itself and everything to do with homophobia of my local church. I think that the procedures simply provide the opportunity to enforce bias and exclusivity. If we are going to make any significant changes, we will not be able to do it as individuals who can be picked off as each separately goes through procedures, but as a group that collectively says no to the injustices we experience.

For some guidance I want to turn to Vashti, a person in Hebrew scripture who has been rendered almost as invisible by traditional readings and biblical commentaries as gay men and lesbians have been in the traditional practices of the church. The Book of Esther opens with the naming of an emperor who is giving an extravagant banquet for all of the princes, army chiefs, noblemen, and governors from all of his provinces to show the riches and the splendor of his majesty. After 180 days of feasting, the emperor gives another banquet, this time for all the men, both great and small, who live in the capital city. This one lasts for 7 days.

During this time, Queen Vashti gives a banquet for the women. When the heart of the emperor becomes merry with wine, he commands his right hand men to bring Vashti before him with her royal crown to show the men her beauty. Then, the good news. Queen Vashti refuses to come at the emperor's command. Of course, the emperor is enraged. His wise men tell him that if the other women in the kingdom hear of what Vashti has done, they too will be encouraged to look with contempt upon their husbands. So that all women will continue to give honor to their husbands, the wise men advise him to issue a decree throughout the land stripping Vashti of her royal position. This advice pleases the emperor, and the emperor does as the wise men propose.

If we are ever pressed to name a role model for ourselves from scripture, I think we have found one in Queen Vashti. Vashti seems simply to have preferred to stay with the women at the banquet she was giving for them and to have had the good sense and self-esteem to refuse to appear before the drunken emperor as a sexual object for display. But Vashti's decision, grounded in good sense, dignity, or independence, threatened the empire's social order.

We are not unlike Vashti, and her story is not unlike ours. As lesbians and gay men, we have decided to restore and establish something as basic as our affectional preference, our dignity, our right to love; and something as simple as our act to decide, think, and feel for ourselves has made the church nervous to the point of fearing that our living our lives as fully human beings threatens the foundations of family structure, the natural order, and traditional social relations.

We may say that it was not our intention to shake the social and religious order to its roots. Who would have thought that affirming our love for each other could wreak such havoc? But that is exactly what it has done. Like Vashti's refusal to stand by her man at the expense of her own personhood, we have refused to be less than who we are. And, like her, we have caused the wise men to scurry, fume, and wonder what is to be done with us for subverting the way things should be.

While it may not have been our intention, I think we have to face squarely that our very lives, when lived openly and fully, fundamentally threaten the social order. When we begin to make decisions for ourselves instead of letting others tell us how we should live, we challenge those who have power at the expense of the disempowered and marginalized.

I find one of the signs of such uneasiness and fear in the UCC's timidity and nervousness to establish and affirm ministry by lesbians and gay men. Initially, when our issues were first surfacing, the denomination was nervous about whether or not it should commit itself to ministry to lesbians and gay men. The question was: Does such a group of people merit the attention and caring concern of the church? The denomination was moving on some fronts from rejecting us as unacceptable people to seeing us as in need of help.

If the UCC has been slow to initiate programs and designate personnel to minister to the needs of lesbians and gay men, it has barely budged either to recognize that lesbians and gay men can themselves be ministers or to place us professionally within the ranks of the denomination. Our denomination's reluctance to accept and be enhanced by the ministry we could provide strikes me not only as exclusive on the part of the denomination, but as detracting from the ministerial potential of the denomination as well.

I suspect that the denomination's reluctance to establish ministry by us has to do with not wanting to give us the power to help and to relate to other people as capable individuals. The church has less trouble seeing us as victims in need of ministry than as fully human people who can respond to and help with the needs of others. For the denomination to accept us as people of equal worth and capable of ministering to the needs of others would signal a change as magnificent and surprising as if the emperor had turned himself around and accepted Vashti as an equal partner with talents, gifts, and interests as important as his own.

For me, the irony of the church's resistance lies in the evidence that many of us already function as ministers in spite of the denomination's refusal to recognize us as such. I am referring not only to those of us who have formal theological training, but to all of us who either in or out of the denomination interact with people with loving concern that is based in caring, sharing, and working to overcome social problems. We have found ways outside of the UCC to engage in ministry both as professionals and as volunteers in places where service and the making of justice are critically needed.

I think that many of us have opted to be ministers in other ways than with denominational approval. Forgoing the energy-draining and dehumanizing battles with church boards and search committees, and frustrated by being assigned nonhuman status, many have chosen to do without the denomination's blessing and have created and become engaged in serious ministerial work in nontraditional settings.

If, for a moment, we turn our attention to the lesbian/gay community outside of our denomination and the organized church, we notice that the leaders and workers in organizations that serve the community's needs are often lesbians and gay men with seminary degrees. In talking with the people who are working in programs for lesbians and gay men — organizations for young people and old people, antiviolence projects and AIDS projects, gay/lesbian rights organizations, counseling services, and efforts to combat racism and sexism, to name a few — I am struck by the number who have responded to calls outside of denominations that have excluded, or else delayed in making up their minds about what to do with the emergence of, qualified lesbian and gay ministers.

I am also encouraged to find that in other areas of ministry that fall outside of denominational organization and are not specifically lesbian/gay-related — for example, in women's shelters, poverty

programs, day care centers, and residences for the mentally re-
tarded—lesbians and gay men are working, leading, ministering.
The point is that, even though the denomination has not recognized
our gifts, skills, and intentions to minister, we are engaged in ministry that is very much in line with that spoken of by the Hebrew
prophets and by Jesus. What has been a priority for us has been to
respond to the needs of the needy and to liberate the oppressed.

And that response has occupied us more than dealing with the
nonsense of the church's waffling on whether or not we are qualified to minister. We already are ministers. We have proven that in
our practice and commitment to others, to justice, to sharing in our
work. Why, then, do some of us still hold onto the denomination?

The tenacity with which I have endured the indifference and lack
of support of my denomination reminds me of certain attachments I
have had to reluctant lovers. Wanting someone to accept me and
love me has sometimes made me hang on beyond the point of maintaining self-esteem, personal integrity, and well-being.

The desire for mutuality and reciprocity from unlikely and unwilling sources that has often tied us to unhealthy relationships has
also cost us dearly in our experiences with our biological families.
We have hidden, lied, fabricated, pleaded, and twisted ourselves to
preserve the love or to get the approval of our families. It was not
until I stopped wanting my family's approval and started building a
new family of friends and lovers that I was able to relate to my
biological family as an equal, and that they began to take seriously
my needs, desires, and interests. When I started making decisions
and behaving without the fear of disgracing them, when I stopped
engineering and designing my life to please them or to get them to
like me for who I am, when I was finally willing, able, and ready to
live without them, they started treating me as a gay man and a
whole person.

I would suggest that the unwise compromises we have made for
reluctant lovers and biological families are not unlike the second-
class status we have accepted within our denomination. I look back
over my history with the UCC and see myself bending every which
way to get accepted, affirmed, ordained, employed. And as in any
nonreciprocating relationship, I have had no power to get the denomination to do any of these things I want. I have not had recourse

to rules, agencies, or commissions devoted to establishing, maintaining, and protecting my rights.

The only tactic open to those who stay in a relationship in which they have no power is to scream loudly, to make a point of saying: "We are in pain. Don't you feel sorry for us? How can you so cruelly exclude us?"

I am tired of waiting and begging. I am tired of my only power being the outside chance that I can get someone to feel sorry for my pain, frustration, and sorrow. It is not easy to do as Vashti did, but if we do not we become immobilized by the hope that things will get better, just as we have been by the hope that someday, if we hold on long enough, the reluctant lover will shower us with all the attention and affection we want. We become immobilized by feeling obligated to work things out and to make adjustments within the denomination, just as we have been when we have tried to fit ourselves into what our biological families have expected us to be. We become immobilized if we feel that we owe our denomination our patience to endure and make it more inclusive slowly, especially if our patience only encourages a lack of concern and responsibility from the denomination. We know that in healthy relationships there must be mutuality and reciprocity. If lesbians and gay men are not included as equals, we need to consider seriously ending the relationship with our denomination.

I do not think we can make the denomination more inclusive until we establish our own standards and learn to stand and live without depending on our denomination's approval. I think it is time that we move ourselves beyond the roller-coaster ride of expectations and disappointments that rest on unfulfilled promises of being included eventually. I think it is time we placed ourselves in a context in which we give ourselves the status of fully human beings. It is time for us to draw on the tradition we have already started, a tradition of lesbians and gay men doing ministry and church work in areas and settings where the denomination has not ventured. I think we should validate our efforts and establish them as the center of our faith community and religious life.

The basis of our relationship with our denomination can no longer be our pain and frustration, but our actual work, the positive, constructive efforts that are the center of our lives.

I suggest that in the year that follows we move into the promised land in two ways. Hebrew scripture tells two stories of moving into the promised land. The Book of Joshua tells the story of conquest, fighting, battle, and confrontation; the Book of Judges tells the story of settling in and living as equals among neighbors, integrating and sharing ourselves as independent people with other independent people. I think we need to do both.

Efforts to confront and negotiate will be easier than the other approach by which we must set out to live as equals, define ourselves independently, and let go of the need to be approved of by our denomination. I think it will be harder, but more important, to develop ourselves and prepare for eventually ending our dependency on the denomination. If the UCC cannot find a way to ordain us, to take our struggle seriously, then we will have to be the ones to take ourselves seriously. We will have to ordain ourselves, form our own churches, recognize ourselves, and interact with the world with a new independence. Because we have been surviving and maintaining against great odds, we have developed skills with which we can live, learn, and love freely without the permission and approval of the denomination. We have the enormous task before us of changing a heterosexist world. I am not sure we can be diverted by the task of having to change our denomination from the inside. While an active, ongoing critique of its practices is necessary, investing ourselves totally or primarily in its response to us is not. If our denomination is not ready to join us in the task of freeing the captives from heterosexism and homophobia, perhaps it is time to end a relationship that is not mutual and reciprocal. Perhaps in time they will join us.

REFERENCE

Westerhoff, J. H. III. (1976). *Will our children have faith?* New York: Seabury Press.

A Bonding of Choice:
Values and Identity Among Lesbian and Gay Religious Leaders

Clare B. Fischer, PhD

Starr King School for the Ministry

SUMMARY. In this preliminary study of values and attitudes of a select number of lesbian and gay religious leaders, respondents reflected on the meaning of family, church, and community. Although the survey is modest in scope, several themes emerge that locate this study in the context of gender analysis. Female respondents had greater similarity in their emphasis upon relationality than did lesbian and gay respondents within the same denominational tradition. For male respondents, the "coming out" narrative was a central event and deepened the meaning of telling another about self.

In spite of the ambitious scope of the title, this article has a modest intent and is written as a preliminary report concerning the value expression of a small group of religious leaders who identify themselves as lesbian and gay. The literature bearing on gay and lesbian contributions to the religious community is sparse. Although much attention has been given to the matter of homophobia in the church and to the gay and lesbian response to this, little information has been published that tells the reader about the active religious leader

---

Clare Benedicks Fischer is Aurelia Reinhardt Professor of Religion and Culture at Starr King School for the Ministry. She presented a paper on lesbian ethics at the American Academy of Religion in 1985, and participated in a published roundtable on "Lesbianism and Feminist Theology," *Journal of Feminist Studies in Religion* (Fall, 1986).

Correspondence may be addressed to the author at Starr King School for the Ministry, 2441 LeConte Avenue, Berkeley, CA 94709.

145

whose sexual identity is labeled as homosexual. There is very little that introduces the reading public to the value and moral reasonings of lesbian and gay religious leaders, lifting their perspectives out of the context of institutional exclusivity.[1]

My concern is to redress this lack by offering a review of testimonies from men and women who are attached to the church in leadership positions, who understand their respective aspirations and contributions as grounded in religious vocation, and who understand this call as deeply nourished by their sexual orientation. It is important to listen to gay and lesbian leaders as persons who are struggling with others for a common good that is not narrowly construed as single-issue politics. All of the respondents of my study displayed a constructive posture toward institutional life and felt uneasy with an "over against" mentality or defensive perspective. They identified their sexual orientation as foundational to attitude and activity but emphasized that vocation and vision of religious leadership was never reducible to the matter of homosexuality in the church.

METHOD

In the conclusion to *Habits of the Heart*, Robert Bellah and his collaborators in the writing of this important report of American moral life invited the reader to continue the dialogue they had initiated (Bellah et al., 1985). They affirmed a conversational mode, asserting that "any living tradition is a conversation, an argument in the best sense, about the meaning and value of our common life" (p. 303). Their approach to the inquiry about middle American moral life was exemplary.[2] I have embraced the notion of an "active interview," that assumes the participation of the interviewer in the conversation. This is a departure from the standard approach to information gathering, which has asked for distance between subject and interrogator and demanded a detachment from the process. In my eliciting of responses, I attempted to ask, listen, and engage with a sense of presence. This was an inviting modality focused on understanding rather than "pure data."

The Bellah et al. (1985) study helped prepare me for this small survey in several ways. Not only was the conversational interview an inspiration, but *Habits of the Heart* demonstrated how vital narrative can be to the study of moral reasoning. "Narrative is a primary and powerful way to know about a whole. In an important sense, what a society [or a person] is, is its history" (p. 302).[3]

Carol Gilligan's now classic analysis of engendered moral discourse has also been useful in the general interpretation of my material (Gilligan, 1982).[4] Her perspective pointed to the function of gender socialization in the construction of ethical positions. Although Bellah et al. and Gilligan functioned as catalytic readings, this study offers no refinement or modification of either. Bellah et al. and Gilligan provided insight and research strategies that I have woven into my analysis.

My work is not scientific in the sense that I have not attempted to create a method that is replicable or a position that brings closure on the subject. It is a semi-informal glimpse of the value expressions of a selected group of men and women living and working in the San Francisco Bay Area. They were not chosen randomly, nor is my report anecdotal.

Each of the 11 subjects was asked to give me at least an hour of time in order to explore an open-ended set of questions. I promised confidentiality but was informed by all but one that it was unnecessary. (I have chosen pseudonyms, nonetheless.) The interviews were conducted in various places over a 2-month period. During that time I hesitated to chart or analyze the responses, wanting to complete the interview phase with a fresh perspective on whatever was to be expressed. The interview as such consisted of two parts: a story section and a set of questions tapping values regarding family, church and theology, politics and community. I am not surprised that the material related to church and theology is, in my opinion, the most interesting, and so it seemed to the interviewees as well.

The narrative segment began with a simple request for a story that would tell me about the *self* and how self is revealed in relation to the values and moral perspectives of the subject. All cooperated with this request.

The second part of the interview, which took most of our time together, began with a drawing I made of a spiral with a core labeled "self." (See Figure 1.) The spiral identified each of the relationships I wished to have responses to, from family to community.

Figure 1
Spiral Questionnaire

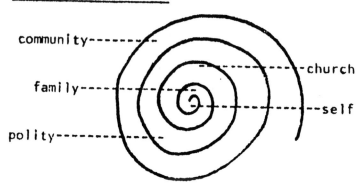

Within each concentric area I placed certain cues that I hoped would provide focus. Under church, for example, I noted polity, theology, spirituality, and liturgy; under family, in addition to the phrase "shape of," I listed abortion, euthanasia, and suicide. I showed this drawing to each respondent before I began our conversation.

Many respondents spoke of the difficulty with one or another aspect of the interview, indicating that they had not expressed themselves on that issue prior to our exchange. In spite of this difficulty, most interviewees thanked me for probing further into a particular area and for disclosing something of myself. (While I was careful not to lead the response, I remained present to the interviewee and indicated something about the question and my own value position *after* the interviewee had spoken.)

With the completion of interviews, I summed up responses on a chart. Initially, this was done without an eye to pattern. After the first effort, I discovered some clear gender patterns and recharted the material according to the sex of the respondent. It is on the basis of this later charting that I developed the analysis I offer here.

Although I had known some of the interviewees prior to this study, at least a third were new contacts. I had planned to speak with 12 people, half of the group to be male respondents. In the implementation of my research plan, I saw only five women and six men. They shared much, including common geographic location, educational preparation for ministry, and attachment to the liberal religious (principally Protestant) tradition. Eight belonged to either the United Church of Christ or Unitarian Universalism; the balance to the Presbyterian (two males) and United Methodist (a woman) tradition. All had earned a master's degree in Divinity or comparable educational training (that is, courses in the seminary but an M.A. rather than an M.Div.); one was completing his degree program. Eight were ordained and one was struggling with his denomination to overcome obstacles to his ordination because he is openly gay. All knew of the Metropolitan Community Church and supported its efforts on behalf of the homosexual religious community, but none expressed interest in leaving their respective traditions for it. Three were employed as professional parish ministers, four worked in related "nonprofits," and two in denominationally related agencies. Two were involved in PhD programs in religion or theology and one, as noted, was completing his education for parish ministry. The median age of the 11 was 39.8 years. The women on average were a few years younger than this median and had had less experience with the institutional church of their profession.

Marriage and partnership commitments were highly varied from the perspective of the interviewees' past relationships, but most currently lived in coupled situations. Four of the five lesbian respondents were in partnered relationships at the time of the interview; two had been involved in a covenant ceremony within the past 3 years. Men in this sample had a wider experience with respect to long term same-sex relationships; three had been involved in heterosexual marriages, whereas only one woman had been. However, the gay interviewees had a median duration of partnership with the same person greater than that of women—12, 10, and 9 years for four of the men responding to the inquiry.

While sweeping generalizations are not appropriate to a study of this scale, it is noteworthy that I selected a close sample. I was clear about not including persons whom I could not speak directly with, thus limiting the sample to persons in the immediate environs of San Francisco. All but one were white with a self-defined sense of belonging to the "middle class." The 11th was a Hawaiian who was emphatic that his cultural and racial reality made a great deal of difference in his experience of the life of Continental Americans and particularly mainstream church activists and functionaries. In the section of responses to questions about church and theology, his voice was distinctive.

Although in the seminary environment many second and third generation professional ministers or ministers in preparation are present, this sample included only two who came from ministerial family backgrounds. In both cases the father was or had been a parish minister. The daughter of a minister was on very good terms with her family and admired her father, finding him completely open to her sexual identity. On the other hand, the gay respondent whose father was a minister had been alienated from him since he spoke of his sexual identity. As I noted earlier, four of the sample had been involved in heterosexual marriages. At the time of the study one continued in this arrangement, although he identified himself as a gay man. There were children from the heterosexual marriages, and the relationships between parent respondents and children were warm and rewarding in all cases. One shared an adopted child with her partner.

A word about language is in order. The distinction between a moral judgment, a value perspective, or a position on a particular issue was left open to each respondent to clarify or define. I resisted shaping the discussion in terms of my understandings but held to a sense that the questions called upon responses where language is not interchangeable. When I asked about the optimum character of the family, I believed I was inquiring into a value; by contrast, abortion and euthanasia represent ethical dilemmas. Issues included such matters as AIDS and church homophobia. I did not develop these distinctions in my analysis, nor did I believe it to be useful for the approach I took here. But I hasten to emphasize that the interview process involved some probing about language and a general interest on the part of the respondents in whether their answers were revealing of moral or value perspectives. This exchange might well have been pursued and studied in relation to the Bellah et al. thesis of first and second languages.[3] I did not inquire in this direction because the study was perceived from the start as a preliminary one, but I believe that this would be a fruitful approach to take in a more elaborate investigation of gay and lesbian religious leadership.

STORIES

Although 11 stories from the respondents represent that number of individual accounts of self and pivotal value perspectives, limitations of space preclude a full reporting of the narratives offered by lesbian and gay religious leaders concerning selfhood. As I listened to the stories I made abbreviated notes rather than a taped testimony, jotting down those facets of the narrative that provided form and emphasis. After the interview, I wrote a brief summary of the story and reviewed my notes to make more readable the quoted material. In reading over this material and charting the same by asking questions of the spoken text, I discovered a pattern. The questions were rather journalistic: What happened? When? Where? What is the significance for the narrator? How have implications or consequences been expressed? Much to my surprise, the material drawn from interviews with the gay narrators conformed to the questions of my chart; the women's stories did not. In short, a gender difference emerged that bore some comparison with the findings reported by Gilligan.[4]

One story offered by a gay respondent illustrates my point with respect to conformity to my preliminary chart. (I had a story form in mind that is rather formal: a definitive beginning and end with a midpoint crisis that gets defined, resolved, completed.) Paul told of the announcement to his father that he could not marry his fiancee because he "has a quirk in his personality." He explained to me that this happened over 20 years ago, but he remembered well the "prelude" to his admission—the sense of "puzzlement and disaster" regarding his situation (a parish minister soon to marry a woman). He had had no experience in talking openly with his family about intimate matters and had given no indication of his increasing awareness of gay orientation. When he spoke to his father he was greeted with silence and, shortly thereafter, his father's illness (which was medically diagnosed as trauma related). For Paul, the telling was essential to his integrity; honesty and its communication subsumed all other claims.

In general, the six gay men's stories shared these characteristics: (a) a specificity regarding the stories' historical setting, (b) an identification of self as the central figure and a recognition or admission of gay orientation as the pivotal moment (a "coming out story") or both, (c) a dimension of vocational crisis in the telling, (d) an evaluation of the telling as an ending to one way of being and a sense of new beginning, and (e) an incorporation into the narrative of some symbolic or real experience of journey. Although I had not requested a story related to sexual orientation, but asked only for a narrative that would reveal the self and pivotal experiences regarding values, all six men provided veritable retellings of the first telling.

Here are some illustrations of the points enumerated above. Matthew explained that he was parked in a van struggling in conversation with a male friend over his recognition of desire for that friend. He recalled, in telling me, that it was then that he recognized his gay identity fully and the implications it held for him. Matthew spoke of the anguish of this recognition and his worry that his acknowledgement of gay identity would put an end to his aspiration for professional parish ministry. The sense of impasse overwhelmed him at first and a depression held him from seeing how he could serve his denomination and not be truthful about his gay orientation. Not a trailblazer or a pioneer was he, but a committed religious leader, and he was not able to see how his conflict would be resolved. However, in rereading the story of Moses, Matthew identified with the strength of calling and began a pilgrimage some years ago that permitted reconciliation in his actual work of parish ministry.

The telling of the coming out narratives reached a depth that was reminiscent of the ritual experience of religious people narrating tales of the community's origin. The tapping into a core truth reaches past the mere psychological release of secret knowledge. Charles' story exemplified this. During a long car trip that he took with his wife at Christmas time, he became increasingly restless with himself and struggled to tell her that their marriage could not continue. In speaking, he felt great contempt for himself; his was a selfish, sinful, and immature position. But to his surprise his wife quickly embraced his words and his person after he blurted, "I am a god-damned queer!" She stated that she loved him for himself, not in spite of his sexual identification. Her affirmation reached through

Charles' long experienced sense of being "bad," wrong, deviant, and allowed him to see for the first time that he was "truly lovable." When Charles narrated this experience, he referred to the powerful character of the moment; the recognition of his truth spoken aloud and accepted by someone whom he loved was a veritable conversion from dark to light for him. To acknowledge the self as lovable, honest, or courageous seems to be a consequence of speaking with another about homosexuality and the constitution of the self.

John shared with Paul a negative consequence of coming out. Having served in a team ministry for some years, he decided to tell all of the congregation's families of his sexual identity. He did this with each household and with great care. However, his colleague in the church was deeply opposed to this, and John explained that he was soon to be betrayed by him, as well as other members of the church's hierarchy. Some insisted that he take back what he had announced and return "to the closet." The bitterness of that moment continued for John, who later left professional ministry but still wanted to engage again in some form of Protestant ministerial work.

Vocational crisis of the sort John experienced is dramatic compared to the stories of others interviewed here. However, Frank and Craig both told of vocational ambiguity and the discomfort with this because of their sexual orientation. Craig told two stories, each pointing to a hope for greater clarity in his religious quest. He spoke of a long bicycle trip taken after he realized that he was gay. He had hoped that by the end of the trip he would discover some insight about himself and how to diminish his unhappiness. He did not. He told another story too, one which reached into his family history and indicated his restlessness with what it means to belong. In speaking with me, Craig noted that he told the second story as a metaphorical narrative pointing to the ambiguity in self-understanding and how that shaped his attitude toward the structures of the church.

Craig told of his coming out to a therapist many years ago, and added that this telling did not modify either his marital arrangement (heterosexual) or the way he approached the work of ministry. He explained that his recognition of being a gay man allowed him finally to feel comfortable with the sense of "difference" that had been with him since childhood.

Frank's narrative came closer to those told by the lesbian storytellers of my study. They shared an approach that had negligible highs or lows in the shape of the story; there was neither a crisis to be faced nor a challenge to be overcome. On the contrary, every one of the narratives communicated by the women eluded a concise start or finish, although all could be placed in a general space/time. One indicated that hers was an action-less story, a telling of image in a regional setting that had great meaning for her. Another spoke of a continuity in life experience formed by the acknowledgement of being "special." Although I did not have difficulty describing gay men's stories of a pivotal value experience in terms of the five characteristics listed earlier, I found that none of the same applied to the women's narratives. They spoke to a different set of characteristics; four are listed here. The first facet of lesbian narrative referred to the "flow," that is, that beginning and end are not limited to the definition of an event. The other three characteristics were: (a) an emphasis upon the meaning of relationship, (b) an integration of the relational experience into an understanding of transformation, and (c) a sense of the importance of nature and human community in the revelation of self. Unlike the gay men's stories, these stories did not tell of the drama of "coming out," nor was the self depicted as the center of the story.

Nancy's story illustrated the point on flow. She moved back and forth in time between childhood and the present in talking about selfhood as the recognition of "difference." She recalled that in 4th or 5th grade she would say things nobody else would mention. "I experienced myself as a part of but not really there." Nancy stated that her family was experienced as different, too, because they were more tolerant than their neighbors. She wove this theme of "outsidedness" into contemporary examples of the same sense of here-but not-here. That which kept her from loneliness in the past was the church and, today, the women's church. In her teen years she had had the support of the minister's wife and several other women who encouraged her. She was currently depending upon the support of other women in her denomination and in the feminist movement within the church world. Perhaps the singular event in her narrative was in the recollection that her mother followed her into the new church of her choice.

This telling of another's support resonated throughout the lesbian stories. Susan's had a more precise shape, in terms of time and place, and attested to the positive consequences of living in a women's community. She told of a summer job at a camp as a married woman with a teenaged daughter. During that time (the whole summer, rather than a specific day), Susan came to acknowledge her tolerance, overcome her stereotypes about lesbian women, and discover that she was not only a homophobic person but was attracted to other women. Susan did not describe the experience as incongruent with her other experiences or aspirations, but instead spoke of herself as being in a transformative process that began in that place and was continuing. Her awakening was connected to the sensory reality of the camp and the communal warmth of the camp residence. There she learned to trust herself, in part because her supervisor encouraged her and gave her confidence in risking new experiences and putting her ideas to work.

An aesthetic of transformation attached to natural surroundings was also central to Alice's narrative. Having resisted the idea of story at first, Alice told me that she wanted to relate the importance of an image to her spiritual self-understanding. Her emphasis was surviving in and through friendships. She spoke of a tree that is on the grounds of her grandparents' home, which years before had been split by lightning. This tree, from which she took strength, was an image of rootedness, strength, and familiarity. Even in the tree's jeopardy there was the ever-present representation of its perseverance. She told me that her image-story was about the co-existence of both, and that it symbolized solitude and community for her. I understood Alice's story as spiritual narrative, rather than non-narrative; perhaps it was a minimalist structure that pointed to a depth of the narrator's vocational core.

While Mary spoke mainly of her family life history in large brushstrokes, her story revolved around her sense of call to the ministry. She emphasized that "part of what I need to be doing is speaking the truth and serving justice." This telling was repeated in Elizabeth's response, although hers was more closely tied to an event than the other lesbian narratives. The words "leap of faith" were threaded throughout Elizabeth's story of her recent adoption of an infant with her partner. Once again, the idea of a particular beginning was questioned. She wondered aloud whether she would start with her partnership, which was completely linked to the idea of parenting, or whether she should begin with how they came to adopt the son they now lived with. She opted for the fuller account, indicating to me that lesbian narrative has an expansive, web-like form. The leap was undertaken several times, but the pivotal one was in staying with the birth mother and developing a relationship with the child before its actual placement with her. The narrative was dramatic but not because it moved to a singular moment; the drama was in the ordinary staying-with that Elizabeth described.

In a sense, Elizabeth's story had a coming out dimension, but it was different from the experience of telling another. She described the steps in which the adoption was undertaken and stated, rather matter-of-factly, that there was a peeling away of any pretense regarding her sexual orientation. With each formal encounter (hospital, adoption agency, court), her lesbianism was announced. "You can't be a good parent and present yourself in hypocritical ways."

Elizabeth's story was a relational one that exemplified the flow from one event to another and the flow as transforming. In her description of the leap of faith, she spoke of moving through unchartered territory with the support of numerous friends and the good will of institutions. The lesson she took from this "rite of passage," as she described it, was that she learned to present herself in a nonapologetic manner, and this confidence seemingly convinced others of her integrity.

There were gender distinctions in the form and content of stories given by gay and lesbian respondents, but I am hesitant to conclude that this difference provided further evidence of Gilligan's (1982) thesis regarding "different voices." In her work, males approached a narrative in terms of the question of autonomous action, while her female subjects indicated something about the value of relationship. The polarity Gilligan wrote of suggests a radical separation in discourse concerning moral issues that places emphasis upon male expression of abstract principle (and a legalistic perspective of rights) as contrasted with a female emphasis upon compassionate mediation. In my small sample, gay respondents clearly identified the coming out narrative as central and implied something that I believe to be congruent with a traditional understanding of heroic action. In these stories, conflict or crisis shaped the action and required risky response on the part of the storyteller. Not so in the case of lesbian narrators, who spoke warmly of the times when support was offered to them or of the reassuring reality of natural environments.

THE PATTERN PRODUCED BY THE SPIRAL

Each interviewee was introduced to the set of open-ended questions by a spiral picture that incorporated four circular dimensions representing family, church/theology, political life, and community experiences. Of these categories, the church/theology responses occupied a significantly greater part of the interview and proved to be highly illuminating. Although I will review all of the sections in an abbreviated manner, I want to elaborate upon this category at the outset.

Obviously, all of the respondents had lively concerns with the religious dimensions of their lives and were very articulate about their respective understandings of the professional ministry. Most answered my inquiry about church polity with minimal criticism of denominational structure and a rather high regard for its tradition. What I was unprepared for was the relative absence of talk about the particular church principles and practices regarding homosexuality. I had anticipated that respondents would volunteer thoughts about their denomination's approach, especially as it pertains to the professional ministry. Few spoke of this subject, and those who offered the most substantial responses were gay men who had been directly and negatively involved in this question. (I would suspect that there would have been more conversation on this topic if my interviews had been conducted after the Roman Catholic encyclical on homosexuality was published.)

Gender differences emerged in this section of the interview. Lesbian respondents gave voice to a notion of church that resembled familial relationship; gay respondents tended to answer more crisply and institutionally. The language of polity seemingly served as a cue to most of the male interviewees for reflection on the national offices and hierarchical authority. Women answered, for the most part, in terms of local settings and their presence with particular groups in the congregation.

I asked questions following the spiral from the core "self" through concentric sections to the peripheral segment on community, indicating that this last led back to the middle with respect to sexual identity and support groups for the individual. The inquiry into self remained both core and thread through each part of the interview.

My questions regarding family followed our exchange about story, and involved three concerns that I hoped would elicit both value and ethical judgments. I first asked respondents to talk about the "desirable shape of the family." I regarded this as an "ought" question, but most responded initially by speaking about their lived experience as family members. Every lesbian interviewee indicated that family embraced both biological and extended members — that is, sustained and trustworthy friendships. Two volunteered that family held both an intimate and a more generous meaning, involving a spiralling out from the former to the latter. Although some of the gay respondents echoed some of this sense of a larger family, there was considerable variation in the response. At one end, two spoke of family as small and closed (either the particular biological arrangement and cultural sharing that marks a traditional sense of family or the sole relationship to partner); at the other end, a familial shape that reflected celebrative times together (important festive dates in the year when particular people come together, biologically and experientially, or else friendship related). The subject of biological family estrangement was almost absent in the female responses but was repeated by several of the men.

Working within the large rubric of family, I asked two questions related to ultimate matters, that is, those of birth and death. I specifically asked for responses about abortion, using language that did not suggest rights or policy implications. However, five of the six gay respondents referred to the language of rights, affirming women's reproductive rights, several employing such terms as "absolute" and "fundamental." Two gay interviewees modified their position once they expressed that their understanding of "right" was associated with the inappropriateness of men's engagement in the discussion of abortion. Their ambivalence was articulated in terms that displayed ethical reasoning about the taking of life. One asserted that he was paying closer attention to the Roman Catholic Church's position today, particularly as it embraces opposition to both personal and institutional life-taking. The other respondent spoke from a philosophical stance: "I'm so against death as a solution to anything."

Ambivalence toward abortion as an ethically warranted action was also expressed by two of the lesbian interviewees. Each indicated that the right to reproductive choice ought to be secure but added that the issue itself is shaped within and debated from a cultural context marred by misogyny. Said one respondent, "I wonder how abortion would be judged if we lived in a society open to women having children independent of spousal relationships." Elizabeth, the other respondent, said:

> There should not be a legal dimension; it is really an intensely personal decision—serious, weighty, having gravity. I feel that men don't carry their share of the decision; sexuality is just more connected for women—we are reminded every month.

She added that the church community could serve as a supportive agent in this decision by finding options for women. She alluded to her own experience as an adoptive mother whose infant son was made available through church connections.

Men and women seemed to agree that abortion is a serious consideration in pastoral counseling situations and that the parish minister has responsibility for understanding both the decision to seek abortion and the consequences for the woman post-abortion, that is, the need for some form of grief counseling. But few respondents, lesbian or gay, believed the pulpit was an appropriate place for responsible ministerial counsel. Alice commented that the pulpit can be misused as the site for "prophetic statement"; abortion ought to be talked about in close relationship and not as a subject of controversy from a privileged position of expression.

Discussion of euthanasia tended to become an exchange about suicide as well, with half of the respondents (of both sexes) indicating that the consequences of the latter often prove to be tragic for survivors. My probe into the matter of choice and death was an extension of the abortion discussion. I attempted to elicit moral reasoning about the questions of who decides and when decision is necessary. Responses to the abortion inquiry were basically direct and brief in contrast to those I listened to regarding euthanasia. Most respondents asked whether there are no other options. Lesbians in the sample tended to reflect on family histories and personal experiences with the terminal illnesses of loved ones. Susan spoke, for instance, of her mother's struggle with Alzheimer's disease and the hardship such illness exacts upon a family.

Frank's reflections on euthanasia shifted to cultural facets of death and dying, noting his disagreement with the coverage devoted by the press to a story about a Japanese woman's attempted suicide after the death of her child. He stated that a western view of life's absolute value ought not be superimposed upon differing cultural perceptions and expectations about correct behavior in the face of despair. He followed this thought by distinguishing between pain and depression and noting that this distinction allowed him to understand where and when intervention should occur. "If a person is despairing," he said, "that's one thing and I could do something, intervene somehow. I am less certain about pain."

The suffering of AIDS patients was introduced by many of the respondents. Several of the gay interviewees spoke of their concern for friends, and one indicated that he was still grieving from the death of a close friend who had succumbed to the disease. Although fewer women spoke of AIDS, one volunteered that the lesbian community had played a pivotal role in offering support to the disease's victims. She noted that lesbians had taught gay men about community: "It is something we have had long experience with, and AIDS has made it critically important for gay individuals to learn what we have known and practiced." She offered that her experience with the dying, particularly AIDS patients, has also been a learning experience. "Something mysterious in dying teaches me about mortality. It has been tremendously important; we all have hearts and I've learned something about the spiritual depths of life."

My questions regarding theology followed the exchange about euthanasia and suicide. This part of the inquiry was particularly illuminating and yielded further evidence of gender difference in response. With respect to the general question of theological belief, lesbians differed from gay respondents in their emphasis upon the relational experience. This was well illustrated in Alice's reflection on transcendence. "Transcendence," she stated, "is a process, a relationship. It isn't getting out of oneself. I believe that it happens when I am present for you." Her words were echoed in Mary's brief assessment of theology as a "process of working together which allows us to get beyond ourselves." This expression of theology as transcendent process of community was expanded by Susan, who spoke of her theology as community that reaches beyond the limits of time, connecting past and present and inviting an integrated consciousness of a shared future. She marveled at the "torch-bearing" function of religious community, an honoring of those who have passed, and the meaning of their efforts. Her theology was infused with cosmological symbol and revealed the centrality of "abundance and touching." She concluded that this theology shapes community "where people of like spirit gather — moving and primordial — embracing life."

Although Susan's rich answer to this question did not identify the native American religious tradition as fundamental to her understanding, she spoke of natural elements and music as essential dimensions of religious gathering. Two of the women in the sample expressly identified other religious traditions as integral to or enhancing of their respective theological understandings. Nancy, observing that she had been influenced in her spirituality by native American mythology and ritual, attested to her "creation orientation." "I am more pantheistic and spirit-oriented than most Christians." Hers was a concern with the "quality of presence." Elizabeth also identified inclusiveness of other religious teachings into her theology. A Unitarian Universalist minister, she spoke of her integration of an eclectic-pragmatic belief that "is a dance, or perhaps a true combination of Buddhism and western teachings." The idea of nonattachment had deepened her understanding of the human condition.

God-language and the meaning of Jesus Christ threaded through the responses of the three lesbian respondents who belonged to either the United Church of Christ or the United Methodist Church. All of the women in the sample were identified with feminism, but the two Unitarian Universalist women did not address either of these dimensions of theology. I can only speculate that those more closely associated with Protestant Christianity find that more attention must be given to matters of exclusive and patriarchal language. Mary announced that her theology was strongly shaped by an incarnational understanding. She stated that the Gospel teaches humanity about God's embodied word. "There is something quite remarkable about the human being who showed us how to be God's love in this world." Alice did not echo this position, but expressed a worry about the uses of Gospel and the "idolatry of fact" she associated with the strong emphasis upon the Jesus of history. She spoke of her theology as an expression of shared engagement in the discovery of a Christology free of masculinist bias and contemporary efforts to emphasize a heroic political Jesus figure.

Nancy was the least patient of the five with respect to Christianity and its tradition of a familial language of God as father and son; she also rejected the implicit notion of hierarchy of "son embraced in the feudal language of lordship." "It makes no sense," she observed, "to accept a radical presence among us and then separate 'Him' from humankind as an elite figure."

Only one gay respondent echoed the women's sentiment regarding community and relationality with respect to theology. Frank, who was struggling to integrate his cultural heritage as a Hawaiian into Protestantism, spoke of a belief he perceived to be outside of the mainstream. His emphasis upon the spirit and the church's veritable marginalization of this expression of divinity was not repeated by any of the men in the sample. He explained: "Christianity's biggest problem is its obsession with Jesus as God; Jesus is human, God is spirit and we've choked off the flow of the spirit." Although Frank's criticism of Protestant Christology was sharp, he did not conclude with a negative assessment. On the contrary, he noted that the spirit will prevail because "the spirit reaches to our deepest source and promotes our being authentically together." I suspect that Frank's quest for cultural integration of his roots had much in common with the women of the sample who were also struggling to stay within a tradition that has historically ignored women's contribution to the church. However, several of the lesbian respondents spoke of reaching beyond their cultural and religious experience (to native American and Buddhist teachings). Frank was concerned with the recognition and integration of his own cultural life; he was currently studying Hawaiian cosmological and mythological material and engaged in traditional dance (Hula).

I have characterized lesbian responses to the theological question as primarily relational, addressing the limitation of traditional religious teaching and envisioning a larger understanding of community. Gay responses focused around how the self experiences God. This personal discovery is not without social implications but resembles a quality of male narrative: a telling of the self in grasping a fundamental and ultimate truth. The language of several respondents illustrated this point. One spoke of theology as "being alone with God"; another offered theology as "a welling up from who I am." A third indicated that theological reflection concerns "the discovery of the inner self."

Several respondents observed that their theological understandings would be incomplete without self-recognition of their sexual identity. John stated this succinctly: "Being gay is the ground." In his case, after 15 years of religious questing, a veritable pilgrimage through major religious traditions including Greek Orthodoxy, Roman Catholicism, and Judaism, he finally grasped that "truth." He noted that Tillich's theological teachings had been essential to his understanding and integration of sexual identity into his own theology. Matthew also spoke of a period of theological searching that had become an harmonious weave of mystical teachings and self-acknowledgment of homosexuality.

Five of the six gay respondents made some reference to theology as relevant to the social order, particularly in its assessment of justice and equality. Matthew observed that theological "practice" embraces three concerns: (a) the definition of the underdog, (b) the legitimation of authority, and (c) the location of the poetic. He explained that the first two go together, prompting him to be suspicious of declared authority that may have no base but proves dangerous to a group of people who emerge as second-class citizens. He added that he was always "with the underdog." The poetic function serves as a means to lift his spirit and that of his congregants and encourages a more prophetic vision. Craig's understanding of theology and social justice was grounded on his understanding of Jesus Christ as "the lover of people; he loved people who are in love." This truth has enabled Craig to work with the poor and dispossessed for more than 20 years.

Half of the gay respondents mentioned the role of sexual identity in their respective expressions of theology, but only one addressed how this theology provided a new point of departure for the church. John stated that he has begun to construct a theology embracing gay and lesbian sexuality and spirituality. He spoke of the necessity to rid the church of its categories and its ambivalence toward homosexual persons. He pointed out that it is unhealthy for the gay community to continue to offer an apologetic for themselves.

I followed my probe into theology with a general question about the shape and meaning of worship and liturgical activity. Men and women provided little that would distinguish their preferences. I had thought that women might be more critical of the spoken word in celebration and that men would emphasize the power of preaching. This did not emerge from the sample. In fact, three of the five women spoke of the positive function of sermon, its role in creating focus and cohesiveness during the service. Lesbian respondents did volunteer, however, that they were often dissatisfied with the order of worship and the way in which preaching is traditionally undertaken. Several spoke of their experimentation with shorter sermons, or with congregational participation in song or litany at the midpoint of a sermon. All the women emphasized the importance of music, indicating that song enhances and deepens the meaning of the word. Several added that movement and symbolic ritualization, including visual material, added to the celebrative character of Sunday worship.

The men and women I interviewed agreed that liturgy is the work of the people and that involvement of the gathered assembly is essential in creating a sense of the unity of theology with worship. Charles addressed the mystery of such events. "Although as a minister I have some control, the experience transcends me and every person gathered; there is a mysterious dimension which takes on a life of its own."

It is unclear whether a gender difference might be found with respect to who takes responsibility for worship on Sundays. I noted that women tended to speak of what they thought would engage the assembly more fully but did not explicitly refer to collaboration with the community in planning liturgy. On the other hand, three of the gay respondents mentioned their respective leadership activities in worship. Frank offered that he believed that he had responsibility for "making connections" both within the service (i.e., between the parts—sermon, hymn, and so on) and in relation to the cultural realities of those worshipping together. Matthew pointed to the failure of many liturgical events because there was neither internal integrity nor an ongoing sense of the church's continuity. He has taken the lead in knitting together these parts and dates by writing material for worship that fosters this liturgical integration. He summed up his remarks on liturgy with these words: "Every celebration is a witness to life in the face of God and should display the integrity of all celebration."

Responses to my inquiry into attitudes about the institutional church yielded the most clear-cut expression of gender difference. The ambiguity regarding professional leadership roles in the creation of liturgy among women of this sample may be better understood in reading answers to this section of the interview. Although I did not ask either how church is defined or what type of relationship there should be between local congregations and the national church hierarchy, men and women responded as if I had made such an inquiry. Women tended to respond in language that distinguished church from other social arrangements. Men, by contrast, offered views about the usefulness of or tensions with church polity. Several alluded to institutional practices or statements supporting or betraying gay religious leadership.

Elizabeth's testimony best exemplified lesbian expressions of the church as a special community within a larger community. She spoke of the church as "a cooperative venture involving members in a variety of efforts and permitting them to set limits and put aside differences in order to get the job done." This collective energy, she added, teaches us how the church is more fulfilling than the family to the extent that it embraces diversity in the shared hopes and common activities of the community. Alice supported this view, observing that the church "is a group of people in an ongoing relationship that commits the members to mutual exploration, in the deepest sense, of who they are alone and together."

These articulate statements about the church emphasize (a) membership as diverse, and (b) activity as intimate but expansive. No mention of committees or structures of authority were introduced by most of the lesbian respondents. Charles, on the other hand, joined the women in his sense of church as an extended family, but turned to the question of authority and how ministers differ from members of the congregation. He was emphatic that a tension between the professional responsibilities of the minister and the congregation's participation in church polity was healthy and ordinary, but that it can become a problem when the interdependence of minister and congregation falls out of equilibrium. The minister's particular authority, according to Charles, is to "call the 'yes' to memory." This affirming work enables the congregation to return to the source of all authority.

Matthew was more adamant in his attachment to an institutional understanding of church. In our conversation, he explored the character of congregational polity of Unitarian Universalism and explained that it was the best possible arrangement for his disposition and vocational expression. He noted that the connection between the local congregations and the national offices of the denomination are important ones, with strengths and weaknesses that need to be sorted out. Principles and policies move from grassroots to center (the annual General Assembly) and back again, providing guidelines that do not diminish the local church's accountability and action. At the core of polity, Matthew observed, is a commitment to a covenant between the people and the church as an expression of God's presence in history.

Several men spoke of their differences with denominational efforts. They indicated there was a gap between intention and action, proclamation and deed. Most irksome for these gay respondents was the apparent acceptance of a policy of inclusiveness (of gays, of women, of people of color or differing cultural backgrounds) that in practice is not implemented. Some referred to tokenism, others to covert discrimination; all of these critics expressed some suspicion for hierarchy and the church's distance from routine practice.

Only two women volunteered responses about the institutional church as a national structure of power and influence. Susan, whose ministry has been located outside the parish and who understood noninclusion of alternate approaches to professional religious leadership as discriminatory, spoke of the "old boy network" that persists in her denomination. This group of influential male ministers has effectively hindered women's placement in churches and maintained control of the church's structures. She added that many women have not chosen to challenge this pattern and have preferred to adapt to and "cast themselves into a male ministerial mode." What this means is that women ministers have failed to experiment with the character of religious community and the nature of worship. Susan concluded that this has not been true with respect to lesbian ministers, who have much in common with one another and have the strength of their convictions about the integrity of theology, worship, and church structure.

Nancy, a United Methodist minister, also spoke of the church structure and offered that she was of "two minds" with respect to the regional structures of her denomination. On the one hand, the Methodist appointment scheme of ministers demonstrates the value and vitality of local connection, fostering a high degree of communication among laity and professional religious leadership in a particular religious setting. This has permitted women to come together routinely and, at the annual regional conferences, to develop continuous dialogue with one another. Nancy's enthusiasm for this aspect of the denomination's structural expression was not ambivalent. However, the other side of this approach is the maintenance of an hierarchical arrangement that diminishes local communication and grassroots activity. "I have trouble balancing my antihierarchy views," she added, "with the church's everyday administrative practice."

I have noted that women answered the church question with attention to the character of local religious community. They responded with appreciation of membership diversity and a dynamic process that allowed individual members to grow. This relational concern echoes the way in which lesbian interviewees told their respective stories at the outset of my inquiry. It also amplifies the discussion of worship organization and responsibility. Women seem to concern themselves with "doing," being in the presence of others, and experiencing change through persistent activity. Men, answering the church inquiry, were inclined to talk mainly about the sources and implications of church authority. They spoke of the local church community but tended to locate this community within the national denominational structure. Theirs was an answer that appreciated institutional arrangements or found denominational practices wanting. Obviously my generalization has exceptions, but I am satisfied that a thread of gender-shaped expression weaved throughout the interviews.

Before concluding my remarks on this section of the inquiry, I want to report that there was some denominational clustering around church involvement that cut across gender lines. All four of the United Church of Christ respondents (two women, two men) had sought out alternative churches for their personal membership. That is, they have remained within the denomination but also participate in churches that are not strictly constituted of denominational members. John joined a house church, that meets his worship needs and is a caring community. Yet he did not feel completely "at home" in this small church. Two of the women participated in an alternative church that is connected with the denomination but open to gay and lesbian members and to those who cannot find spiritual comfort in other churches. Frank has remained interested in ordination, but is alienated from his local church community because the Hawaiian hierarchy has taken exception to his "out of the closet" sexual identity. His exploration has continued within the denomination but with greater attention to the integration of Polynesian cultural understandings into the theology and worship of the United Church of Christ.

I asked each respondent about secular politics and the church in my effort to understand how religious leaders integrate church and state. I discovered no apparent gender distinctions in the responses to this inquiry but found that they fell neatly into two positions. The first argues for strong church visibility in the political realm and perceives the pulpit as an appropriate site for the encouragement of this vision. This position, expressed equally by men and women, indicated basically that "citizenship is not abandoned at the moment of ordination." Several voiced a commitment to the prophetic ministry, that assumes that matters of political life must be addressed, especially on behalf of those who have no audible position in the public realm. Thus, the minister's prophetic role includes speaking for those citizens who are undervalued by political decision-makers. Obviously, this understanding is strongly correlated with the response of those who spoke of their theological practice as expressive of social justice work. Matthew asserted that the local church is the site for citizenship encouragement, and one of the tasks of the professional religious leader is to foster civil obedience or disobedience after a good case has been made for one or the other.

The other position, which essentially denied the political work of the church, was virtually anticipated by many respondents who favored political activism. They expressed some anxiety about proselytizing from the pulpit, and all agreed that they would not publicly favor one political candidate over another. This hesitancy was amplified by the group of respondents who did not feel that the religious community ought to mingle with the affairs of the public realm. Two women offered that there was some danger in embracing political causes, but they reasoned differently from one another. The first pointed to the church's historical embrace of conservative and sometime violent stances. The other spoke of her worry about imposing notions of preference on the people in the pews. She spoke suspiciously of hierarchical declarations and proclamations, seeing them as having little to do with the opinions held by the members of individual and the assault of particular congregations. Her opposition was less a matter of church and state relationship than of intrachurch authority. She held to a radically democratic view of the people's responsibility to pursue such matters without the intervention of leaders in influential position, and without the manipulation of influential argument.

Had I thought about it at the time of the interview, I would have pressed my respondents for answers regarding the sources of political initiative. Although the sample yielded something about the ambiguity of local church in the immediate political community, it remained unclear how this group looked upon the national denominational offices and the efforts of the National and World Council of Churches. I would have inquired into "citizenship" education and whether these interdenominational structures provide useful resources. I also would have asked about the gulf between local congregations and professional religious administrators and probed whether their leadership roles were strengthened or weakened by these associations.

I concluded the interview with some questions about community, particularly as it defines, enhances, or is ineffective with respect to, homosexuality. I hoped to gather some material both on how community is understood for gay and lesbian persons and if gender is significant here. There is an assumption of women's greater facility in creating and nourishing groups of supportive persons. Would this hold true for my sample? The other perspective reflects a point made in *Habits of the Heart* (Bellah et al.) regarding "lifestyle enclaves." Those authors distinguished community (which is inclusive of difference) from those "enclaves" that gather people who are similar in experience and value position. My findings proved little with respect to the character of groups singularly identified with homosexuality. Rather, friendship seemed to be the key term in this discussion, men and women agreeing that the warmth and dependability of good friends satisfies the need for sociability. Lesbians, however, indicated that such friendships were associated with women's groups, not lesbian women's groups, and that sexual identity was an irrelevant factor in the community of support they experienced. One respondent answered, however, that she had found the lesbian religious leadership (in ministry and in the academy) very important for her "spiritual survival." Gay respondents also spoke of the role of good friends and indicated that they did not have much experience with the gay community as such. All agreed that a sense of feeling at home was fostered in gay bars, at gay concerts, and at dances.

Three of the lesbian respondents spoke of the danger of grouping homosexual women into the category of "lesbian." They argued that there is no definitive group or community, although there are, of course, particular lesbian gatherings of friends. This assertion is important as a fundamental notion in studying persons categorized into a group: affinity or likeness is insufficient warrant for assuming a monolithic reality of homosexual identity. Mary, for example, distinguished herself from those women who remain bitter or alienated and who "batter themselves" with the notion of difference. Elizabeth clarified this point by speaking about her own development and consciousness. In the early phases of her self-recognition as a lesbian she wanted to associate with lesbians to the exclusion of others. This served to diminish her loneliness and the awkward belief that she was ill-suited to the dominant culture. However at the time of this study, Elizabeth was wary of any "ghetto" association that separates persons from one another in the common struggle for human liberation. She spoke emphatically of the power of women's support activity that includes a variety of sexual attitude and practice and embraces more than a working tolerance for whatever minority participates within the group. Alice echoed this sentiment and affirmed that friendship flourished where there was recognition of diversity and appreciation of its function within a group.

Few of the gay respondents contributed to this exchange regarding friends as fundamentally different and challenging. John admitted that he had experienced too much disappointment in the so-called gay community. He spoke of fractionalization in the political efforts of gay activists and a lack of cohesiveness in the various campaigns mounted on behalf of the gay liberation movement. He observed that "you can't build community around lifestyle." His somewhat melancholy reflection paralleled the Bellah et al. conclusion regarding enclaves.

CONCLUSION

In reviewing the words of 11 women and men in an effort to summarize how their testimonies illuminated ethical and value understandings, I am unprepared to draw any dramatic conclusions. There are several tentative understandings derived from the interview study that help bring this article to a close and suggest the starting point for a more elaborate comparison. Perhaps no one generalization is more important than this: Lesbian and gay religious leaders are not single-issue believers or activists. I noted this earlier in the context of my assertion about religious vocation as the ground from which each of the respondents drew sustenance. Although the reality of homosexuality in the church remains controversial, all the respondents replied that their calling was shaped by a sense of the human condition in God's world. They have engaged in education and ministerial efforts that foster a vision of an egalitarian and socially just order, a perspective that is expansive and energetic, and that requires a good deal of optimism and belief in the efficacy of religious leadership. As I indicated, in spite of institutional disappointment and personal experiences with church bigotry, none of the respondents chose to work outside of the religious traditions to which they felt a deep belonging.

The gender differences that I found in the interviews were unexpected, but not surprising in light of the current feminist analysis of distinctive moral reasoning, socialization, and assumptions of leadership expression and style. Women did seem to communicate the priority of relationship in their stories and in their statements regarding theological content and church activity. Whether their presence in the church will eventually shift expectations about worship, pastoral responsibility, and congregational religious leadership remains to be seen. The men in this study did not negate the value of relationship in their individual expression of theology or ministerial practice. Rather, they placed their emphasis on the self. Much of their reflection, including the content of the six gay men's narratives, revealed a concern with personal presence and freedom from arbitrary authority. In the retelling of coming out, each of the gay interviewees understood that an impasse had been met and overcome and that the telling had had a freeing effect. It would be possible to conclude that the veritable act of narration (both for the first time and to me) was a relational effort. Nonetheless, the stories and the responses disclosed what I perceived as an essential struggle "to be." By contrast, the women seemed to express a satisfaction in "being with."

The patterns I refer to here are preliminary assessments of men's and women's responses to a limited number of questions. What was important in the testimony gathered was the process by which I initiated an exchange about pivotal dimensions of these individuals' shared life. All respondents listened to my questions carefully and responded seriously, in ways that expressed their understandings and experience. Not a silent notetaker, I indulged in active conversation and found myself wishing for more time.

I have offered here some of the reflections provided by the interviewees and, in recalling those responses, have attempted to organize some preliminary thoughts that began during the interview phase. I am left with more questions than answers. Among these, veritable building blocks for another study, I list just a few:

1. How representative are these expressions of lesbians and gays?
2. Does the vocational commitment of these respondents provide a greater commonality among gay and lesbian religious leaders?
3. How would respondents answer the questions if I asked them to apply the content of their respective stories to the questions?
4. Would nonlesbian and nongay religious leaders from the same denominational groups respond similarly to church and theology questions?

And the inquiry goes on.

NOTES

1. Although there are a number of publications concerned with the church and homosexuality, and a growing number of books providing information about the experiences of gay and lesbian persons in relation to religious tradition (e.g., John Boswell's classic 1980 study or Jeannine Gramick's 1983 edited collection), these do not disclose information about religious leadership and value understandings. David Kelsey's 1983 essay is a useful overview of the theological context of church understandings of homosexuality.

2. The appendix of *Habits of the Heart*, entitled "Social Science as Public Philosophy" (Bellah et al., 297-307), is a brilliant statement of methodology as social engagement.

3. Bellah and his colleagues distinguished first language from second language. The former refers to a way of speaking about morality in contemporary America that reveals a commitment to utilitarian and expressive individualism; the latter is attached to the traditions of church, expressive of rooted experience within a historically continuous religious environment.

4. Gilligan (1982) discovered that her female respondents expressed a position of caring, while male respondents in her study and of earlier moral development studies gave voice to a position emphasizing rights and principles. This difference in discourse was attributed to personality development in males and females that were summarized as gender differences between attachment (female) and separation (male).

REFERENCES

Bellah, R. and R. Madsea, W. Sullivan, A. Swidler, and S. Tipton (Eds.). (1985). *Habits of the Heart, Individualism and Commitment in American Life*. Berkeley: University of California.

Boswell, J. (1980). *Christianity, Social Tolerance and Homosexuality*. Chicago: University of Chicago Press.

Gramick, J., ed. (1983). *Homosexuality and the Catholic Church*. Chicago: Thomas More Press.

Gilligan, C. (1982). *In a Different Voice*. Cambridge, MA: Harvard University Press.

Kelsey, D. (1983, April). Homosexuality and the church: Theological issues. *Yale Divinity School Reflection*, pp. 9-12.

Psychodynamic Theory
and Pastoral Theology:
An Integrated Model

Michael J. Garanzini, SJ

Saint Louis University
St. Louis, Missouri

SUMMARY. The article proposes that a pastoral concern for gay and lesbian individuals must be sensitive to the psychological and social dynamics involved in their attachments, separations, and losses. Drawing on object relations theory and insights from self-psychology, a model is proposed whereby counselor and counselee can examine the cycle of attachment, separation, loss and reattachment that characterizes all important relationships. The suggestion is made that this cycle is applicable to the development and reformulation of life-giving myths and ways of being in the world. Finally, an analysis of the role of early narcissistic wounds and the healing process in therapy is presented.

The Christian churches have not been known for their openness and objectivity when it comes to understanding and helping gay men and women. There are, of course, notable exceptions, but most ministers and theologians, no matter how they feel about the issue of homosexuality and Christian doctrine, agree that a defensive posture characterizes most religious groups. The Roman Catholic tradition has been adamant in its stand on gay sexuality, its documents stressing three positions: (a) a reluctance to accept what has been described as a "homosexual lifestyle," although that has never

---

Michael J. Garanzini is a Jesuit priest who teaches child development, child and family counseling, and pastoral counseling courses at Saint Louis University. He is the author of *The Attachment Cycle: Object Relations and Healing in Therapy*, published by Paulist Press.

175

been defined; (b) a growing appreciation that sexual orientation may not be chosen or willed and that it is to be distinguished from sexual practice; and (c) an instruction to those with teaching authority and responsibility that sexual activity can only be condoned when it is between two legitimately married persons [National Conference of Catholic Bishops (NCCB), 1976].

The point here is not to argue with either the positions themselves or the assumptions upon which they are based. Rather, what follows is the broad outline of a theory of psychological development-in-relationship that (a) describes the developmental themes and issues that are especially important in the lives of gay men and women, and (b) attempts to combine sound psychodynamic theory with relevant pastoral theory and practice. This should be especially useful in understanding the therapeutic process from a pastoral perspective; in other words, it tries to give pastorally oriented counselors a language and theory that makes sense theologically, psychologically, and therapeutically. Again, this is a broad outline and such a project cannot hope to address all the issues that are raised in the pastoral counseling of gay men and women. Still, a model that helps in understanding the normal developmental process and the healing process in therapy and echoes the Judeo-Christian scriptures can be useful to pastoral counselors in their attempts to communicate the genuine love and acceptance that makes self-acceptance and honesty possible.

Within this discussion, special attention will be given to the fundamental dynamic of relationship development and the role that early wounds play in hindering that process. It is assumed here that therapy concerns the healing process and that pastoral counseling, when it is truly therapeutic and truly pastoral, concerns the communication of acceptance and the healing of the person on the physical, psychological, and spiritual levels. In so doing, the pastoral counselor carries out the injunction to all disciples to "heal the sick" and "preach the kingdom of God" (Mt. 9:35, Lk. 9:6).

THE ATTACHMENT CYCLE IN HUMAN DEVELOPMENT

Research and theory in the bonding process and the nature of instincts has progressed rapidly in the years following World War

II. It is not a sophisticated and complex field of study. Object Relations theory has drawn on attachment and bonding studies of infants and children to support a psychodynamic theory of the nature and goals of human relationships that stresses the fundamental drive for attachment as opposed to pleasure and satisfaction, a cornerstone of more traditional Freudian theory. The attachment cycle proposed here is based heavily on the work of Object Relations theory and the work of the Self psychologists, an even newer branch of psychoanalysis (Greenberg & Mitchell, 1983).

The attachment cycle can be defined as follows. Individuals are naturally, even instinctively, drawn to those who are perceived as better able to manage the world and thereby care for them. Development, however, means that separation from those to whom one is bonded is necessary, even if painful, on the psychological and physical levels. Eventually, all individuals must accept the loss of the individual to whom one is attached, at least in the terms that produced the attachment. When the loss of the important individual is accepted and successfully mourned, then reattachment is possible, this time on a different, more adequate or mature basis. One does not progress psychologically, physically, even spiritually, without negotiating this attachment, separation, loss, and reattachment cycle with important individuals. Renewal of relationships, or at least a coming-to-terms with their meaning, is necessary for increased maturity, and this renewal process obliges one to experience first the anxiety of separation and then the grief of loss. Without traversing the cycle, individuals remain immaturely and unhealthily dependent. Renewal of the terms of relationships produces a renewal of the sense of identity in that the self experiences itself as having survived a kind of death—the death of a former, less mature self.

The mother-infant bond is the first attachment relationship for most, and in this primal relationship, the child experiences not only important lessons in care, anticipation, joy, and other positive emotions, but also negative feelings such as anger, jealousy, and disappointment. Both sets of emotions aid in the development of a sense of belonging as well as separateness, difference, and uniqueness. Harry Stack Sullivan believed that the developmental history of a person is more accurately described as the "developmental history of the possibilities of interpersonal relationships'' (Sullivan, 1953, p. 30).

Two important postulates follow from Sullivan's basic tenet. First, the need for tenderness and belonging is fundamental and innate, or biologically rooted. In other words, Freud's assumption of instinctual libidinal energy or drive as the source of human motivation is challenged because it cannot explain bonding when no gratification is forthcoming. Second, anxiety is communicated in both directions of each relationship. Anxiety in one party will be felt, or "picked up" by those with whom the individual is related or attached.

Because relationship is fundamental and necessary, isolation is deadly. Motivation is most accurately described in the context of securing proximity and closeness, or maintaining bonds. Anxiety then is the "signal" alerting the individual to the threat of separation and estrangement. From the earliest days of human life to the last, humans are motivated by a desire to build a self-in-relationship. The work of psychologists who studied the human infant in its relational contexts, such as Melanie Klein, support this contention (Klein, 1948). From her observations of children, Klein believed that complex emotions such as resentment, envy, gratitude, joy, and disappointment are visible in the mother-infant dyad. These emotions are related to the child's chief desire to be attached and the fear of annihilation in the sundering of attachment bonds.

Others, like Margaret Mahler and her associates, have noticed how through separation the individual learns to develop as an autonomous person (Mahler, Fine, & Bergman, 1975). In normal development, the infant and mother progress through stages of attachment and detachment, or separation. This separation process is resisted by the child, and occasionally by the mother, because both feel the anxiety of possible loss. The first such experience occurs when the child is weaned. Both mother and child experience the anxiety of separation, but the child must accept the loss of mother as sole source of food and nourishment if the child is to mature to the next stage of interdependence. If the child is not weaned, then the child would be unhealthily dependent on the mother for food. By separating from her—losing her as sole source of food—the child is in a position to accept the help of other potential "feeders" and can reattach to her for other purposes. Now, mother can play other roles and the child develops a certain autonomy from her.

Paradoxically, by giving up the relationship under its old terms, the relationship is reborn and renewed, given a new focus and new possibilities. Mother can now be teacher, for example, because teaching the child to dress, walk, or feed itself will necessitate a certain independence and self-reliance that is the by-product of the former separation or individuating process. Both parties, moreover, experience the anxiety and fear of a too early separation. Both fear the change of identity that such separation would produce. Both die a little to an old self in that child and mother are defined by this bonded relationship.

To Mahler, an infant is indistinguishable from the relationship in which it is bonded until this separation-individuation process begins. Without this painful separation process, one or both of the individuals are "stuck" in an unhealthy relationship. It is important for the child to experience both the inevitability of loss of the former terms upon which the relational ties were built and to experience the ability to stop that process for some time — until it is ready.

When the pain of separation becomes acute, in other words, the child ought to be able to stop such anxiety by winning back to itself the detaching, absent, or negligent caretaker. When those experiences have not been at times possible or positive, as in the case of inconsistent parenting, then defense mechanisms such as denial, compulsion, obsession, and so on, develop to an unhealthy degree. They ward off the anxiety but do so by sacrificing a realistic assessment of the environment and at serious expense to the child's own self-assessment, his or her feelings of value and worth. In later life, investment of one's "self" in a relationship becomes impossible or at least extremely difficult because a foundation in this cyclic process is missing. Without the early and continual experience of the reformation of the terms of relationship toward increased mutual interdependence, based on a positive assessment of one's lovability, intimacy in relationship is too painful to endure.

Over time, the child sheds a perception of being one with the mother and through the cycle of separation, loss, and reattachment, comes to appreciate the distinctness of the other. Important others, moreover, are carried "inside" when they are physically absent.

The tolerance of another's physical absence grows in time, providing a defense against the anxiety of separation.

Again, Mahler's work, as well as that of D. W. Winnicott, has pointed to the importance of internalizing the loved other as a way of remaining attached when physical presence is not possible (Mahler, 1975; Winnicott, 1965). Nevertheless, an experience of alienation is inevitable when the bonds of relationships are broken as one or the other individual senses the need to become more autonomous and less dependent. Thus, the role of loss cannot be overemphasized.

When resentments, anger, frustration, and fear are endured, when old relationships are mourned as not likely to return, then a new relationship can rise from the ashes of the old. The self is experienced as stronger, as a survivor, as somehow more whole. Indeed, the self is new because its identity has been reformed.

Over time, relationships traverse these attachment, separation, loss, and rebirth cycles. McWhirter and Mattison's work on the stages of gay relationships is an excellent example of how this growth process takes place within gay relationships. Attachments are in need of regular, periodic renewal—not so that they can become what they were before, but so that they can become something different (McWhirter & Mattison, 1984). Maturation in relationship, or maturity itself, is mutual and healthy dependency in a stage-appropriate manner. Independence is both a fiction and an unhealthy state. It is the quality of one's attachments that determine maturity—in the physical, psychological, and spiritual senses—and these attachments are not only to people.

The process outlined here holds true for attachments to ideas and to ways of seeing the world, especially myths of what constitutes healthy and happy living. Painful separations and disappointments brought on by the inadequacy of opinions and beliefs force the individual to reexamine the fundamentals upon which one's values, world, and self-concept are built. At first, these are inherited products. That is, they are passed on through one's social milieu, but in time need to be tested for their adequacy and merit, especially in adolescence. Values, world-views, beliefs, even self-concepts, are altered or even discarded when found to be inadequate or incorrect.

For example, most children grow up with the myth that happiness and wholeness in life necessitates the finding of one life-time partner, having a family, earning a decent income, and so on. Gay men and women discover that the myths of the straight world are not only inadequate for many nongay individuals but are especially debilitating. Suffering the loss of these myths is a frightening process. The more one separates from the lifestyle and the customary activities that secure the myths that were inherited, the more anxious one feels. Denials, obsessions, compulsions, and other defenses may ward off anxiety for a time, but prove to be destructive over time.

Attempts at living a "straight" life consume the time, energy, and emotional repertoire of many gay individuals. Believing their sexual orientation is a "mistake" or an "unfortunate accident" or a positive evil—all attitudes supported by institutions such as the churches, but more importantly by the social fabric in which young people are raised in most Western cultures—some seek to purge themselves of this part of their lives. Ego-dystonic homosexuality is as much an indictment of the culture as it is the sign that inappropriate and impossible myths have not been shed, and that the individual is in the throes of separation anxiety.

Those who find their sexual orientation difficult to accept must be helped to have the courage to face not only the part of themselves that they do not like but, more importantly, to face the fact that they are the victim of a myth, or myths, that they need to shed. In the process of shedding such a myth they will experience a real death-like state and will need to appreciate the sometimes long mourning process that will follow. John Fortunato's autobiographic account is an excellent testament to this painful process and the implications for the therapeutic process. He described well assisting the mourning and grieving process (Fortunato, 1982).

In pastoral counseling, a unique opportunity arises for helping in this separation and mourning process. By listening to and accepting the story of the significant relationships where care or a lack of it shaped the counselee's history, the pastoral counselor communicates a message of reconciliation and aids in the healing process. This is so because the story of the individual will offer clues as to the chief psychological barriers to self-acceptance, the necessary foundation for courage, and to intimacy with others. Unhealthy dependencies, overly anxious and unsuccessful separations, or unmourned and unaccepted losses will likely be the chief obstacles to building mature attachments. In other words, failures to mature in the life-long struggle with intimacy, or healthy interdependence, have their roots in significant failures in traversing the attachment-separation-loss cycle with others. While the cycle may become "stuck" at any one time in a life history, each relationship holds the potential for correcting and healing past wounds. Pastoral counseling is, then, a psychology of hope, not one of determinism or defeatism, and characterizes the pastoral therapists' fundamental offer.

Because past relationships with caregivers have such a powerful impact on future health and self-definition, it is important to understand the way a "self" develops and the way wounds to that self can make progress difficult when it comes to the important task of maintaining healthy attachments. It is maintained here that many gay men and women, precisely because of their sexual orientation, have suffered under a suspicion that they are not as fortunate, lucky, or healthy as nongay men and women. Sometimes this stems from early wounds to the psyche and thus astunting of the development of the self. The psyche is especially vulnerable in the first 3 years of life, but can be seriously affected throughout the years of psychic dependence on caretakers, such as in early adolescence. In the next section, the insights of those psychologists who have theorized about the development or the wounding of the "self" will be taken up. The section ends up with a reflection on how the attachment cycle and the psychology of early wounds can be seen from a theological and scriptural perspective.

PROBLEMS WITH INTIMACY
AND THE FAILURE
OF THE ATTACHMENT BOND

Philosopher Hanna Arendt has written that to know someone is to know the story in which he or she functions as the main character (Arendt, 1958). This succinctly describes the dilemma in pastoral counseling: how to get to the heart of a counselee's story where the self that is on-the-line in the history of the individual's relationship is visible. Many of the chief insights of the psychologists of the self have come through work with individuals diagnosed as narcissistically wounded. The literature has tended to stress the more extreme examples of adult narcissism. Yet much of what has been learned from work with these individuals, many of whom are gay, is potentially useful for understanding the difficulties encountered in the normal developmental process. Symptoms that characterize narcissistically wounded people — a grandiose sense of self, a heightened sensitivity to criticism, an inability to maintain lasting relationships, a feeling of emptiness and estrangement from one's surroundings — amount to an inability to maintain intimacy and to a poor sense of self-worth (Kohut, 1971; Kernberg, 1980).

According to Miller and Kohut, two of the outstanding theorists of the nature and source of narcissistic disturbance, early traumatic events, or inconsistent or unavailable parents to emotionally needy children, can cause a split in the development of the child's sense of self (Kohut, 1971; Miller, 1981). In most cases, an ego develops on a normal course as the child learns to get along in the world of family, school and, later on, career. But, believing that something is truly wrong with their "selves" they develop only superficial relationships out of a fear that if truly known, they would be unacceptable or unlovable as they are or were with the primary caretaker. This results from an interpretation that the absence, disappointment, or abuse of one's parents was somehow caused by or related to who and what they are, not simply something they did.

In narcissism, then, the issue is not excessive love of self, but fear of an unlovable self. Such individuals make great strides in developing their skills and in "pushing" themselves forward, shoring up this fragile self by overcompensation and by a preoccupation with themselves. They can be successful. They are usually very proud of their accomplishments. But they remain isolated and unattached to individuals around them, who find it impossible to relate to them or take them seriously. Their self-centeredness is their chief liability.

In more traditional psychoanalytic language, an ego develops at the expense of a self. The self remains infantile. It is "split off" from the ego, remaining weak, unconvinced of its worth. A "false self" communicates with the world while a "true self" remains hidden. Only a loving, empathic, and accepting therapeutic relationship with someone who is willing to endure the long hours of feeling, at times, unimportant and incidental in the counselee's life can break through to this hidden self.

Clinical evidence put forward by Miller, Kohut, Kernberg, and others confirms what Morgenthaler has proposed: Homosexuality can function in some individuals as a cover or "seal" over a wounded self. (See Dannecker, 1981, chapter 13.) The reasoning goes as follows.

Early on, a child who senses his or her difference looks for reasons and explanations. Unable to understand these differences, but sensing that attractions are in some instances unacceptable, the child is deeply hurt by what is perceived as a condemnation. In early adolescence, when the search for others with whom one can be affectionate becomes important, a fundamental part of the psyche must be driven underground. Attachments continue to be painful and complete investment of the self more and more impossible.

If early relationships with primary caretakers have been difficult, painful, and experienced as "rejecting," then a person may lack the ability to form relationships where risking intimacy is possible. Later·on, one may idealize a potential partner and then discover flaws that provide the excuse for retreat from investment. One may develop a cynical attitude that intimacy is not possible between members of the same sex and so indulge in promiscuous activity, or simply remain aloof from getting involved with anyone. The result of early debilitating wounds, then, is to make intimacy impossible and to allow excuses, rationalizations, or unconsciously motivated actions to sabotage relationships.

HEALING PROCESS IN THERAPY:
A PASTORAL PERSPECTIVE

Pastoral counselors often are faced with the problem of how to help seriously wounded individuals gain confidence to heal or accept the healing of their past hurts. In short, they are called on to help clients learn how to form and maintain healthy relationships. Early wounds may be the chief obstacle to this healing process. The inability to complete cycles of separation and loss that, when endured, are life-giving, lies at the heart of the counselee's dilemma and pain. Before proposing a model of healing in therapy based on the theory that the counselor offers the courage to reveal past hurts and to traverse the attachment cycle by modeling it (that is, by living it with the counselee), a brief look at the scriptural foundations for such a model may be helpful. It is hoped that this discussion situates the above theoretical discussions in a theological and pastoral light by showing that the fundamental laws of human relationships are those in evidence in the scriptures.

The Hebrew and Christian scriptures are the story of God's attachment to creation. They recount the journey of a specially chosen people who were free to reject or separate themselves from the life-giving relationships that they discovered they had inherited. The covenantal relationship, or bond between God and his people, forms the history of Israel's possibilities for growth and insight into its own identity and destiny as well as the identity and nature of God.

In the New Testament, Christians believe that the story of that life-giving search is given fuller, richer accounting as the nature of God and the bond between the Creator and creation unfolds in the life and teaching of Jesus. For example, the parables of Jesus often point to the way this God is best understood as a caring parent, as a protector intimately involved with his children. Or, the parables speak of the way all human beings are bonded and so need to treat one another as extensions of themselves. The parables of the Prodigal Son or the Good Samaritan are parables of bonding and thus reveal something about the real nature of the Divinity as well as the divine-like behavior to which human beings are called.

In the Gospel of John, the attachment, separation, and loss cycle is given special attention. One might say that the entire Gospel is a meditation on the way Jesus discovers his identity as bound up with that of his Father and how all followers of Jesus are caught in this same reality. The story of Jesus' passion and death is the story of the separation and loss of that relationship as experienced by the human Jesus. The necessity of suffering that alienation from life through death on a cross is a hallmark of the Johanine gospel. To "live in the Father" means, for Jesus, risking the loss of everything, including and especially one's life—putting one's very "self" on the line—for the higher, more substantial, more fulfilling reward of union with God.

The history of the Jewish people, then, is the history of their attachment, their separation (sometimes through their own fault), and their experience of loss, desolation, and annihilation. In each reunion, each renewal of the covenantal bond, they in fact became a different people, more mature, more spiritually aware. The story of the life of Jesus is the story of a human being who, while divine, was able to accept the inevitability of separation and loss as he became more and more convinced of his profound union with a God he could call Father. His life, death, and resurrection are the cornerstone of Christian belief and echo the profound human experience of suffering and rebirth discovered in all life-giving relationships. Every encounter between a Christian and another human being will be, then, an encounter with this mystery. Healing grace is communicated when one human being risks the pain and hurt of rejection possible in every contact of intimacy. The pastoral encounter can be understood only in light of this mystery of suffering because the pastoral relationship reenacts the saving mystery of the life, death, and resurrection of Jesus. In psychological terms, we understand it as attachment, separation, loss, and rebirth or more mature reattachment. Obviously, much more can be and needs to be said about the scriptural ties of the model of attachment proposed here. But for the purposes of this brief discussion it will, perhaps, be more important to examine the way the cycle is reflected in the therapeutic encounter. The pastoral counselor will be more effective and more able to risk the demands of the healing relationship that he or she encounters if, as the previous discussion attempted to show, a sound theory and a theological resonance underlie the counselor's perceptions and interpretations. In sum, one can communicate the courage to face a kind of dying if one is convinced of the power of grace to overcome the forces of sin and death encountered in each authentic dying—whether to others, to one's past, one's myths, or to one's self.

A MODEL FOR PASTORAL COUNSELING

In his book, *Embracing the Exile*, John Fortunato, a therapist interested in the spiritual as well as the psychological dimensions of human wholeness, described pastoral counseling with the image of the DNA double helix (Fortunato, 1982). He saw ego strength and the growth of the individual's social life along one strand, and spiritual growth along another. But if the goal of counseling along the ego or psychological strand is gaining control over one's life, then the goal of pastoral or spiritual counseling is helping the counselee let go of trying to gain so much control. This latter goal necessitates faith. Yet both movements are dependent on one another.

Many homosexual men and women must contend with a self that has been devalued as a result of growing up in a world that has not valued them for who they are, as opposed to what they are or can do. Such a devalued self can be the chief obstacle to maturation and growth at several levels. It may be more useful, therefore, to conceptualize that three strands constitute the total life of the person—an ego, a self, and a spirit, all which are in need of progressive differentiation and then integration. Before progress can be made on the spiritual strand, in other words, one must have experienced wholeness and healing at one's core, the self, as well as success, mastery, and minimal competence in the ego dimensions of social interaction.

Healing the wounded self, then, becomes the aim of much of pastoral counseling, especially where fundamental issues of relationship and intimacy are concerned. In counseling we can identify four phases of this healing process. These phases mirror, in a more protracted way, the healing ministry of Jesus where encounter, interaction, a sharing of fundamental concerns and issues, and finally a self-communication on the part of both healer and the person healed enables or fosters the courage that makes abandonment of the debilitating condition possible.

The therapist's identification of these phases serves as a guidepost for the reception, clarification, and participation in the counselee's story. The word "phase" is used below to suggest the fluid nature of these healing periods and to suggest that regression is not unlikely, nor a sign of failure. The counseling relationship will have as its goal the creation of an environment whereby the early, unpleasant, unacceptable residue of experiences that shaped the perception of the self can be examined. This can only be done in an atmosphere of intimacy, that is, of honest and complete sharing.

Phase One

Despite their level of sophistication and accomplishment, those with early wounds may appear shallow when initially discussing themselves. They may project, for long periods of time, a distant, aloof attitude, attempting to convince the counselor of stability. They are often successful but complain of a lack of intimacy, real friendships, or self-satisfaction. Sometimes a pattern of anonymous encounters or short-term relationships encouraged by the gay sub-culture characterizes past liaisons. In counseling a certain distance remains even in the counselor-counselee relationship. The counselor, in fact, may feel unimportant, unappreciated, as if his or her presence in the room is not terribly important to the counselee. Some are constant complainers and will drain the counselor with a seemingly endless barrage of disappointments, resentments, and criticisms. During this early phase, the counselor is experiencing the mechanisms of defense against intimacy that are habitual for the counselee. Constant complaining or an endless litany of self-praise or self-reference ward off others and can make genuine communication impossible.

Should the counselor challenge the counselee too quickly in such an early phase, the counselee may well feel put off and thus place the counselor in the category of those not to be trusted. The counselor may be perceived to be homophobic and will need to evaluate his or her attitudes and behavior honestly so as not to reinforce this misinterpretation. Patient waiting is crucial at this phase because the counselor is being tested. When the counselee feels that the counselor has proven him or herself to be worthy, having sufficiently reserved judgment to merit the investment of something more than what the usual defenses were willing to share, the counselee will open up to reveal the more unpleasant, the darker side of the psyche. This phase can last for several months. If the counselor is found worthy, then the relationship moves on to a new phase.

Phase Two

The second phase brings more testing, but this time the testing is of a direct nature. The rage and disappointment felt at those who did not provide sufficient care is vented on the counselor. Here the counselor's patience may be pushed to the limits. Believing themselves unworthy of love and acceptance, counselees will prove this unworthiness by making unreasonable demands designed to push the counselor away. Lateness, disagreements during the session, forgetting appointments, and so on, conspire to make the therapeutic encounter unpleasant for the counselor. The neurotic style of the individual — paranoia, impulsiveness, hysteria, passive-agressiveness, obsessive-compulsiveness — will complicate the healing process and will either sidetrack the agenda by forcing counselor and counselee to examine issues unrelated to the wounded self, or will be used by a skillful counselor to press further into the hidden attitudes and feelings about the self that such neurotic behavior masks.

Some counselees will even suggest that the counseling relationship be terminated during this phase. Sensing the frustration of the counselor and unconsciously perceiving that this is no doubt due to their own unworthy state, some offer to end the counseling relationship, citing a lack of progress, a lack of time, or some other excuse. If such excuses are explored by the counselor with the counselee, they often end in admissions of a poor self-image and a feeling of unworthiness and guilt over taking up the counselor's time and energy. This can be the first admission of a fragile and fragmented self that underlies the self-defeating behavior of the counselee.

It is important that the counselor keep in mind the counselee's fear of becoming attached to the counselor and the unconscious way the counselee drives the counselor away in order to avoid a repetition of an incomplete attachment, separation, loss, and reattachment cycle. Having missed out on the opportunity to complete the cycle successfully in the past, or having become stuck in an impossible attachment, an incomplete separation, or an unmourned loss, the counselee is caught in the dilemma of both wanting to create a bond of genuine affection and openness and not wanting to risk the hurt that comes from an inability to tolerate ambivalence in relationships, accept distance and change, or accept termination. In any event, the counselor's refusal to allow or acquiesce in a termination before the counselee has experienced real healing becomes a strong statement of affirmation and communicates unconditional acceptance. For some counselees, this is the first experience of unconditional acceptance in a relationship. It can, in turn, form a new basis for future relating. The narcissistic wound can begin to heal because the counselee has, perhaps for the first time, an awareness that it is safe to trust another human being. The stage is now set for the third phase.

Phase Three

During the third phase, old injuries, experiences, and events are recalled and shared with the counselor. A new awareness of feelings, the motives behind actions, unexamined resentments, and fears all surface during the sessions. Defensiveness, hypersensitivity, and occasional bouts of grandiosity will be evident, but gradually these defense mechanisms are put aside. The counseling relationship is the reality that allows the counselee the freedom and courage to drop those defenses. Insight alone into the poor way these mechanisms function does not translate into courage to abandon them. A relationship of care does.

Over time, a self grows from the infantile and neglected self hidden from view due to painful encounters with others. The counselee will appear childish and will feel childish, often confessing so to the counselor. In one respect, the self communicated in the counseling relationship is a younger self, a child in most cases, but as the counseling relationship progresses, the split between ego and self is healed, ambivalence in relationships is tolerated, and the possibility for relationships where distance, separation and termination, or letting go, increases. With this possibility, the experience of renewal in relationship is also possible. A relationship can die to its present form and rise again to become something new, something more hopeful and more healthy for the individuals involved. In some cases this will mean that two people go their separate ways; in others, it will mean that they experience and struggle within a closer, more spiritual bond.

For far from being distinct entities, the ego, self, and spirit strands are interwoven. Relationships require the ability to communicate, share intimacies, and transcend the self and external world. Pastoral counseling attends to all three dimensions and uses as its laboratory the normal cycle of attachment, separation, loss, and rebirth that occurs in relationships important to the individual, whether those be with one's parents, friends, lovers, or counselor.

By focusing on the quality of attachments, the expectations and hopes of the counselee for love and care, the anxieties and fears of separation and loss, the pastoral encounter is concerned with the central issues of human life, both secular and religious. In the final phase of healing, the counseling relationship itself becomes the prototype for future relationships.

Phase Four

Although the relationship between counselor and counselee has not been one of equals, nor one of total intimacy, still it has been by this phase one of complete and honest sharing. An attachment has been formed, and it has passed the testing period whereby the counselee attempted to prove his or her unworthiness. It has progressed further into a sharing of historical information and, over time, has become a significant element in the history of the counselee. The counselor has entered into the story of the counselee as one of the most important persons in the counselee's life.

Disagreements and differences have helped awaken within the counselee the sense of uniqueness and difference that does not mean isolation and estrangement. A tolerance of this difference in the counselor has helped forge a sense of fundamental unity and union previously unknown to the counselee. The final phase must now concern termination.

The experience of the loss of the therapeutic relationship with the pastoral counselor will become an important, perhaps, the most important lesson of the counseling experience. By giving up the counselor, the counselee endures a dying that had been previously impossible and unacceptable. The ultimate lesson, that relationships we allow to die are then able to become new-born, cannot be learned outside of the experience of the grief of loss. In this final phase, the counselor helps the counselee prepare for this grieving process by exploring the general reactions, feelings, and specific worries that the counselee experiences at the thought of ending the counseling relationship. Even though the relationship may continue, as when the counselor is still available or accessible should he or she be needed, the counselor must not play down the significant issue that it will be essentially changed; that it will not be the same. A carefully negotiated separation and eventual ending of the counseling relationship becomes a sign of hope for the counselee, who now experiences the courage to move on. It is as if the counselee appreciates for the first time that he or she can lose the presence of another without losing him or herself: I can let go of my attachment to this important person because I can hope and expect something new to rise from the ashes of the former relationship.

With this, the cycle is completed. The counselee reappropriates the counselor and the meaning of their relationship in memory and in living a freer existence. A freer existence means being capable of giving onself in relationships without fear of intimacy.

The pastoral counselor recognizes that this healing event and process is essentially described in the Gospel accounts of the healing miracles of Jesus. An encounter translates into an invitation and exchange about the desire and motivation for healing. Courage is communicated in the offer of Jesus, an offer of his very self to one in need of salvation from the chains of sickness and sin. For a cure means, inevitably, the leaving of a former way of life and an inaccurate self-perception. One need only examine the story of the man born blind, the encounter with the Samaritan woman at the well, the raising of Lazarus—all in John's Gospel—to see these dynamics played out in the offer of new life or healing.

CONCLUSION

The pastoral counseling of gay men and women constitutes a special challenge today. Society's misunderstanding and suspicion of the motives and values of gay men and women have produced suspicion and anger on the parts of gays toward the churches, in many instances justifiably. Compassion is needed on both sides. The churches are changing slowly, but they are changing.

In Roman Catholicism, for example, reforms since the Second Vatican Council have produced a renewed interest in engagement with the secular world, and an emphasis on the healing, reconciling mission of the People of God (Gadium et Spes, 1966/1982). These developments all run counter to an older tradition that emphasized juridical structures and moral codes.

Still, the newly reaffirmed mission of the Church has heightened sensitivity to the duty to help reconcile individuals with God, their fellow human beings, and their selves, a duty that extends to all members of the community, not just to ministers. This has helped place pastoral counseling in an esteemed light as an important work of the Church. The reforms have also brought into clearer focus the teaching of the sanctity of the conscience and the duty of each individual to grow in an appreciation of the demands of the Gospel injunction to love honestly and courageously. Finally, the Church has grown in its appreciation of the role and value of the social sciences. The disciplines of psychology, psychotherapy, sociology, and so on, are now seen as indispensable aids in identifying the needs of persons and the direction of pastoral ministry.

In an address before the College of Cardinals on November 5, 1979, John Paul II said:

> The Church is a big community within which there are different situations in the individual communities. There is no lack of people suffering oppression and persecution. In the whole Catholic community, in the individual local Churches, there must be an increase in the sense of solidarity with these brothers and sisters suffering in faith. . . . Solidarity means, above all, a proper understanding and then a proper action, not on the basis of what corresponds to the concept of the person offering help, but on the basis of the real needs of the person being helped, and what corresponds to his or her dignity.

Such statements, including those of San Francisco's Archbishop John Quinn, whose 1980 letter to the clergy and laity of the Archdiocese stressed the right to pastoral care, respect, and justice of the gay members of the Church, have produced a quiet revolution in the thoughts and in the hearts of many (Quinn, 1980). The change and development of moral theology and pastoral teaching will in some sense be tied to pastoral practice, just as it is tied to the reflection on the scriptures and the tradition of the Church. As pastoral practice with and among gays becomes increasingly sound and theologically informed, it will inevitably have an impact on the development of the moral teaching and perception of Christians—especially if such pastoral care is based not on "what corresponds to the concept of the person offering help," but rather on "the needs of the person being helped."

REFERENCES

Arendt, H. (1958). *The human condition.* New York: Doubleday.

Dannecker, M. (1981). *Theories of homosexuality.* London: Gay Men's Press.

Fortunato, J. (1982). *Embracing the exile: The healing journey of gay Christians.* New York: Seabury Press.

Gadium et Spes. (1982). *The constitution on the church in the modern world, documents of Vatican II* (W. Abbot, Ed.). Piscataway, NY: Association Press. (Original work published 1966)

Greenberg, J. R., & Mitchell, S. A. (1983). *Object relations in psychoanalytic theory.* Cambridge, MA: Harvard University Press.

Kernberg, O. (1980). *Inner world and external reality.* New York: Delacorte.

Klein, M. (1948). *Envy and gratitude and other works.* New York: Delacorte.

Kohut, H. (1971). *The analysis of the self.* New York: International University Press.

Mahler, M., Fine, F., & Bergman, A. (1975). *The psychological birth of the human infant: Symbiosis and individuation.* New York: Basic Books.

McWhirter, D., & Mattison, A. (1984). Psychotherapy with male couples: An application of staging theory. In E. Hetrick & T. Stein (Eds.), *Innovation in psychotherapy with homosexuals* (pp. 115-131). Washington, DC: American Psychiatric Press.

Miller, A. (1981). *The drama of the gifted child.* New York: Basic Books.

National Conference of Catholic Bishops. (1976). *To Live in Christ Jesus: A pastoral reflection on the moral life.* Washington, DC: Author.

Quinn, J. (1980, May 5). *Pastoral letter on homosexuality.* San Francisco, CA: Archdiocese of San Francisco.

Sullivan, H. S. (1953). *The interpersonal theory of psychiatry.* New York: Norton.

Winnicott, D. W. (1965). *The family and individual development.* London: Hogarth.

Pastoral Counseling and Homosexuality

John A. Struzzo, PhD

San Francisco, California

SUMMARY. The Judaeo-Christian religious tradition has generally been mistrustful of sexuality, wherein homosexuality is not even a legitimate discussion. The psychological tradition has been hetero-sexist and homophobic. It is argued that only a creation-centered spirituality and a transpersonal psychotherapy can be truly supportive of gay men and lesbian women. A transpersonal model is presented that is integrated with creation spirituality. This model is applied to specific situations of gay men and lesbians with clinical examples. In this inquiry, the special gifts of homosexuals are noted.

Most pastoral counselors are a product of a Judaeo-Christian tradition dominated by what Matthew Fox (1984) has termed a fall/redemption theology, which is both patriarchal and dualistic. At the same time, most approaches to psychotherapy stop at the level of the ego. Concerns with the transcendence of the ego or a spiritual approach have often been considered escapist and even, by some, pathological (Vaughan, 1986).

This article proposes that only a creation-centered, incarnational spirituality and transpersonal psychotherapy can truly be supportive of gays and lesbians. In this latter approach, sexuality and homo-

---

John A. Struzzo is a licensed marriage, family and child counselor, and a pastoral psychotherapist in private practice in San Francisco, CA. He also has been a professor of sociology and psychology at several universities and colleges, most recently at the College of Notre Dame in Belmont, CA. John Struzzo also has lectured widely across the United States on issues pertaining to psychology and spirituality.

Correspondence may be sent to the author at 547 Pennsylvania, San Francisco, CA 94107.

sexuality are both a blessing and a gift. This approach is applicable to all people, but is especially relevant to homosexuals.

CULTURAL CONTEXT OF PASTORAL COUNSELING

Religious Tradition

The Judaeo-Christian tradition that has informed most pastoral counselors has been, for the most part, hierarchial, patriarchal, generally mistrustful of sexuality, and negative toward homosexuality in particular. This background becomes a filter through which the counselor listens to the client, and determines how he or she interprets data, and what questions and issues will be focused on in the counseling process. To the extent counselors have internalized these beliefs, they tend to look upon homosexuals as abnormal and perverse in a basic way. At a deeper level, they tend towards a basic mistrust of sexuality grounded in a dualistic world-view. According to this dualism, influenced by the gnostic and stoic teachings, all humans are spirits imprisoned in a material body. Body and spirit are antagonists. The material realm, which includes the body and sex, is considered evil. Sexual pleasure is the result of original sin and manifests the basic disorder between the body and soul. All pleasure, and especially sexual pleasure, is tainted with sin, and the only justification for sexual expression is procreation. In this context, homosexuality does not even become a legitimate topic of ethical discourse (Boswell, 1980).

In the fall/redemption model of spiritual growth, death and illness are the wages of sin. Sin for the most part involves some aspect of sexuality. Spiritual growth demands that one must mortify the senses and body, and avoid even the occasions that might stimulate sexual desire. In practice, the control of passions and pleasure has meant repression and denial. The goal of the holy person in this context is one of humility and obedience. These are virtues, but in practice, humility has tended toward self-depreciation, and obedience has frequently meant renouncing one's self-esteem through passive resignation. Thus a fall/redemption model begins with original sin, man and woman's fall from grace, consequent punishment, and struggle for redemption (Fox, 1984).

Creation-centered spirituality begins with God's creative energy and original blessings. There is one divine, "creative energy which flows through all things. We are part of that flow and need to listen to it" (Fox, 1984, p. 38). Thus the universe itself is the starting point for creation spirituality.

One of the great spokespersons for creation spirituality has been Meister Eckhart, and more recently Thomas Merton and theologians of liberation theology. In this perspective, everything in creation is part of God and a source of blessing, including sexuality in its various manifestations. Creation spirituality, instead of being dualistic (either-or), is dialectical (both/and). Body and spirit are seen as integrated and mutually interdependent. Spirituality demands befriending and celebrating one's earthiness and humanity; it requires discipline and love, rather than control. Pleasure is sharing in the divine ecstasy. Creation-centered spirituality is aware that humans enter into a broken world and has an understanding of sin. However, it holds with Dr. Haag,

> No man enters the world a sinner. As the creature and image of God he is from the first hour surrounded by God's fatherly love. . . . A man becomes a sinner only through his own individual and responsible action. (Fox, 1984, p. 47)

Creation spirituality includes the feminist in perceiving God as Mother and Child, as well as Father. God has primarily been presented in Western religions as male, which has served to legitimate male dominance and to oppress women. Societies that conceive of their deities as father figures tend to be more repressive of homosexuality than those that treat them as mother figures (Taylor, 1965). Thus, lesbians contend with both the oppression of being female as well as being homosexual.

Psychological Tradition

The psychological tradition has been heterosexist in that heterosexuality has been assumed to be superior to homosexuality. It has been homophobic in its irrational fear of homosexuality. These heterosexist and homophobic biases have led to an assumed psychopathology of lesbianism and male homosexuality. Although the

American Psychiatric Association in 1973 removed homosexuality from the list of mental disorders, many psychiatrists personally continue to believe that homosexuality is a pathological adaptation (Bayer, 1981). In the place of homosexuality, psychiatrists substituted ego-dystonic homosexuality in the list of mental disorders. The fact that ego-dystonic heterosexuality was omitted clearly reflects a homophobic bias that remains in the mental health professions.

In my experience as a psychotherapist, gays and lesbians tend to be overdiagnosed as having paranoid, narcissistic, and borderline personality disorders, and tend to be considered more seriously disturbed than they are. John Gonsiorek (1982) has argued that some gays and lesbians will manifest considerable symptoms of pathology during the coming-out process. These may be manifestations of an intrapsychic pathology, or a precipitating trigger for underlying problems. However, they also may represent coping techniques in a repressive society with no underlying pathology. Gordon Allport (1954), in writing about the victims of prejudice, declared that there are several common traits present in persecuted groups. These traits include excessive concern and preoccupation with minority or deviant group membership; feelings of insecurity; withdrawal; passivity; neuroticism; strong in-group ties coupled with prejudice against out-groups; slyness and cunning; acting out self-fulfilling prophecies about one's inferiority; secrecy; and self-hatred. These characteristics are what writers like Bergler (1956), Socarides (1978), and Hatterer (1970), among others, describe as inherently pathological features of homosexuals, and which led them to conclude that homosexuality is a mental disease. Thus psychotherapists need to distinguish between intrapsychic pathology and what is a manifestation of subcultural adaptation.

Furthermore, if counselors begin with a stereotyped belief, they will selectively perceive data in a way that justifies current beliefs and reconstruct the past to rationalize the stereotype. This process may take at least two forms: (a) preferential remembering of information that is consistent with the stereotyped beliefs regarding the target, and (b) selective reinterpretation of past events to give them meaning congruent with current stereotyped beliefs about the target (Gonsiorek, 1982). It is, therefore important for pastoral counselors to be clear and explicit about their beliefs regarding homosexuality, and to understand which beliefs are culturally determined, which they have personalized, and which are objectively valid.

Spiritual Journey of Gays and Lesbians

Gays and lesbians often experience a sense of crisis as they begin their spiritual journeys. Because they have been labeled immature, unnatural, sick and illegal by the major institutions, and with these factors compounded by the AIDS crisis, they have difficulty appreciating the fundamental goodness of creation and the giftedness of homosexuality. The dualistic influences of their religious heritage and societal intolerance lead many to reject their bodies and feelings. What they deny and reject, they project outward on others. This is the basis for homophobia. Those who have a fear and revulsion of their own homosexual capacity tend to perceive in others what they despise and have often repressed in themselves.

The fundamental spiritual challenge for gays and lesbians is to appreciate and celebrate the basic goodness of all creation, including their sexuality, without becoming possessive and addictive. The spiritual task is to be in the world but not of the world. This stance may at first seem a return to the fall/redemption negativism toward the world (Fox, 1983). Just as it is unhealthy and self-deceiving to deny the body, sexuality, and materiality, and to live primarily on an intellectual and spiritual level, so is it a myth to deny the spiritual and look to the material world for meaning and fulfillment. To perceive oneself as merely a personality seeking ego-gratification fails to provide answers to the deeper questions about purpose and meaning in one's life (Small, 1984).

Creation spirituality is a spirituality of the oppressed. The Jews who were exiled, poor, and rejected were special instruments in the fulfillment of the Messianic prophecy. Gay men and lesbians can be seen as the sexual anawin, the sexual poor; the oppressed whom God calls to special favor (Fortunato, 1982). John Boswell(1985), in a recent lecture to gay and lesbian religious professionals, discussed the special oppressed status of homosexuals. He distinguished three categories of the socially oppressed: (a) the inferior insiders; (b) the outsiders; and (c) those in no category. Women would be most characteristic of the first group. No one would say it is wrong to be a woman or try to get rid of them, even though many consider them to be inferior. The second group would be represented by blacks and Jews. Although there have been attempts to annihilate blacks and Jews, at least outsiders know who they are, and there are bridges to the wider society. For example, the dominant society recognizes that Jews and blacks have experiences that parallel their own. However, the most oppressed are those who are invisible, those without a category. Homosexuals fall within this group as left-handed people did in primitive societies. Most heterosexuals do not consider gays and lesbians as a distinct subculture with separate needs, desires, and beliefs. As Boswell (1985) argued, most heterosexuals believe that homosexuals are like them but have chosen sinful and perverse lifestyles and behaviors that they, the heterosexuals, would never choose, even though they believe they could so choose. The fact that homosexuals are different does not place them in a different category, but simply proves how deviant and degenerate they are. Because average heterosexuals do not consciously experience strong erotic attraction to the same sex or an erotic need of affirmation from the same sex, they thus assume· that gays and lesbians have disordered desires, rather than different ones, or that homosexuals are people who like to flaunt traditional norms and laws.

As Fortunato (1982) wrote, embracing the exile is the heart and opportunity of the spiritual journey of gays and lesbians. When confronted with negativity, most people tend either to resign themselves passively or try to get rid of the negative object. However, neither of these approaches works in the long run. The ultimate solution is a transpersonal one: to accept and embrace the negative.

TRANSPERSONAL PERSPECTIVE

Traditional psychology and psychotherapy have focused on the personality, concentrating on raising the client's self-awareness. The paradigm of wellness is a strong conscious ego that is self-determined and autonomous. The client is primarily concerned with developing ego-strength, raising self-esteem, and letting go of negative patterns of self-invalidation. As one begins to identify and own the feelings, thoughts, and beliefs that were previously denied and repressed, one assumes responsibility for who one is, and the choices he makes. Thus, psychotherapy at the level of ego is concerned with identification. One shifts from other directedness to inner determination (Vaughan, 1986).

Once the ego has been strengthened, the goal of pastoral counseling is to assist clients to disidentify from the restrictions of their personality, and to realize their identity with their total self. Clients tend to identify with their bodies, feelings, and minds. In doing so, they believe they are as smart as their mind thinks, and as happy as their bodies feel. Thus, every person is consigned to the limitations of his ego. Most religious traditions teach that there is a higher state of being that transcends the limitations and confinements of the mind, feelings, body, and ego. Humans are spiritual realities manifest in material forms in space and time. Men and women are spirit with individuality, unique meaning, and a special purpose. The purpose of life is to disidentify from one's false self, and realize one's true nature. To realize one's true nature entails dying to the control of one's limited ego, and then transcending it. This process of self-realization leads to an expansion of the self (Wilber, 1982). Pastoral counseling does not strive for reformation, but transformation of the person. Such transformation does not occur from changes in the outer circumstances, but from creation from within. One's outer life is a mirror of one's inner self; without understanding one's inner world, one's outer experiences are ultimately meaningless and disconnected (Small, 1982; Vaughan, 1986).

When one begins to ask deeper questions about the purpose and meaning of life, success in terms of personal gratification and ego goals appear to be meaningless. In the early part of one's life, one looks for meaning outside of oneself. Some accept prepared formulas provided by society, religion, or the family in which they were born. However, without some deep inner experience that validates those beliefs, their adherence is usually superficial and perfunctory. One is stifled, rather than liberated (Arpita, 1986). Others attempt to deal with the question by avoiding any committed adherence to beliefs or tenets. They tend to argue that they are open to all beliefs and systems. However in practice this approach lacks vitality and is frequently characterized by cynicism. Many deal with the problem of meaning in life by avoiding it. They focus on keeping so busy that they have no time to realize that there is no foundation or purpose beneath their fury of activity. These people constantly distract themselves from inner uncertainties by looking for meaning in the external world. They work constantly to attain external goals such as security, wholesome relationships, status, power, and so on. They also sometimes seek external stimuli such as drugs, alcohol, compulsive smoking, and overeating to further the distraction. They have no time to confront the deeper issues of life. If one does not confront this question of meaning on one's own, however, life itself will eventually destroy these protective distractions, attachments, and interpretations, and force one to face the reality of one's own mortality and the meaning of one's life (Arpita, 1986).

The AIDS crisis has provided gays and lesbians with an opportunity to confront these deeper questions, to reassess the truth about life. In facing the fragility of existence and addressing the basic question of meaning, gays and lesbians are challenged to reach beyond their own limits into a deeper fellowship with all men and women. To cope with hostility, rejection, and nonacceptance from outside individuals and institutions, gays and lesbians are invited to look inward and enter into a deeper spiritual journey. In accepting one's finiteness and limitations, one can become aware of a reality beyond the limits of this world and become revitalized. The paradox is that when one embraces death, one realizes that death is an illusion, and one instead experiences the fullness of life. One realizes that although one has a body, feelings, mind, and ego, a person is more than these and not identified with any of these. Thus, one begins to disidentify from the ego and identify with a transcendent and transpersonal self (Walsh & Vaughan, 1980). The entire process of human development can be understood from the transpersonal perspective as the expansion and transformation of one's consciousness.

TRANSFORMATION OF CONSCIOUSNESS

In exploring the basic levels of consciousness, I will use a model from the Yoga tradition which postulates seven basic centers of consciousness within the human person. As Ken Wilber (1982) pointed out, "consciousness is a spectrum" (p. 16). Each center is called a chakra, and may be likened to a hub of a wheel with spokes radiating out that affect one's physical, emotional, psychological, and spiritual functioning. Each chakra represents a different level of vibration and a different level of consciousness. Each chakra corresponds roughly to the endocrine glands within the body (Bethards, 1977). These centers are located at the base of the spine, in the sexual organs, the solar plexus, the heart, the throat, the spiritual eye, and the crown of the head.

Each of the seven chakras represents a distinct level of existence and perception. At each center, one becomes identified with the mode of consciousness it represents and sees the world through that mode. When one evolves to a higher level of consciousness, one's perspective changes, and what once seemed so important becomes insubstantial and unimportant. As one evolves to a higher level of consciousness, one vibrates at a more intense level of energy. The way we see others is an explicit measure of our vibration level.

Most psychotherapies have focused only on the lower levels of consciousness. Behaviorism has focused on the first chakra, Freudianism on the second, Adlerian on the third, and Jungian psychology and humanistic approaches on the fourth. Both Jung and Maslow began a consideration of transcendence of the ego as an important aspect of health and growth (Wilber, 1982). However, mastery of the states of higher consciousness has been associated more with spirituality than psychology (Vaughan, 1986). Mystical theology in the West, and Vedanta in the East, from which Yoga psychology is derived, discuss the higher levels of consciousness. Transpersonal approaches to psychology and psychotherapy is an integration of the Eastern and Western approaches.

As Wilber (1982) pointed out, most people in Western society are not ready to pursue mystical experiences and therefore should not be pushed into them. The goal of most Western approaches to growth and health is to strengthen the ego, integrate the self and correct one's self-image, and build self-esteem. The goal of Eastern approaches is to transcend the ego and attain enlightenment. Eastern approaches claim to release the individual from the root cause of suffering, whereas Western approaches tend to deal with the alleviation of symptoms. It is not a question of which is better; they simply are focusing on different levels of consciousness.

However, a transpersonal approach seems especially useful for gays and lesbians for two reasons. First, Jung wrote that homosexuals are often "endowed with a wealth of religious feelings . . . and a spiritual receptivity which makes them responsive to revelation" (quoted in Kelsey & Kelsey, 1986, p. 203). Jung's hypothesis is based on the assumed presence of a stronger feminine side in the homosexual male than in a heterosexual one, and the integration of the feminine with the masculine. When men are in touch with their feminine side, they create the space to be deeply spiritual. Transpersonal psychology incorporates the religious sentiment into its approach to psychotherapy. Ego-oriented psychotherapy tends to focus on adaptation to one's culture as a criterion of health. The very culture from which the homosexual emerges is homophobic and heterosexist, and therefore part of the problem that gays and lesbians struggle with; it does not make sense to encourage adaptation to that which is unhealthy in the first place. Thus, an approach that transcends culture and ego is more suited to the specific needs of gays and lesbians. Being marginal to society can be an opportunity rather than a problem.

In the developmental process of raising one's consciousness, there are three basic tasks: (a) open up each chakra, (b) balance the energy at each chakra, and (c) raise that energy upward. Before exploring this process of transformation, I will first discuss in more depth each individual chakra (Ajaya, 1983; Small, 1984; Vaughan, 1986).

In the most primitive mode of consciousness, humans are absorbed with survival, with coping with life-threatening situations. At this first level of consciousness, fear predominates. The main task is to learn to be grounded. The basic task in life is to survive and to know it is safe to be here. Physical well-being is the focus of the first chakra.

At the second level of consciousness, one's personality becomes more fluid and less rigid. One is dominated by the pleasure principle, to maximize pleasure and minimize pain. Physical sensation is primary. One searches for pleasure outside of him- or herself— sexually attractive partners, delicious foods, stimulants, or any experience that will afford sensory pleasure. Some become addicted at this level and constantly seek more intense experiences to fill the void. However because one's search is external, it does not lead to lasting satisfaction but only to temporary appeasement. The goal at this level is to learn to master one's emotions and the sensory realm, including one's sexuality.

At the third chakra, the pursuit of pleasure is replaced with concern about power. At this level of consciousness, others are seen as rivals and one becomes absorbed in issues of success and failure, dominance and submission, heroism and cowardice. At this level one is goal oriented and finds it difficult to live in the present moment. The goal at this level is to strengthen one's ego so as to function competently in the world.

The fourth center, the heart chakra, is the integrating link between the lower and higher chakras. The focus at each of the lower chakras is one's basic needs; one is concerned with others only in so far as they are aids for satisfying those needs. At the heart center, one becomes concerned about meeting the needs of others. When functioning at the lower centers, one feels incomplete and seeks something outside of oneself for fulfillment. At the heart center one's fullness begins to overflow to others. One shifts from "I need you, therefore I love you" to "I love you, therefore I need you." At the lower centers, one tends to feel a victim of extrinsic circumstances, whereas at the heart center, one begins to feel a sense of mastery over one's external world. One still operates from an egoic level and experiences incompleteness and discontent, but one also begins to transcend the ego.

At the heart level, dualities that were once considered polar opposites become a creative dialectic and can now reside in the same space. One realizes that one can become both spiritual and sexual, committed and flexible. The key to transformation at the heart level is acceptance. One surrenders the need to control and judge and becomes more accepting of self and others. Love and acceptance are not enough for total transformation to take place however. One needs to become aware of another dimension where the meaning and purpose of a larger reality, a higher self exists. As one evolves to a higher level of consciousness, one gradually disidentifies from the ego and surrenders to a more universal center of nurturing love and wisdom.

The fifth chakra, located at the throat, is the center of creative expression in all forms. At this level of consciousness, one assumes responsibility for creating one's own reality. This is done in surrender to a higher power from which creative expression flows.

At the sixth level of consciousness, one attains a power of understanding that goes beyond form. This is the opening of the spiritual eye. At this level of consciousness, one knows through intuition, as a direct comprehension of the nature of reality that transcends sense knowledge. This is the level of the superconscious mind. Intuition often expresses itself in the form of symbolic language and requires one to go beyond a literal interpretation.

The seventh chakra represents the highest level of consciousness. Here, one experiences a unity of consciousness and completion. One experiences inner unity, unity with all creation and with one's creator. Self-mastery and mastery over one's environment is complete. At this level, one experiences the realm of Being, a state of pure consciousness.

Consciousness is like a filter through which one views the world. For example, if one is operating out of the second chakra, one will see the world through a need for sensual pleasure. If one is at a bank and the teller smiles, one may interpret that as a sexual come on. If that same person is operating from the third chakra, one may interpret the smile as an attempt at control. And if that same person were operating from the heart chakra, then the smile would simply mean that the teller was being friendly.

At the lower levels of consciousness, people are run by their feelings and desires without much realization of the meaning of their behavior. Without the energy of the higher self, the lower-self experiences are devoid of meaning and purpose, and one continues to look outside of oneself for that meaning and purpose. Lower and higher are not evaluative terms, but simply refer to levels of consciousness. When one is stuck in the lower chakras, the person is addicted and is operating out of a limited perspective. Addictions cannot be controlled; they need to be transformed, freeing up their constricted energy so that it might flow in a different direction. However, if a person does not accept oneself at the level of current consciousness, that energy becomes supercharged into the very characteristic one is trying to change. One becomes what one resists. For example, if one is stuck at the first chakra and is dominated by fear, and tries to act as if there were no fear, or tries to get rid of the fear, that fear will be increased rather than transformed (Small, 1982).

Each level of consciousness is good and necessary. Persons cannot move to a higher level of functioning until they meet their needs at a lower level. Until people experience basic security and trust they will not be able to meet their sexual needs. Growth does not occur in a straight line, but in a saccadic and spiral process.

The ultimate goal of transpersonal growth and development is to transform all one's energy into higher consciousness. One does this by opening up each chakra, balancing its energy, and raising that energy upward.

Process of Sexual Transformation

Opening up a chakra means experiencing and accepting its level of consciousness. When the second chakra is closed, sexual energy is rooted in anxiety and tends to be either compulsive or repressed. One feels alone, unsafe, and unprotected. One experiences the natural yearning for self-gratification as bad. For gays and lesbians, there is a deeper crisis. They learn early in life that it is not safe or acceptable to explore their sexuality. Sex is a dark secret to be kept from others.

To experience and accept one's sexuality is the first task in the process of transformation of one's sexuality. To do so demands making conscious one's basic sexual feelings and desires and being open to their messages. One first, then, acknowledges one's sexuality, and comes to know it by experiencing the self as sexual, whatever the particular sexual orientation.

Sexual Identity:
Awareness and Acceptance

Most people learn to trust their body, their feelings, and their sexuality through the response of others to them. Sexual awakening is a confusing process for most. However, society and families usually provide role models to facilitate sexual awareness and sexual identity. For the gay and lesbian, there are no role models. For every other minority group, there is a place to go where its members can be affirmed in their identity. Blacks, for example, even if not acknowledged or affirmed by the larger society, can be black at home and be so defined. Gays and lesbians usually have no one who will help clarify their sexual emergence, or tell them who they are. When they begin to discover their same-sex orientation, they do not greet it with joy. Even before they discover their unique sexual identity, they know that society considers homosexuality a negative value. Thus, homosexuals are encouraged to fragment themselves and appear normal. They begin to live in two worlds — one inside their mind and feelings, and one they share with others. They feel pressure to enclose their sexuality in a private prison to preserve it from external threats and judgments. The effect of this double life are feelings of fear, anger, guilt, and confusion. At the same time, they feel mistrustful of their own families and friends, as well as social institutions that label them negatively. At first, gays and lesbians not only conceal their identity from others, but also from themselves through denial and repression. They tend to think of themselves as heterosexual, but at the same time have feelings, thoughts, fantasies, or behaviors that could be defined as homosexual. Because there is denial and repudiation of their own sexuality, gays and lesbians will project this part of themselves onto others and react negatively to or avoid other homosexuals (Struzzo, 1983).

Once homosexuals begin to realize and acknowledge their unique identity, they tend to distance themselves from significant others with whom they had previously identified, as well as from those institutions that labeled them negatively. If gays and lesbians are to explore their unique identity, they need the support of other homosexuals with whom they can identify. Obtaining this affirmation and confirmation usually entails "coming out" not only to themselves, but also to other homosexuals and ultimately to the heterosexual world. Coming out means to acknowledge, experience, and accept one's homosexual feelings and attractions. The function of coming out is to assist gays and lesbians to believe in and accept the rightness of their own sexual identity and to foster self-respect. Because identity is first realized through identification with others, it is important for gays and lesbians to find a homosexual support group that can help them to clarify and affirm their own identity (Struzzo, 1983).

Acceptance and rejection are crucial at this stage. Rejection at this time can be experienced as powerfully negative and can do severe damage to one's self-concept. Those who experience rejection in the initial coming out process may return to the closet and experience guilt, anger, and chronic depression. Because of the vulnerability of their self-concept, it is important for lesbians and gays to choose carefully those to whom they come out, and to select those who they believe will respond positively. For lesbians, there is an added obstacle in the coming out process. In contrast to gay males, she has been largely ignored by the churches, media, and scientific literature. Consequently, she experiences an even greater lack of role models. Also because the homosexual world, like the larger society, is male dominated, lesbians may face hostility and ostracism from gay organizations as a result of sexism. This is often manifest in sexist language that pervades rituals of male dominated institutions, especially religious ones. This is an area in which the pastoral counselor especially needs to be sensitive. Sometimes lesbians' identity, in contrast to gay males, is a political statement regarding gender roles rather than reflecting sexual attraction. For some women, the choice is perceived to be between nonsexist, emotional and sexual relationships with women, and sexist relationships with men.

Once one gets in touch with and accepts one's sexuality, one realizes it is unbalanced. As one identifies with sensual gratification, the person begins to define the self by the degree or type of sensation one is either feeling or missing. If one is not high, then one feels depressed. One lacks balance—when one feels intense energy, one is uncomfortable and looks for ways to release it. Once that energy is released, one feels empty and looks for ways to restimulate oneself. The result is a vicious circle of stimulation, release, restimulation, and so on (Bubba Free John, 1978). People feel victim to external circumstances to get their sexual needs met. Likewise, they are run by their inner impulses. Balance is necessary for the mastery of sexual energy.

CONTEXT OF TRANSFORMATION

Mindfulness

The starting point of balancing and mastery over one's energy is awareness. Through the process of self-observation, one learns to observe one's sexual feelings, thoughts, desires, and fantasies as they are experienced, and learn what triggered them, and from what connections they arose. One gradually realizes that he turns himself on and off sexually rather than being simply a reactor to external stimuli. The process of self-observation without judgement is called mindfulness (Small, 1984; Goldstein, 1983). Some live their lives as observers rather than as participants. They learn to dissociate their feelings from their experiences. This is distinct from mindfulness. Through mindfulness, one is actually involved in life, but consciously observes one's body processes, feelings, thoughts, behaviors, and so on as one continues to be involved. In so doing, one assumes total responsibility for those experiences.

If a person is stuck at the sexual level of consciousness where one continually craves sexual gratification, mindfulness can be particularly helpful. One continues to crave something until one fully experiences the object with total involvement and consciousness (Small, 1984). This is a slow, gradual, but necessary aspect of transformation. Prematurely withdrawing from negative compulsive behavior, while remaining fascinated by it, feeds the habit. If people try to be celibate before mastering their sexual energy, they will only reinforce its demands, often unconsciously and negatively (Haich, 1972).

Letting Go

Once a person has mastered the tasks of the lower chakras, security, sexual awareness and gratification, and power, and has developed a strong ego and self-esteem, then the further task of transformation is a letting go. "Letting go" is a "letting be" — the entering into darkness, and pain, and letting the pain be pain. It is not that security, sensate pleasures, and power are wrong or problematic, or that they in themselves inhibit happiness and fulfillment. Rather, it is one's attachments and inner addictions that create unhappiness and emotional and mental illness. The problem lies in the grasping. Letting go is unclenching one's grasp, the letting go of the attachment. One does not let go of security, sensate pleasures, and power, but of striving and wanting. Ultimately it means letting go of the not having. One then enters the void and lets the void be void. With Rilke, one lives the question. One then relinquishes control over life and allows the self to be led. In this path of surrender, one attains true security, pleasure and power. The letting go does not take away the desire, but enables a person to attain a new relationship to the desire. Thus, saying yes to loneliness does not take away the loneliness, but enables wholeness to emerge. Loneliness then becomes transformed into hospitality (Struzzo, 1982; Fox, 1984).

Letting go is a difficult concept for most to grasp. Western culture encourages either resignation or getting rid of that which is undesirable and uncontrollable. In letting go, one enters into one's own inner emptiness. The immediate experience is often one of anxiety, depression, and discomfort. One feels the pain of deprivation and a quiet desperation. Letting go can sometimes be a resignation rather than a true acceptance and surrender, and can lead to further depression and perhaps suicide. Thus, surrender also demands a waiting for. To wait for means to discern an unknown path. It becomes an invitation to a spiritual journey. Growth and transformation of consciousness demands taking responsibility for the pain and darkness and exploring the meaning of it.

In Arthur Miller's 1964 play, *After the Fall*, Helga, in a recurring dream gives birth to an idiot. The child keeps trying to climb on her lap. She feels horrified and repulsed. Finally, she bends down and kisses the broken face of the child. Transformation demands that a person continually bring into awareness parts of oneself that previously were regarded as repulsive and wrong so they can be integrated. When Helga is able to say yes to her dark side, symbolized by the idiot child, she becomes able to say yes to life.

On the other hand, when a person represses and refuses to acknowledge parts of the self that are uncomfortable, or refuses to accept external circumstances over which one has no control, then one sets the stage for a sterile and meaningless future. When people refuse to acknowledge, experience, and accept their anger they also stifle their passion and deaden themselves into a gutless, lifeless conformity. The more people refuse to accept their sexuality, the more they suppress their creative potential.

Letting go, then, is befriending one's pain, whether it be loneliness, anger, AIDS, or any limit over which one feels helpless. In doing so, compassion and empathy can emerge. It links one with others who suffer and thus opens up one's capacity as healer. When one enters into the void and nothingness of life, one experiences the fullness of life. In that confrontation, one's creative energy is nurtured and expanded. Ultimately, in that embrace one lets go of one's ego. In doing so, one realizes a larger reality, that one is part of the cosmos, part of God, and that God is part of one's self. This realization transforms one's entire life (Struzzo, 1982; Ballentine, 1986; Miller, 1981).

Conservation of Energy

Transformation is the work of the higher self. However, the energy from the lower self is the stuff of transformation. To be able to raise one's energy means a prior conservation of energy. As one develops a higher level of consciousness, one vibrates at a more intense level of energy. Therefore one's nervous system needs to be developed to sustain such intensity. If one puts 220 volts of electricity into a 110-volt line, it will be shortcircuited. Likewise, if one tries to develop a higher level of energy before one's nervous system is ready for it, one burns out (Haich, 1972; Small, 1984).

To conserve energy, one needs to learn to express it inwardly rather than outwardly. For example, when one feels anger, one can express it externally by screaming or fighting, or one can sit with the feeling and simply experience it without judgment. The latter approach is inward expression (Struzzo, 1985). By learning to focus and sit with one's feelings, one begins to realize the distinction between having feelings and being run by one's feelings. Realizing and living the truth that we are not our feelings is the basis of disidentification. Also, as one withdraws energy from the objects of desire through this process of focusing and inward expression, one becomes more integrated.

If one prematurely withdraws energy from an unmet need, then one will suffer a downfall. There is a basic law of descendence whereby energy moves downward to the direction of its densest point. Thus, if one is trying to conserve sexual energy by expressing it inwardly and yet becomes more irritable, fearful, depressed, and restless, then it is not working. One needs to look at what is blocking the energy. If one is acting out of negative feelings like fear or guilt, then one is pulling energy downward and one is probably repressing energy rather than conserving it. Conservation of energy is not a passive withdrawal or negation, but a positive transformation (Small, 1984; Haich, 1978). However, when one is operating from a higher level of consciousness, then outward expression can be energizing. Therefore sexual experiences that express love and a spiritual bond can nurture one's energy rather than deplete it.

Service

Another important aid in transformation is service and love. When one is centered in one of the three lower chakras, one is preoccupied with self. One will greatly benefit from having someone to concentrate on besides the self. This is especially important for those gays and lesbians who do not have lovers. Also, having a vision or project that is larger than oneself will pull one's energy upward.

As one enters into an inward journey of transformation, one learns compassion for oneself, which can then spill outward to others. One learns that gratification ultimately comes from within, rather than from extrinsic objects, and that it is in serving others that one receives true gratification. There is a basic spiritual law that says that a person can only hold on to something by giving it away. A person learns love by loving. Compassion and service transforms sexual energy into love. This is the task of opening up the fourth chakra, the heart center.

Creativity

The fifth chakra is the creative center. Expressing one's creativity also transforms sexual energy. It is in how one does things, rather than what one does that creativity lies. One can cook, read a book, write, paint, sing, and so on, in a creative way or not. Creation comes from embracing the nothingness, the void in one's life.

Gays and lesbians especially have the opportunity to be creative in that the circumstances of their life often confront them with loneliness, darkness, and the void. Creativity also comes from diversity. Gays and lesbians in their diverse lifestyles from the majority, offer the possibility of greater creativity than those who tend to be conformist.

Meditation

The work of transformation involves expanding one's consciousness, raising one's energy upward through the higher chakras. The sixth and seventh chakras are spiritual centers that enable people to tune into total transforming cosmic and divine energy. One of the most important aids in this work is meditation. Meditation enables one to surrender one's absorption in one's own personality, desires, and egoic concerns, and turn to transcendant realities and God. By tuning in to one's own experience of the divine, one becomes a channel for the expression of divine love. Then, everything that person does becomes such a channel including sexual expression.

Meditation has three pre-requisites. First, it demands silence and solitude, so that one can tune out environmental stimuli. Then, internal stimuli will take center stage. At first, such stimuli are quite intense, and one is restless and easily distracted. The second pre-requisite is to learn to quiet the body and mind. Meditation is first concentrating one's energy, and then focusing that energy on a transcendental object. It is like taking a magnifying glass and focusing the sunlight at one point. Likewise, by focusing all one's energy at the spiritual eye, the sixth chakra, one creates the potential for great power. Meditation assists one to live fully in the present. As one learns to experience centeredness and concentration, her outer life becomes transformed. One is better able to concentrate on tasks without distraction, emotionalism, or daydreaming. One becomes more effective in carrying out the tasks of everyday life. One develops a meditation in action whereby one achieves a neutral observing attitude toward thoughts and feelings that show up in one's daily life. One finds an emotional balance and serenity that begins to pervade all behavior.

Meditation greatly assists both mindfulness and letting go. Because of the greater awareness realized, a person becomes more aware of the connection between thoughts and emotions, and between emotions and physiological responses. Ultimately, one realizes that the outer circumstances of life are results of inner choices. Because one creates one's own reality, one can create health at every level, as well as disease. This capacity is everyone's to develop. Thus people can learn to experience joy in the midst of sorrow. They learn that joy comes from experiencing life as it is, rather than trying to make it what they think it should be. When people accept and surrender to life as it is, which has nothing to do with approval or agreement, they experience the fullness of joy (Ballentine, 1986; Sri Chinmoy, 1985). Meditation is the main key to transformation.

Prior to meditating, it is useful to do relaxation exercises, such as hatha Yoga, and also breathing exercises. Breath is almost synonymous with energy. By learning to control and direct one's breath, one learns to master all energy. Control is not attained by will power or repression, but by awareness, by paying attention to and focusing on it. The more one becomes conscious of something and takes full responsibility for it, the more one is in control. The more control one has over one's energy, the more he can direct it upwards (Davis, 1976; Ballentine, 1986).

The ultimate goal of transformation is the union of the personality with the spiritual self. The consciousness of the spiritual domain has its own special quality. "The transmuted energies reach up to it from below, as it were, and give it added vitality and heat, but they neither create nor explain the higher life" (Assagioli, 1977, p. 272).

The energy one radiates is crucial in determining what one attracts to oneself. Every particle of matter vibrates at a certain rate. The slower the vibrations, the more unpleasant one's life, and the more conflict and pain one will experience. Events will happen too fast to be in our control and will run us. When a person raises one's vibratory level, one can sidestep collisions, both physical and psychic, and literally change the world for the better (Golas, 1972).

SPECIAL OPPORTUNITY
THAT GAY AND LESBIAN IS

The gay and lesbian has a unique challange to transform into opportunities what have prior been perceived as hindrances. Being an outsider and marginal to society can be a creative edge. To look at a village from its center gives a totally different view than that from the edge. Because gay men and lesbians are marginal, they have less of an investment to maintain the status quo. In questioning society's rules and definitions around homosexual issues, it is easier to question other rules and values. In letting go of heterosexual projects, homosexuals are challenged to create their own models, lifestyles, values, and beliefs around their identity.

Likewise homosexuals have the opportunity to reeducate and revitalize major institutions, especially those which have been most repressive. For example, by sharing their lived experiences, lesbians and gay men can offer religious institutions assistance in the transformation of theology. They can offer the institutions of marriage and the family different models to help redefine sexual roles and equality of relationships, and they question the societal myth that men and women are incomplete without the opposite sex. Homosexuals can help all to understand that masculine and feminine are inner energies that can be united within the person and lead to wholeness. All possess the capacity for psychological wholeness within themselves (Kelsey & Kelsey, 1986). Likewise the more balanced male and female energies are within individuals, the greater their creative potential, as well as the potential to be healers (Sanford, 1980). Gay men and lesbians can also teach married couples that commitment and love, rather than legality is the essence of relationships. In another area, homosexuals have already revitalized the mental health professions by challenging the homosexuality-as-sickness model.

The AIDS crisis not only is an opportunity for a spiritual journey, but also can aid the transformation of the health professions. Because AIDS is such a stigma, and because there is of yet no cure for the disease, many who have contracted the disease are confronted with totally letting go. In doing so, they are forced to rely upon their own resources, especially mental and spiritual ones. This challenges the traditional medical model, which tends to view disease as an outside force invading an organism and victimizing people. By letting go of the victim role, people with AIDS can help others to learn the role the mind and spirit play in the healing process.

Because external relationships are a mirror of internal ones, the more gay men and lesbians transform their own lives, the more they will transform all relationships and institutions. Being an outsider and minority can thus lead either to a greater addiction to this world, or a real detachment that leads to autonomy, liberation, and a more expansive world-view that embraces and celebrates all creation. As Matthew Fox (1984) put it:

> who can teach us more about celebration than those who have learned to celebrate in the midst of sadness and oppression? Who will know more about the value and purposelessness of savoring pleasure than those who have had to face the critical question of whether life is beautiful or not? Who know more about the beauty of creation and New Creation than those who have been told verbally and nonverbally by religion and society that the way they were created is a mistake or even sinful? (p. 200)

CLINICAL ILLUSTRATION

Jim is a 25-year-old gay male who was a former client of mine. The presenting problem was that since the age of 14 he had been a drug and sex addict and an alcoholic. Six months prior to coming to me, he had entered a treatment program for substance abuse, and had joined a 12-step program for sexual addicts. However, because he now was sober, he was feeling the underlying anxiety and depression that had previously been covered up by his addictions.

Jim was the youngest of three, having two older sisters. His parents were also alcoholics and frequently abused Jim as a child. He was put in a juvenile detention home when his parents felt they could no longer control him. Jim had been arrested for theft and illegal entry. The personal and family history revealed serious pathology which in traditional therapy usually suggests a poor prognosis. Early in the process, Jim asked me if he could be cured. I suggested he could have anything he was willing to stand for and commit himself to. I suggested that he was more than his history. So often, the limits placed on the client by the therapist's prognosis actually limits the possibilities of the client. A transpersonal perspective transcends those limits. It does not ignore the real scars and brokenness of the past. Rather it goes beyond the cause and effect of linear thinking and allows for the possibility of breakthroughs.

First, I assisted Jim in getting in touch with his feelings, especially those of guilt, anger, and fear. As a child of a disorganized family, he had learned not to feel. I used both gestalt techniques and age regression through hypnosis to assist that process. Also, I taught Jim meditation early in the therapy. At first, Jim perceived the problem as being outside of himself, primarily blaming his parents. Little by little, he was able to assume responsibility for his present situation and look at the lessons he needed to learn from them. He began to observe his inner dialogue to learn how he continued to create anxiety and depression. In the past, Jim's relationships were highly volatile and unstable. He began to work on communication and assertive skills. Through the use of mindfulness, he learned to let go of self-blame and self-judgement, and learned to accept his feelings. Also, Jim became more intimate with friends and began to experience control in the area of sexual expression. Much of the early part of therapy involved listening to Jim tell his story. However, eventually we looked at the payoffs and costs of continuing to tell that story. He began to realize that the continued telling of his story to himself continued the original feelings. Thus I could begin to ask when he was going to get off of it and tell a different story.

In general, Jim made tremendous progress by realizing that he was more than his feelings, thoughts, or the melodramas of his past. In realizing that, he could transcend them. Traditional therapies would have us believe that Jim was not capable of such growth. Because we took a transpersonal approach, Jim came to realize that the limitations on his development were primarily due to the limits of his thinking and beliefs, rather than due to historical and external circumstances.

Jim was raised Roman Catholic, but had repudiated any religious affiliation since age 12. Working through his feelings toward authority figures through therapy, and through regular meditation, Jim rediscovered God within himself. Frequently, Jim experienced a sense of darkness and intense alienation and abandonment. Sometimes the fear would be so intense as to run him totally at the time. Jim learned more and more to focus on those fears without judgment and without trying to get rid of them. He simply let them be and realized there was a distinction between having the feeling of fear and being afraid. He could observe his fears, as if he were watching a movie, and just let them be. The result was a diminution of their hold on him. Also, Jim slowly felt more alive. His depression lifted and his anxiety subsided.

Another useful tool in assisting Jim was interpreting the transference between him and me. Jim saw me as his father, and as a religious authority. Jim projected onto me a judgmental and vindictive authority figure who was not to be trusted. Eventually, we established a strong trusting bond where I became the father he never had and wished he had. Eventually, he removed all projections from me and saw me as a guide and friend. Jim came to realize that he was the parent of his own inner child and needed to nurture and give to his own child what was missing. One of the important aspects of therapy was working on forgiveness of his parents, and of himself.

After one year of intense weekly therapy, Jim terminated, realizing his special giftedness. Working through much of his story led him to become compassionate toward others who suffer, and also to realize that his marginal status with his family was an opportunity for autonomy. He ultimately realized that he had within himself everything he needed to be whole.

In Jim's case being gay was not a central issue, but was part of a deeper issue of accepting himself as sexual and more basically, being able to accept himself at all. Jim had been suicidal during his addiction period. Jim and I took the approach that the primary task was to embark on a spiritual journey, and to put everything on that path, including his sexual orientation. In that context, he was able to look at his problems more as lessons to be learned and as opportunities, rather than as obstacles to be overcome. In that focus being gay became a nonissue.

Clients like Jim are instructive. First, Jim demonstrates that a transpersonal approach to counseling can open up unlimited possibilities. However, there are no particular formulas or techniques that can create transformation. If one could attain transformation through techniques, then it would be the ego that would be expanded. Techniques can create a context in which transformation can be realized. However, addition or deletion of knowledge or behavior in a linear sense is not transformation. Transformation is an unlearning. The real task is to stop trying to change the world in accordance with any image, and instead go within the center of oneself to see anew what already is. To do this requires trust and surrender. There comes a point in one's journey where there are no logical answers. One enters a realm of consciousness that operates beyond the ordinary reality which we perceive. There is no particular formula or technique that can be taught. The process itself is the teacher. role is to guide clients

The pastoral counselor's role is to guide clients to clear the space so their true self and potential can appear. This will demand that the counselor is also on the path of transformation and is in tune with her clients. In this process, distinctions such as gay or straight or male and female will fade, and rigid beliefs erode. What emerges is a tremendous sense of freedom and empowerment. The more they experience inner transformation, the more they will manifest that change in eternal transformation.

What follows is quoted from a gay man whom Matthew Fox (1983) wrote about in his discussion of the spiritual journey of the homosexual.

> It is only by finally coming to terms with being gay — and otherwise letting myself be gay that I have begun to see the incredible pain and magnificent pleasures of being a living person. . . . That struggle — which I fought the whole time — is opening my life in a way I never thought possible. It has given me a chance to work at my whole life and to say I don't have to be like everyone else in the rest of my life's aspects either. Living as a gay man has let me feel love and passion and pain, I didn't know I was capable of. (p. 202)

REFERENCES

Ajaya, S. (1983). *Psychotherapy East and West: A Unifying Paradigm*. Honesdale, PA: Himalayan Institute of Yoga Science & Philosophy.

Allport, G. (1954). *The Nature of Prejudice*. Reading, MA: Addison-Wesley.

Arpita. (1986). *Meditation and Meaning in Life*. In R. Ballentine (Ed.). *The Theory and Practice of Meditation* (pp. 93-108). Honesdale, PA: The Himalayan Institute of Yoga Science & Philosophy.

Assagioli, R. (1977). *Psychosynthesis*. New York: Penguin Books.

Ballentine, R. (Ed.). (1986). *The Theory and Practice of Meditation*. Honesdale, PA: Himalayan Institute of Yoga Science & Philosophy.

Bayer, R. (1981). *Homosexuality and American Psychiatry: The Politics of Diagnosis*. NY: Basic Books.

Bergler, E. (1956). *Homosexuality: Disease or Way of Life*. New York: Hill & Wang.

Bethards, B. (1977). *Sex and Psychic Energy*. Novato, CA: Inner Light Foundation.

Boswell, J. (1980). *Christianity, Social Tolerance, and Homosexuality*. Chicago: University of Chicago Press.

Boswell, J. (1985). "Homosexuality, Religious Life and the Clergy: An Historical Overview." New Ways Ministry Symposium Lecture, Mt. Rainier, MD, Nov. 8-10, 1985.

Chinmoy, S. (1985). *Meditation*. Jamaica, NY: Agni Books.

Davis, R. E. (1976). *The Philosophy and Practice of Yoga*. Lakemont, GA: C. S. A. Press.

Fortunato, J. (1982) *Embracing the Exile*. New York: Seabury Press.

Fox, M. (1983). The Spiritual Journey of the Homosexual and Just About Everyone Else. In R. Nugent (Ed.), *A Challenge to Love: Gay and Lesbian Catholics in the Church* (pp. 189-204). New York: Crossroad.

Fox, M. (1984). *Original Blessing*. Santa Fe, NM: Bear.

Golas, T. (1972). *The Lazy Man's Guide to Enlightenment*. Palo Alto, CA: Seed Center.

Goldstein, J. (1983). *The Experience of Insight*. Boston: Shambala Books.

Gonsiorek, J. (Ed.). (1985). *Homosexuality & Psychotherapy: A Practitioners Handbook of Affirmative Models*. New York: The Haworth Press. *Journal of Homosexuality*. 7 (2/3).

Haick, E. (1972). *Sexual Energy and Yoga*. New York: ASI Publications.

Hatterer, L. (1970). *Changing Homosexuality in the Male*. New York: McGraw-Hill.

John, Bubba Free. (1978). *Love of the Two-Armed Form*. Middleton, CA: Dawn Horse Press.

Kelsey, M., & Kelsey, B. (1986). *Sacrament of Sexuality: The Spirituality and Psychology of Sex*. Warwick, NY: Amity House.

Miller, W. A. (1981). *Make Friends With Your Shadow: How to Accept and Use the Negative Side of Your Personality.* Minneapolis: Augsburg.

Sanford, J. (1980). *The Invisible Partners: How the Male and Female in Each of Us Affects our Relationships.* New York: Paulist Press.

Socarides, C. W. (1978). *Homosexuality.* New York: Jason Aronson.

Small, J. (1984). *Transformers: The Therapists of the Future.* Del Ray, CA: DeVorss.

Struzzo, J. (1982). Happiness: A Developmental Perspective. In T. Kane (Ed.), *Happiness* (pp. 113-127). Whitinsville, MA: Affirmation Books.

Struzzo, J. (1983). Intimate Relationships: Heterosexual and Homosexual. In S. Sammon (Ed.), *Relationships* (pp. 91-112). Whitinsville, MA: Affirmation Books.

Struzzo, J. (1985). Anger: Destructive and Life-giving Energy. In B. Riordan (Ed.), *Anger* (pp. 116-131). Whitinsville, MA: Affirmation Books.

Vaughan, F. (1986). *The Inward Arc: Healing and Wholeness in Psychotherapy and Spirituality.* Boston: New Science Library.

Walsh, R. & Vaughan, F. (Eds.). *Beyond Ego: Transpersonal Dimensions in Psychology.* Los Angeles: J. P. Tarcher.

Wilber, K. (1982). *The Spectrum of Consciousness.* Wheaton, IL: Theosophical.

Index

Abelard, 123
abortion, 107, 158-159
Abraham, 100
abstinence, sexual, 15,34,35
acquired immune deficiency syndrome
    (AIDS)
  Baptist Church's position on, 25
  as God's punishment, 8-9,31
  lesbian/homosexual clergy's attitudes
    towards, 160
  pastoral counseling implications, 199,
    202,216-217
  Roman Catholic Church's position on, 8
acquired immune deficiency
    syndrome-related complex (ARC), 8
Adam, 106,112-113
adultery, 100
Affirmation, 9
After the Fall (Miller), 211
American Baptists Concerned, 25
American-Israeli Civil Liberties Coalition,
    115n.
American Jewish Congress, 90-91
American Life Lobby, 1
American Lutheran Church, 24
American Psychiatric Association, 35,101,
    197-198
Amos, 135
anal intercourse, 72,104
androgyny, 111-115
animals, homosexuality among, 67
anxiety, separation-related, 177,178,179,
    180
Aquinas, Thomas, 28,34
Archdiocese of San Francisco, 27
Athens, 113
attachment cycle, 176-184
  definition, 177
  failure of, 182-184

pastoral counseling implications, 189,
    190-191
  in scripture, 185-186
autonomy, sexual freedom and, 52
Avita, Beatrice, 124-125

Babylonian exile, 96,97
Bailey, D.S., 14-15
Baptist Church, AIDS policy statement, 25
bar mitzvah, 62
bat mitzvah, 62
Baucis, 102-103
beauty, 113
behaviorism, 203
Bennett, Allen B., 17,89
Beth Ahavah, 86
Beth Chayim Chadashim, 84-85,86,87-88,
    93
  Union of American Hebrew
    Congregations membership, 58,59,
    60,85,87
B'nai Haskalah, 86
bisexuality, in Greco-Roman culture, 113
Blue, Lionel, 17
bonding, mother-infant, 177,178-179
Book of Esther, 139
Boswell, John, 14,24
breathing exercises, 215
Brueggeman, Walter, 96,97-98
Bryant, Anita, 1,87

Cain, 104
Canaanites, 104
Capponi, Giovanni Batista, 124,125
Carlini, Benedetta, 119-123,125,126,127,
    128,129